YORK

ANIMATED FILMS

virgin

film

James Clarke

For Stephen and Justine. Happy trails.

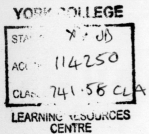
First published in Great Britain in 2004
by Virgin Books Ltd
Thames Wharf Studios
Rainville Road
London
W6 9HA

A catalogue record for this book is available from the British Library.

ISBN 0 7535 0804 4

Typeset by TW Typesetting, Plymouth, Devon
Printed and bound in Great Britain by Mackays of Chatham PLC

Contents

Acknowledgements

Thanks as always to my editor, Kirstie Addis, and a special thanks to my agent, Laura Morris.

Introduction

Ray Harryhausen perhaps put it best when he said of animating his stop-motion models: 'It's almost metaphysical in a sense. It's controlling another object's life force.'

While Harryhausen was addressing the intrigue and charm of his particular branch of the expansive and glorious animation tree, namely making models rather than drawings or found objects move, the observation is true of all types of animation. In spirit animation reaches back far beyond the modern age to a more primal graphic and illustrative power present in the human imagination and heart.

In fact, this looking back is a key feature of what comes to mind when most people think of animation, because animation is everything from Pinocchio learning to walk, skeletons fighting classical heroes, a Pumpkin King ditching Halloween for Christmas and a truckload of Agent Smiths brawling with Neo in a dingy part of the Matrix.

Despite the rich variety of animation worldwide, most audiences will equate the word animation with childhood visits to the cinema where their first movie was probably a Disney feature. Alternatively, television continues screening the vintage short animated films produced by Hollywood in the 1940s and 1950s. What all of this is bound up in, then, is a powerful quality of nostalgia. Get talking to an adult about childhood and the chances are animated films (long or short) will come into the conversation soon enough. At its best, nostalgia can help reveal the effects of time's passing and the two hugely popular, widely seen animated features *Toy Story* (John Lasseter, 1995) and *Toy Story 2* (John Lasseter, 2000) very consciously appealed to this nostalgic spirit and the importance of childhood memories and treasures.

Being such a part of many people's young years, recollections of favourite animated characters and films is a popular pastime and certainly the collection of animation art has quite a following. Significant, too, is that countless stories that form the basis of animation are themselves strongly tied into a sense of nostalgia, frequently being adaptations of fairy tales and old-time stories, whether from oral traditions, legends, folktales or the more recent iteration, the comic strip.

Undoubtedly, one of the most compelling aspects of animation is its power to remind audiences of the importance of play and imagination in a world that increasingly sidelines such necessities. You could even boldly state that animation is one of the most popular forms in which the spirit of true anarchy and the antic spirit live on.

In Native American mythology, the coyote figure is a central force, playfully and wilfully at odds with the established order that it seeks to mock and undermine. Animation plays this same coyote-like role so perhaps it is no surprise that the American animation idiom has led such a vivid and popular life.

Animation, then, is a liberating form that free associates like crazy and makes audiences see the world afresh and, clichéd though it sounds, with the eyes of a child again.

In the light of this it is easier to see why animation so readily lends itself to investing the worlds of inanimate objects, of animals and of nature with real spirit and character. For thousands of years nature and the animal world were considered to possess these qualities. Only in more recent ages has the pursuit of reason weakened our perceptions. Animation helps resuscitate the human imagination's more ancient vision and reminds the adult imagination of that world of possibility that most people get drilled out of them by the necessary evil of having to 'grow up'. Animation reminds us that seeing isn't believing. Believing is seeing.

Animated films are the biggest special effect cinema has yet given us. In animation anything can happen. Animated movies are also an immensely common source of reference for people. Even the most casual film-goer probably had their first film-going experience at an animated feature. For many lifelong film fans their love of movies was tattooed on their heart by an animated feature.

The tradition of the animated film is also, in part, the starting point for people's understanding, appreciation and sheer enjoyment of the magic of what we now think of as special effects. It makes perfect sense when, for example, we remember that George Lucas, who has done so much for the legitimacy of the visual effects format, began his filmmaking career as an animator. Given the continued prevalence of special-effects-orientated films in mainstream movie-going, animation's legacy is immense. Yet still, there is probably an unhealthy association of the word 'animation' with the phrase 'for kids'. An animated film can be as resonant and meaningful and artful as *Citizen Kane* (Orson Welles, 1941) or *The Godfather* (Francis Ford Coppola, 1972).

A product of the mechanised, modern age, animation often tells stories that play up the usually hapless relationship between humans and their inventions. It is a relationship that cinema has always depicted. Think of Charlie Chaplin being pulled through all those cogs and gears in *Modern Times* (Charlie Chaplin, 1936), or Buster Keaton in *The General* (Clyde Bruckman, 1927) or Laurel and Hardy endlessly trying to fix something and failing hilariously in all that they did, their friendship miraculously enduring every tribulation.

Somewhat ironically, it was by mocking and parodying the modern world of machines that animation really broke into mainstream culture, itself becoming a mass-produced form involving huge numbers of animators, painters, designers and technicians. The assembly-line model of mass production as espoused by Henry Ford was at once the source of many animated shorts' humour but also the very reason that so many animated shorts could be produced.

Initially, animation had begun as the playful domain of individuals such as George Melies, Emile Cohl and Winsor McCay. A hundred or so years later quality work continues to be produced by small teams of animators far from the imposing shadow of the big-budgeted animated features. Czech animator Jan Svankmajer and the London-based Brothers Quay are examples of work on the smaller palette with very vivid and powerful effect.

Many would find it hard to argue that in most animation there is a spectrum of joyfulness, colour and energy at work. Animation wilfully subverts the accepted physical laws of the world; and the law of the body's fragility. When Tom, chasing Jerry, steps on the wrong end of a rake and it slams up into his face, his pain is temporary. The chase is all, and that chase is rooted in all-too-human jealousies and frustrations.

The fantasy dynamics of animation are overwhelming and it is the one form of cinema that can be designed and planned more than any other. The huge cost and labour implications mean that getting everything measured and calibrated just right for emotional effect is paramount. Even editing animated films is a different process to editing live action. In live action, the director typically covers action from a number of angles and chooses what works best during the edit phase. Not so the animated film where these decisions are mapped out and agreed in pre-production.

Like the best fantasy stories and scenarios, animation needs reality and reality needs animation. This notion of the redemptive possibilities of the imagination and the spirit of the fanciful has been central to countless films over the years. It is an equation that is hard to argue with. Just watch Terry Gilliam's films to see it proved time and again. *Brazil*

(1985), *Baron Munchausen* (1988) and *The Fisher King* (1991) exemplify this compelling belief. It is no big surprise to learn that Gilliam too began as an animator.

Animation has yielded such diversity, in part because it is so craft-based and can healthily exist and develop outside the huge influences of major studios. Animation remains a very home-grown form that can still be the domain of one person. Avant-garde they may have been but the short films of the late Stan Brakhage were certainly invested with the animator's spirit and sense of creative liberty. Animation is a worldwide form that calls to mind people's ancient storytelling roots when paintings on cave walls of animals and humans were a powerful way of thinking about the world. Animation is super ancient and ultra modern all in the same frame, sketch or move of a model.

The kinds of stories that animation seems best suited to expressing tend towards some kind of fantastic connotation, association or wellspring of inspiration. Evidently, the form is very much about transformation and the magic involved in the act of making something move that would not do so by itself (subsequently, is computer animation really animation in the conventional sense of the word?).

Whether it is Elmer Fudd looking for Bugs Bunny (again!) or Gollum talking to Frodo in *The Lord of the Rings: The Two Towers* (Peter Jackson, 2002), animation embodies the potential of the cinema to transcend the real and make believability far more important than realism. After all, when was the last time you were handcuffed to a rabbit wearing red dungarees as happens in *Who Framed Roger Rabbit?* (Robert Zemeckis, 1988)? We *believe* it is happening though.

Animated film has long been associated with childhood and with a sense of warmth and belonging. Animation allows the audience to dream and let their imaginations go, and as such animation is pleasingly anti-realistic. Everyone loves great big tall stories of wonder and amazement and animation excels at telling such tales through a variety of approaches. At whatever level of simplicity or complexity animation works, it is a magical way to make an image, utterly fake yet with the potential to explore very real emotions and desires.

There is the sprawling and impressively naturalistic fairy-tale aura of the Disney studio film *Pinocchio* (1940) and there is, at the other end of the spectrum, the animation of real objects in the Freudian-fuelled work of Jan Svankmajer in his fairy-tale piece, *Alice* (1987). Vastly different in scope and tone, these two disparate examples are, at the very least, unified by being based on pre-existing stories that owe a huge debt to the fairy-tale impulse.

For psychologist, Bruno Bettelheim, in his landmark book *The Uses of Enchantment: the Meaning and Importance of Fairy Tales* (1977), there is an exciting relationship between the mind of young children and the natural, animal world around them. According to Bettelheim, this relationship is dampened and suppressed by adult life. In effect this animistic aspect of our minds informs and gives so much animation its appeal. 'Subjected to the rational teachings of others, the child only buries his "true knowledge" deeper in his soul and it remains untouched by rationality, but it can be formed and informed by what fairy tales have to say.'

Furthermore, the other affinity animation has with the fairy-tale form is the emphasis on anthropomorphism, whereby animals are leant human characteristics in their facial and bodily appearance and their modes of expression.

It is appropriate that, in the period in which this book was being written, the European and North American cinema has been able to see Japan's most successful animated feature ever: *Spirited Away* (Hayao Miyazaki, 2001), a film steeped in the ethos of the fairy tale to dazzling visual and emotional effect.

The bond between film and dream has often been expressed and animation's freedom from certain laws and aesthetic restrictions (notably photographic realism) plunges its potential right into the dream world.

Certainly, enchantment is key to appreciating the form. For sure, animation may be the most artificial form of all cinema, on the surface, yet it repeatedly wires into the most powerfully subconscious circuitry of our emotional lives. As such it is no huge leap of the imagination to equate the essence of animation with the essence of the fairy-tale tradition and undoubtedly the two forms have been mutual friends since cinema began.

Animation functions as the latest iteration of a visual storytelling spirit that creativity has nurtured ever since humans drew bison and ibex in the firelight of caves.

The universality of expression that animation enjoys is unsurprisingly matched by the global interest in animation, so rooted is it in folk traditions, both visual and verbal. Animation offers endless permutations so that even an elementary glance across the terrain takes you from the short piece *Fantasmagorie* (Emile Cohl, 1908) in which stick figures go through a series of dreamlike experiences through to the Chinese animation of the 1920s and 30s with shorts such as the Wan Brothers' *Camel Dance* (1930) and on to the 1962 feature *Havoc in Heaven* in which Chinese folk hero, the Monkey King, must deal with an apocalyptic scenario.

In another direction the work of animators of the 1950s and 1960s such as Oskar Fischinger and Robert Bree displays the versatility of the form. Russian animation, for example, has yielded classics such as *The Snow Queen*, adapted from the Hans Christian Andersen tale as well as *The Magic Horse* and *Mr Wonderbird*.

The list of achievements, experiments and enchantments is seemingly endless.

So much is possible in animation. From the vaudevillian slapstick of early American animation through to the super-seriousness of contemporary Japanese material, animation embraces so much so easily. Its variations are wide-ranging and animation can handle any kind of dream picture. From the narrative-based, classical animation of characters and dialogue that Disney made an art to the work of animators like Yuri Norstein and the less narratively inclined and intense animated shorts of The Brothers Quay, animation contains all.

Interestingly Norman McLaren, the experimental Canadian animator, said of the form: 'It's how it moves that's the important thing . . . What the animator does on each frame of film is not as important as what he or she does in between.'

Animation has always been popular, possessing great novelty value in its early years and by the 1920s fixing itself as a legitimate means of expression. Two of the earliest achievements that paved the way for animation must be recognised at this point. There was the work of a Briton in America, Eadweard Muybridge who famously photographed a horse in motion, capturing in separate frames the phases of its motion. Muybridge did a similar piece with a baseball batter, naked as he hit a baseball, the movement of muscle and flesh evident with poetic clarity.

In France a precursor to what would be considered animation in its most raw form was to be found in Emile Reynaud's animation precursor, Theatre Optique. This device projected moving pictures and backgrounds on to the same screen. This was first seen in 1892 and the shows were called Pantomimes Lumineuses and ran 500 pictures in fifteen minutes. Other experimenters included Etienne-Jules Marey, Thomas Edison, William Friese Green and Martine Evans.

Animation's appeal spread rapidly and in North America and Japan in the 1920s and 1930s the audience for the form grew with ease. Through the 1940s and 1950s animation continued to secure its place in cinema history. By the 1960s, though, the animated feature and short film in its full, classically animated sense (the Disney format is the accepted highest-profile example of it) began to give way to cheaper animation for television and for many what was considered The Golden Age had come to an end. The late 1960s and the 1970s were testing times, though of course shorter, more experimental work that was not dependent on armies of artists and animators continued. The late 1970s and early 1980s saw brave and largely successful (if commercially failed) animated features occasionally being produced, notably *Watership Down* (Martin Rosen, 1977), *Plague Dogs* (Martin Rosen, 1982) and *The Secret of Nimh* (Don Bluth, 1982). Indeed, this period of the early 1980s also saw the emergence of computer animation, notably in the film *Tron* (Steven Lisberger, 1982) that, since its low-key theatrical success, endures on DVD as something of a cult piece.

Without doubt, however, animation has been enjoying a new lease of life since around 1986 and it continues into the early twenty-first century.

This book spans examples of work by the Disney studio, the work of Nick Park and Aardman Animation, the great efforts of Don Bluth and Jan Svankmajer (poles apart in approach but equally committed), the new world wonders of computer animation and the expansive, intricate visions of the Japanese animated form. It goes without saying that this book can only refer to a tiny fraction of all the animated features produced over the years.

This book will endeavour to highlight not just the ways in which these films have been produced but also the thinking behind them in terms of concepts and also be an acknowledgement of the emotional pull of these so-called tall stories.

Certainly the shelves of most homes with video and DVD players will have at least one animated feature in them. It is unlikely, however, that every home-video library will have a Western or a film noir. Yet for all its popularity, animation tends not to have been given the same treatment and respect as other forms of cinema. Animation saturates pop culture and always has done. The massive *The Lord of the Rings* and *The Matrix* trilogies, for example, are films that in large part feature animated characters.

Like all forms of cinema, animation has its pioneers and heroes and their contributions are as important to cinema as any live action or documentary filmmaker's achievements and accomplishments.

So, could it be said that animation is the most aesthetically pure form of cinema there has yet been? After all, the worlds of animation are only able to exist because of the mechanics of movie-making. Animation is not the recording of a reality you can go and look at regardless of a movie camera being there. A cel of animation only exists because a camera is going to record it. Animation offers a world that only exists once an artist sculpts a character in clay and then begins to make it move, to animate it, to give it life. You can't go where an animated movie is set. Animation was virtual reality before virtual reality became a phrase. Famously, Chuck Jones played with this idea in *Duck Amuck*, his legendary Daffy Duck short where Daffy runs off the film and then back into a frame.

At the dawn of its second full century, cinema continues to recognise the commercial viability of animation and its artistic richness. It is a major storytelling format that has certainly transcended any sense of novelty that there may have been when heroes of the form like George Melies and Winsor McCay were at work in the early twentieth century. Animation is exciting, elastic and highly responsive to new technologies.

Animation was massively popular for about forty years from the 1920s when the short animated piece was a staple of cinemas through to the 1960s when it had flourished into a feature length art form. In the 1970s and for most of the 1980s it was hostage to economics and special effects movies before the 1990s saw it healthily revived. In the early twenty-first century, animation is enjoying the kind of enthusiasm last seen in the 1940s and 1950s and as the culture becomes more global, there is an ever-growing variety of animation available.

In summer 2003, for example, the two strongest fantasy films on offer in London were not from Hollywood but were the Japanese animated feature *Spirited Away* and the French-made animated feature *Belleville Rendezvous* (Sylvain Chomet).

Both of these films are classically animated, cel animation features which is the most well-known form of animation and has been part of cinema-going for seventy years. In the early twenty-first century, cel animation and stop-motion animation has been augmented by computer-generated animation which will become the dominant technique by the end of the decade.

Sadly, in summer 2003, DreamWorks animation, in the wake of the commercial failure of their cel feature *Sinbad*, announced it would be producing no more classical ink and paint features. A few years earlier Twentieth Century-Fox had come to the same decision after the commercial failure of several projects. Of course, regardless of whether it is ink and paint or computer generated, the compelling narrative is what is foremost. Certainly, watching the Pixar-produced computer-animated films, one cannot help but be amazed by the storytelling structure, notably in *Toy Story 2* and *Monsters, Inc.* The way the cause and effect pattern clicks and snaps into place is more astonishing even than the believability of the fur on a monster or the action adventure high jinks of Buzz Lightyear as he fights the Emperor Zurg.

Inevitably, the filmmaker most associated with animation was Walt Disney (1901–1966). His name is perhaps now more synonymous with an entertainment empire than with his hands-on supervision of the development of the animated feature and also the creation of a whole cosmology of animated characters for the short form.

Disney was an able illustrator but his real gift was for story development and administrating and organising his company. As noted science-fiction author Jules Verne brilliantly said, 'What one man can imagine others can make real.' Disney's industrial and aesthetic legacy cannot be underestimated but there are others who have been similarly important to the development of the form.

While the burgeoning work of George Melies in the 1890s could be seen as drawing on and advancing animation (and live action) the very use of the phrase 'drawing on' suggests other inventive souls had already been at work. In 1900 James Stuart Blackton of Great Britain produced a film called *The Enchanted Drawing* that featured some drawn characters in what is considered a prototype of animation. (This cannot really be thought of as the first piece of animation as the sequence was not comprised of continuous frame by frame filming.)

In 1906, Blackton produced *The Humorous Phases of Funny Faces*, which is considered the first-known attempt at animation. This time Blackton incorporated drawn sequences that have been shot frame by frame using a combination of blackboard, chalk and cut-outs for his animated forms. The following year, Blackton produced another short that this time worked as stop motion. Entitled *The Haunted Hotel*, the film used stop motion of three-dimensional objects. Wine was poured into a glass, bread was cut and a table was laid without apparent human agency. The film was very successful and helped popularise the potential of animation at its purest, most playful level, exemplifying what Ray

Harryhausen and Jan Svankmajer many years later would acknowledge as its mystical and magical quality.

Before the special effects and animated wonders of George Lucas's space adventure fairy tale *Star Wars* movies, another George was wowing imaginations. He discovered the principle of stop motion by accident when a strip of film jammed in his camera. When he re-spliced the film the subject in front of the camera had changed but the background remained the same. George Melies's iconic film, *Voyage to the Moon* (1902), showed that animation was the perfect way to capture flights of fantasy and match the vivid image-making of picture books. Indeed, much of the most popular animation continues to take us away from surface reality and the best of it invests the fantasy with genuine emotion and sensibility.

George Melies built something of a fantasy film empire in Paris years but again others were also at work helping refine and further the new world of film. Emile Cohl, who had been a successful comic-strip artist, made a short film called *Fantasmagorie* (1908), a simple series of dreamlike images of stick figures. Cohl went on to produce hundreds of shorts but died in poverty. Others continued to explore the form such as Arthur Melbourne Cooper in his film *Dreams of Toyland* (1908), which animated real toys in a long-ago precursor to *Toy Story*. Indeed, comic books are also the source for other animation heroes across the Atlantic.

The strongest animation combines the fabulous and the mundane and finds its magic in the space between them. Today's live-action films are even really becoming increasingly live-action–animation fusions, most notably *Star Wars: Episode I – The Phantom Menace, The Matrix* and *The Lord of the Rings* trilogy.

In the United States it was Winsor McCay, the celebrated comic-strip artist of the beautiful art nouveau adventures of *Little Nemo in Slumberland* who created the first major North American animated character in *Gertie the Dinosaur*.

Tragically, McCay's name is little known today yet he contributed so much to popularising the animation form and certainly showed the value in fantasy as an emotionally rich form for movies to invest in. *Gertie the Dinosaur* was premiered in New York and McCay even appeared on stage giving the illusion he was interacting with Gertie.

To know something of Winsor McCay's life and see something of his thankfully preserved output is to be reminded of the joy and pain of chasing a dream and the joy and fun of the imagination.

Born in Canada in 1871, Winsor McCay was a dreamer and an illustrator who could not stop picture-making as a wide-eyed kid. His parents sent him to a business college but McCay never really showed up that much and never graduated. His artwork for a local amusement park (with the terrific name Sacket and Wiggins Wonderland) got him noticed and soon enough he was at work in Chicago on *The Enquirer* newspaper.

At *The Enquirer* he illustrated the very popular *Tales of the Jungle Imps* and he also had a hit vaudeville show doing 'lightning sketches' on a blackboard. McCay's newspaper employer Randolph Hearst was wary of McCay's success away from the paper and created a golden handcuff contract for the artist, paying him handsomely but having exclusive ownership of his time.

As so often happens, it was a quiet, understated, unheralded moment of discovery that resulted in the thunder of innovation and bold artistry. McCay's young son enjoyed flip books and McCay was inspired. In 1909, McCay set about laying the groundwork for the American take on animation. He found the time to make 4,000 drawings which, when filmed, brought to life his comic-strip creation *Little Nemo*. Intriguingly, the animation for this short animated experiment is bookended by live-action segments featuring McCay himself, a whimsical-looking, slightly built fellow, who agrees to a bet from his friends to make pictures move. A title card announces McCay as 'The first artist to attempt drawing pictures that will move'. The film shows McCay's friends laughing doubtfully at his proposal and then we see McCay at work, painstakingly illustrating each image, surrounded by stacks of paper. McCay reviews his work on a rolodex of images. An overhead shot shows McCay drawing the elegant, bold lines of his characters and inking them in. McCay even takes delivery of barrels of ink for his Herculean task. One character smokes a cigar and then Little Nemo appears and does some squash and stretch exercises that recall the effect of a Hall of Mirrors at a funfair.

Finally, a dragon turns up, its mouth open wide and containing a seat on which Nemo and the princess sit before the dragon turns and moves away, its tail arcing gracefully as it fills the screen and moves into the background. The fluidity of the inked images is incredible as is the subtle use of foreground and background. Perhaps most important is how playful and whimsical the short animated piece is, setting something of a standard for the cheerily inventive style of so much American animation that would follow in the 1920s and beyond.

McCay's second film was the very funny five-minute-long *The Story of a Mosquito* (1912). Again, McCay does more than might be expected, playing with foreground and background as a balding man sleeps and is visited by a big-eyed bloodthirsty mosquito. Every time the mosquito punctures the man's skin there is a real sense of mass present and as the mosquito gets heavier with blood its movement becomes comically clumsy until finally it explodes.

The saying 'third time's a charm' was never more true than with McCay's third animated short. It is the film that assured his legacy and immortality in animation.

Entitled *Gertie the Dinosaur* (1914) the film creates a real animated character with a range of emotions and even manages to integrate live action and animation. It is funny and wondrous throughout. By the time of this film McCay had become aware of his standing and reputation and he acknowledges this in a title card where he describes himself as 'America's Greatest Cartoonist' . Notice the word 'animator' does not come into play. It is quite a claim and it is more than matched by the vision on screen.

As with the Little Nemo short, *Gertie the Dinosaur* is bookended by live action again portraying McCay as the hapless dreamer at the mercy of his friends' scepticism, which will be undone by the end of the film. McCay is out for a ride in a car with his pals when it breaks down outside a museum. While the car is fixed McCay and his friends go into the museum where they look at an immense dinosaur skeleton measuring seventy feet in length and twenty feet in height. McCay bets his friends that he can make the dinosaur live again through a hand-drawn cartoon. The familiar joshing is played out. The youthful genius is shown studying the dinosaur skeleton.

A title card then says that it has taken McCay six months to make the drawings and again he is surrounded by near-skyscrapers of paper. His friend calls in and sees the 10,000 drawings and McCay's young assistant drops a stack of them.

At dinner, McCay 'lightning sketches' a dinosaur but his friends appear to pay scant attention. McCay then shows a previously drawn background image of a lake and cave. McCay tells his friends he will make Gertie come out of her cave and the animation proper begins. Interestingly, the live action around the animation makes the animated material all the more magical.

An intertitle shows McCay's first instruction to Gertie: 'Gertie, come out and make a pretty bow.' Sure enough, Gertie fluidly emerges from her cave in the background and approaches the camera with a very smiley face. She has the quality of a playful, eager-to-please puppy. A sea creature looks on for a moment from the lake. Gertie gulps down a tree (how familiar the first sighting of a computer-animated brachiosaurus in *Jurassic Park* now seems) and then does a little dance to the camera. As promised, Gertie finally bows to the audience. McCay then instructs Gertie to raise her right foot which she does with ease and waves it. McCay then throws her a pumpkin, appearing about the size of a pea as Gertie swallows it. A woolly mammoth called Jumbo walks past, unfazed by Gertie's antics.

McCay's camera remains fixed in one place as the action plays out but it is never dull to watch. There is a sense of space and dynamism. A dinosaur flies by and another title card continues McCay's conversation with his pet dino-pal. Gertie proceeds to drink the lake dry. The topper, though, is when McCay enters the frame as a live-action figure and Gertie lifts him up on to her back. The animation ends and sure enough the live action shows Winsor McCay winning his bet. Imagination and perspiration have won out again over cynicism and too much faith in reality. The dreamer is victorious and McCay becomes a hero of pop culture in twelve minutes flat.

McCay continued producing animation beyond *Gertie* but it is this film that stands as his great work alongside his dazzling *Little Nemo* comic books.

Just as animation began developing its various aesthetic benchmarks (fluidity of movement, realism of backgrounds, characterisation, a shift from being moving comic strips to more cinematic pieces) so too its mechanical and industrial processes were taking shape.

In 1914, John Bray opened an animation studio and patented many aspects of the animation process, though not the use of cels (acetate sheets on to which paintings are applied, one sheet per frame). It was a man named Earl Hurd who patented the use of cels. Bray, though, saw the value in creating a production line ethos, a sensibility already at work in growing mass production. Another individual was responsible for developing the registration peg so that animated sketches could be aligned on the drawing board and easily flipped through to check for consistency. His name was Raoul Barre.

For the 1920s and 1930s, American animation (which today dominates the popular animation market) was centred on New York. This would change by the mid-1930s, certainly, when Walt Disney expanded his work into animated features with his Burbank base in Los Angeles, California.

In 1990 a Japanese-produced animated feature was released called *Little Nemo: Adventures in Slumberland*. It was a conflagration of McCay's work. With a script by science-fiction literature legend Ray Bradbury (author of novels such as *Fahrenheit 451* and *The Martian Chronicles*) and screenwriter and director Chris Columbus (*Home Alone*, 1990 and *Harry Potter and the Philosopher's Stone*, 2001) the film focused on Little Nemo's dream journey and discovery of a power that threatens both the known and the unknown worlds. The character design and preliminary animation on the film was overseen by Roger Allers who went on to direct *The Lion King*. This *Nemo* version had a rather quiet release.

Alongside Disney, the other high-profile animation studio in America during the 1920s and 1930s was that of Dave and Max Fleischer. Indeed, it was the Fleischers who produced the first feature animation (a documentary), *The Einstein Theory of Relativity*. Based in New York, the Fleischer studio aesthetic was founded less on the realism that Disney pursued and much more on what writer Norman Klein in his book *7 Minutes: The Life and Death of the American Cartoon* calls turning the world upside down. The studio's greatest early success was the series *Out of the Inkwell* which combined live action (an animator) and animation (a clown called Ko-Ko who climbed out of an inkwell and interacted with the animator). The studio would go on to produce *Popeye* and *Betty Boop*, which the Hays Code deemed too sexy and so had to be toned down.

For the great Russian animator Yuri Norstein, animation is the place where allegory, entertainment and political comment mesh. This sensibility also fuels the work of Jan Svankmajer, the Czech Surrealist who might not even term himself an animator.

Animation has certainly become famous for its cute and warm side but there is a whole other version of the form that plays up its capacity for spikier, abrasive and unsettling characters and stories and Svankmajer's work does just that. He has become a key figure for many animators, especially those working in stop-motion animation.

Amazingly, for all the pizzazz of computer-generated visual effects and lavish, naturalistic animation, two of the funkiest examples of animation in the 1990s were directed by Henry Selick. His preferred medium was stop-motion animation, and after a long period where stop motion had really been the preserve of live-action features where certain visual effects and creatures were best realised using the medium, stop motion was given a very high profile platform. The audience for it was there, ready and waiting.

The global affinity for animation has yielded an exciting cross fertilisation of stories and ways of telling them which reminds audiences of the richness to be found in an increasingly global and connected culture. Just look at the mega successful live-action science-fiction film *The Matrix*. The film testifies to the arresting influence of Japanese manga and anime on Hollywood since the early 1990s. Watching the Japanese animated feature *The Ghost in the Shell* (Marmoru Oshii, 1995) about a virtual cyber world, one cannot help but see where *The Matrix* sprung from in part. Intriguingly, the debt to anime that *The Matrix* trilogy owes is all the more evident in the anthology of animated shorts, *The Animatrix*.

Indeed, this hunger for something other than cel animation indicates an increasing diversity of animation being made available. Japanese line drawings inspired not just Van Gogh but Hergé's *Tintin* too. In the late 1980s, Europe and America were alerted to the sophistication of Japanese feature animation and Britain's Aardman Animation was beginning to reach audiences and gain recognition for its stop-motion work. In 2002, Texas-based filmmaker Richard Linklater directed *Waking Life* which used a form of animation laid over live-action images to play up the sense of a lucid dream unfolding. There are many other examples of the real and the animated coming together in movie-making harmony.

Animation is typically sold as entertainment. For film writer Richard Dyer entertainment proposes a kind of Utopia which shows the audience something better that our everyday life cannot offer. It shows harmony and abundance. Hence the Hollywood narrative system that underpins so much animation is perfectly suited to it with its high production values, brio and optimism.

From *Snow White* (1937) through to *Shrek* (2001), community and recognising one's place in the world are key concerns that make the fantasy scenarios all the more appealing. Perhaps it is no coincidence that animation's affinity for romance and the nostalgic developed at a time when the modern world, the mechanical world (through which cinema was born) seemed so brutal.

* * *

The animation of the 1930s and 1940s, which largely established an expectation of what the form could be, has been criticised for sustaining stereotypes about gender and the idea of otherness being represented through physical and behavioural tics. There is also the notion that the female form has always been idealised so that from Betty Boop to Jessica Rabbit to all the female figures of anime, they are showgirls to be ogled by men. A 1987 British animated short flips the notion of looking in the animated short *Girl's Night Out* (Joanna Quinn) about a group of women who have headed out for a male strip show.

Animation, then, is not solely the province of fantasy and adventure derived from a comic-strip way of imagining the world. Animation works on its own merits and conventions, as legitimate a medium as live-action cinema. Animation in the short form especially has a liberty to explore and express thoughts and issues that larger-scale films might struggle to handle. Take for example the 2003 Channel 4 series *Animated Minds* or the short film *A is for Autism*, which is narrated by people with autism while images and sequences they have drawn illustrate the kinds of issues autism presents. A visual form makes a very complex psychology somehow understandable in its essentials. Again, that sense of free association that animation has so finely developed is what makes the material work.

In 1992 a collection of animated films was released through the British Film Institute called *Wayward Girls and Wicked Women*, a collection of animated shorts by female directors. It included films such as *The Stain* (Marjut Rimminen and Christine Roche, 1991) and *Daddy's Little Bit of Dresden China* (Karen Watson, 1988), films that both explore incest and abuse. For Jeanette Winterson, writing about this compilation, animation in its broadest application 'is closer to dance in its human delineation. It offers emotion freed from individual association, and yet is not abstract'.

Like humour, animation (which is often humorous) allows for audiences to engage with an otherwise difficult subject. In the early years of the twenty-first century, animation remains immensely popular with audiences finding more opportunities to view a range of styles. A recent hit has been the virtually dialogue-free *Belleville Rendezvous* directed by Sylvain Chomet in which an orphan boy named Champion enters the Tour de France only to be kidnapped by the French Mafia and then rescued by his grandmother and his faithful dog Bruno.

In Canada, the National Film Board of Canada encouraged innovative approaches to animation and this has yielded a treasury of intriguing animation such as *The Street* (Caroline Leaf, 1976) an adaptation of a Mordecai Richler story in which a boy watches his sick grandma eventually die. Other films supported by the National Film Board were *Pas de Deux* (Norman McLaren, 1967), *Top Priority* (Ishu Patel, 1981), *Getting Started* (Richard Condie, 1983), *The Wind* (Ron Travis, 1975). Indeed, it was a Canadian who directed *Yellow Submarine* (1968).

Commercials and music videos have fuelled an appreciation of animation and often their handsome budgets have resourced very vivid pieces of work. The music promo for the Peter Gabriel track *Sledgehammer* is often held up as an enduring example. Directed by Steve R Johnstone, the video placed Gabriel in a range of fantastic scenarios that were created by different teams of animators. This was a collaboration between Aardman Animation, David Anderson and The Brothers Quay, who were responsible for the sequence of Gabriel surrounded by fruit and vegetables for the Fruit Cake sequence. Aardman handled the stop motion of Gabriel hitting himself with hammers. The promo also included pixilation, so that Gabriel had to strike a range of poses round which furniture was moved incrementally. This pixilation approach has also been used to eerie effect in Dave Borthwick's film *The Secret Adventures of Tom Thumb* (1993). Norman McLaren's Cold War allegory, *Neighbours*, also uses this device.

There are countless examples of animation's affinity for symbolism and allegory. In France, animation director and figurehead Paul Grimault adapted Hans Christian Andersen's fairy tale *The Shepherdess and the Chimney Sweep* into an animated feature called *Le Roi et l'Oiseau* (*The King and the Bird*, 1979) which functioned as a satire on contemporary fascism and tyranny.

Walt Disney, a filmmaker who built his legacy on animation, once said of modern society that it had 'lost the sense of play . . .' and that man 'is the victim of a civilization whose ideal is the unbotherable, poker-faced man and the attractive, unruffled woman. They call it poise.' Animation animates the audience's weary, humdrum life. Isn't one of the main responses people have to animation laughter?

Images of the impossible have been central to human visual expression since the beginning of time. Myths, legends, fairy tales and other more ancient artworks are all imbued with images of monsters, halflings, gods, goddesses and fabulous landscapes that map the human soul.

It is one of the joys of cinema that the fairy tale and stories of legend have been so readily appropriated by animation. To borrow from Paul Klee, animation allows the filmmaker to take a line for a very emotive and motion varied walk.

By the mid twentieth century, cinema was seen as a key way of socialising children, and animation played a significant part in this process. In the West, film has heavily influenced people's sense and reception of fairy tales. Certainly, the films of Walt Disney have led the way in this. Feature-length stories either adapting or drawing heavily on fairy-tale forms will inevitably flesh out and detail the source material, which tended to be fairly concise, to meet the running time demands of a feature-length format.

For some, film versions of fairy tales dilute the original material and their form. Alternatively, it is seen as valuable that fairy tales have been picked up by film, allowing the medium to reconfigure the stories for a particular era and culture. The animation tradition has, ultimately, been a part of cinema since its earliest days, pre-dating colour and sound.

The word animation is tightly bound to notions of the miraculous, of breathing life into something lifeless. Richard Thompson notes in his vivid essay *Meep Meep* ' . . . American animation like American comic strips, was full of weird, twisted, surreal versions of the world, impossible to capture with real life photography. It was powered by glorious primitivism, unlike the increasingly sophisticated live-action film.'

The best animation is always absolutely true to its promise of giving a soul to the inanimate and this is why the animated feature format is so well suited to tales of the fantastic. In a society so romanced by new technology and gadgetry, animation is perfectly in synch with this mindset. From its earliest days, animation has embraced new technology; what seem like gimmicks initially, often become legitimate conventions and styles.

From the multiplane camera of the Disney studio to the ever more fluid realities of computer animation, the medium retains a welcome spirit of playfulness and real invention and there remains a punkish strain too. Indeed this quality has always been part of animation.

Legendary American writer L Frank Baum, author of *The Wonderful Wizard of Oz*, believed that daydreams would make the world a better place: 'The imaginative child will become the imaginative man or woman most apt to create, to invent and therefore foster civilization. A prominent educator tells me that fairy tales are of untold value in developing imagination in the young.'

Animation re-imagines the world and revives the sense of wonder that the eyes of a child see the world with. In doing so, animation moves as a miracle.

How To Use This Book

Animated Films points the way towards some of the best examples of the form, the most arresting, fun and accessible. It is not, however, comprehensive.

This book focuses on individual films, typically within the context of a larger body of work. As such the book is divided into parts within which are the film-by-film chapters. This allows for a more thematic than chronological approach. This book cannot claim to be encyclopaedic in any sense – the field of animation is vast. However, the intention is to spotlight the most familiar and accessible and available examples and the hope is that in turn these may lead to other connections with other animation forms, some of which are mentioned and referenced through this book.

Each film is explored according to the following headings, most of which are self-explanatory:

Title of the Film (Year)

Production crew

BUDGET

BOX OFFICE

RELEASE DATE

CERTIFICATE

CAST/VOICES

TAGLINE

STORYLINE

THE DRAWING BOARD: outlining the concept and development of the project

INSPIRATIONS

TOON TEAM: detailing the crew and collaborators involved

VOCAL TALENT: a look at the actors voicing the characters

INK, PAINT AND HARD WORK: detailing the production process

THEME: the key ideas at work in the film

STYLISH TOONS: a consideration of stylistic and special-effects devices that enhance a given film

CHARACTER SKETCH: a look at the development of characters through the films

TOON TUNES: the music and songs featuring in each film

TOON TALK: memorable quotes from each film

OTHER SIMILAR FILMS: films in the same spirit as the one discussed

RECOGNITION: review excerpts

AWARDS

HOME VIEWING: where relevant, each film's availability on VHS and DVD formats

COMMENT: usually from a core creative about the film

VERDICT: how the film shapes up

The book is divided into the following segments, each looking at a particular genre of animation:

The Disney Effect and Classical Animation: a look at a selection of acknowledged Disney studio animated features that developed the form of classical (or full) animation whereby the animation reproduced a sense of realistic movement, expression and gesture, typically within fantasy storylines.

Stop-motion Miracles: a look at some of the figureheads of stop-motion animation and also an exploration of two stop-motion movies by director Henry Selick: *The Nightmare Before Christmas* and *James and the Giant Peach*.

Britoons: an overview of the British animation tradition in features with a focus on the achievements of *Watership Down* and *Chicken Run*.

Japanimation: a consideration of anime, which has long been popular and recognised for its seriousness and willingness to engage with mature social and emotional issues often through vividly designed and animated fantasy and science-fiction worlds. *Akira, Ghost in the Shell* and *Princess Mononoke* are discussed.

Pix and Mix: live action and animation have been friends for many years. The Disney Studio's version of *Mary Poppins* integrated the forms to great effect and the film *Who Framed Roger Rabbit?* continues to stand as the high-water mark for the combination of live action and classical animation.

The Digital Toon: computer animation is currently enjoying great popularity and this chapter charts the development of the form. It explores the integration of computer animation in live-action visual-effects films and also showcases *Star Wars: Episode 1 – The Phantom Menace* for its digital character animation. The chapter zeroes in on the films of industry leader Pixar with three examples of their work and a consideration of the first computer-animated feature to win an Oscar, *Shrek*.

Mavericks: animation has always had its experimenters. Several other less widely known animators are acknowledged in terms of their contributions to animation through their commitment to creative independence.

Appendices:

Two Classically Animated Pieces: *The Lion King* and *The Prince of Egypt*
  Animated Shorts: no book on feature-length animation could ignore the influence and place of the short form and this segment covers the

ANIMATED FILMS How To Use This Book

work of animators such as Tex Avery, Chuck Jones and a range of others.

Animating the Future: a look at what animated features are yet to come.

Index of Quotations

Bibliography

Web Resources

The Disney Effect and Classical Animation

Walt Disney is one of the most significant popular culture figures of all time, both as an artist and as a movie-making industrialist. He has been held up as the perfect example of the American dream whereby hard work yields success. His films might be said to typify this outlook too. In the same breath, though, his storytelling impulse has been criticised for homogenising the fairy-tale narratives his studio adapted into features beginning in 1937 with *Snow White and the Seven Dwarfs*. What is most undeniable is his personal advancement of the medium of classical or full animation in which drawn characters are animated against usually realistic backgrounds using ink and paint. It is perhaps the form of animation that is closest to the tradition of the picture book and certainly the illustrated fairy tale.

In 2003, the Disney name is synonymous with family-orientated entertainment and a range of animated characters immediately come to mind who have been part of the pop culture treasure trove since the 1930s. The roll call is amazing: Mickey Mouse, Minnie Mouse, Donald Duck, Goofy, Pluto, Jiminy Cricket, Dumbo, Bernard and Bianca, Ariel the Little Mermaid and Simba the Lion King to name a few.

In adapting fairy tales and previously existing stories, Disney (both the man and the collective effort of his titular studio) reframed them in the public's imagination to the point where they have come to be thought of as definitive. If one were to read the original *Pinocchio* story or the original *Snow White* tale recorded from the European oral tradition by Jacob and Wilhelm Grimm, the differences in action and tone would astonish.

Walter Elias Disney was born in 1901 and spent the first few years of his life on a farm in Marceline, Missouri where he must have developed his affinity for animals. It was an interest that went on to fuel so much of his creative legacy. The first piece of illustration he was paid for was a sketch of a horse. Combine this with Disney's love of the writings of the great Mark Twain, particularly his novel *Huckleberry Finn*, and also the work of writers like Walter Scott, and one can easily see how Disney's narrative inclinations were shaped. In turn, Disney's influence on popular culture has been immense.

As a young man, Walt served as an ambulance driver on the battlefields of World War One. Surely this exposure to the horrors of war and the worst of human endeavour compelled him to commit to films about gentility and a sense of hope that certainly suited a twentieth century scarred by conflict. In 1919, back home from the war, Disney went to work in Kansas City as an artist.

At The Kansas City Film Ad Company, which remarkably also was the start for Carl Stalling, Ub Iwerks, Hugh Harman and Rudy Ising (who became Warner Brothers' first animators) and Fritz Freleng, the young Disney met his vital early collaborator Ubbe (Ub) Iwerks, the animator and pragmatist who would bring so many of Walt's visions to life alongside the financially acute energies of Walt's brother, Roy.

Iwerks and Disney regularly took guidance from a book called *Animated Cartoons: How They Are Made, Their Origins and Development* by Edwin G Lutz. Disney soon established his own company called *Laugh O Grams* who produced animated shorts such as *Little Red Riding Hood* (1922) and the *Four Musicians of Bremen* (1922). The studio was short lived with film production increasingly based in Los Angeles, and, in 1923, Walt and his brother, Roy, who ran the financial side of their business, moved to Los Angeles and began a studio there producing cartoons for screenings in cinemas.

The Disney Brothers Studio became successful and a crucial moment was their production of the highly successful *Alice in Cartoonland* series, which combined live action (Alice) and animation. The series ran to 56 episodes and when the series ended a new character had to be found that a series could be built around to sustain the studio's productivity. Walt conjured up a little fellow called Oswald the Lucky Rabbit – Disney's first successful animated character. Between 1927 and 1928, Oswald starred in 26 films and was the first Disney character to be merchandised. Trouble loomed however, though like so much bad luck it led only to something better.

When Walt would not agree to a cut in the budget for the Oswald shorts, the distributor sold the character to another studio. The problem for Walt was that he did not own the copyright on the character and so, as before, he had to devise a new character. Necessity beautifully proved itself the mother of invention. The new character Walt created was called Mortimer Mouse. His wife didn't care for the name Mortimer and suggested Mickey, and a film icon was born. Walt defined Mickey's character but it was Ub Iwerks who gave the mouse his visual appearance and animated him.

Mickey Mouse proved instantly popular with his cheery energy. The third Mickey Mouse short, *Steamboat Willie*, released on 18 November 1928, was the first animated short with synchronous sound. The visual humour that had driven the short form was now complemented by the role of humour through sound. Huge amounts of ink and thought were expended on understanding the charm and appeal of Mickey Mouse, whom Walt Disney seemed to care about as though he were a real being.

In the early Mickey Mouse shorts it was Walt himself who provided Mickey's voice. Over the years Mickey came to look younger and younger, ultimately resembling a cheery young child. Studies have revealed that a juvenile body form sparks warm parental feelings in the observer or audience. A psychoanalyst named Fritz Moellenhoff even wrote an article called 'Remarks on the Popularity of Mickey Mouse' for the psychoanalytic journal, *American Imago*, in 1940. Apocryphal or not, such was Disney's affinity for Mickey that when he heard an animator call Mickey a four-letter name, Disney fired him on the spot.

Ub Iwerks was vital to these early years' successes. Disney was a competent illustrator but his real strength emerged in shaping stories and generating concepts and overseeing production. He was the ultimate producer. Critical to Disney's sense of story was the creation of viable character with whom the audience must connect. Famously he stated that, 'Until a character becomes a personality it cannot be believed ... and without personality, a story cannot ring true to the audience.'

In 1929, the Disney studio embarked on a new venture, suggested by the studio's musical director, Carl Stalling. (Stalling would go on to become a legend of animated shorts, scoring many Warner Brothers shorts with strident pianos and often thunderous orchestral accompaniment. A CD was released in the early 1990s called *The Carl Stalling Project*.) *The Silly Symphonies,* as they were titled, were amusing shorts with new characters each time around, whose exploits were based around a piece of music – a concept Disney would expand on hugely with *Fantasia* (1940). *The Skeleton Dance* (1929) was a landmark *Silly Symphony* and the series as a whole served as a real test bed for many techniques that would make their way into the features.

Indeed, Disney's first fairy-tale adaptation was a *Silly Symphony* title, *Babes in the Woods* (1932). Seventy-five *Silly Symphonies* were made between 1929 and 1939 and nearly every year they won the Best Cartoon Academy Award; the first of which went to *Flowers and Trees*. So familiar are these flowers and trees that they even make up much of the pastoral landscape on the edge of Toon town in *Who Framed Roger Rabbit?*

On the back of this great artistic and commercial success, Disney knew he had to expand the ambition of the studio. The move to features was imminent. To quote the man himself he was ever eager to 'get to the future'.

Unsurprisingly, Walt's ambitions were not always aligned with a financial pragmatism. That was provided by his brother Roy. In 1933, Disney achieved an artistic apotheosis with *The Three Little Pigs* short which was regarded as a Depression era allegory, and which won an Academy Award for the Best Short Subject.

As technology improved and the Disney operation expanded, Disney produced the classic short *The Old Mill* (1937), famous for its use of the multiplane camera (designed by the head of the Disney Camera Department William Garity and built by Roger Broggie). It was an upright 'rack' of several horizontal planes on to which backgrounds and pieces of animation could be laid, that allowed for foreground, midground and background layers, adding a sense of spatial realism.

In 1934 Disney had taken the leap of faith and began work on the first animated feature, *Snow White and the Seven Dwarfs*. He was not the only producer to move into this arena. The Fleischer Studio, a major competitor through the 1920s and 1930s released *Gulliver's Travels* in 1939. Though it was popular in America, World War Two minimised its impact overseas.

In November 1933, the Disney studio was more aware than ever that its cute characters from the shorts had become massively popular and the challenge now was to see if they could master human characters and animation in a longer form. By the mid-1930s, Mickey Mouse merchandising was vital to covering studio costs and it allowed the Disney narrative to become increasingly ingrained in the American and eventually global imagination and cinematic genetic code.

Disney is often cited negatively as narrowing an audience's sense of what a fairy tale can be. Disney followed in the tradition of American fairy-tale writer Howard Pyle, investing his fanciful stories with a dose of American common sense.

In Disney's films magic is often explained as being a mechanical process, demystifying royalty, emphasising the age gap between children and parents. Disney's fairy-tale heroines are seen as liking housework and giving care which is certainly what Snow White does when she goes on the run from the Queen. Cleaning pots and pans and baking pies is more important it seems than looking out for the most sinister force in the forest.

Ever since *The Little Mermaid*, the gently rebellious heroine is domesticated by love in the Disney-animated feature. Disney heroes search for happiness and accept responsibility. To quote from the *Oxford Companion to Fairy Tales*, the Disney version of the fairy-tale idiom tends to focus on 'the privilege of innocence, the valorisation of sentiment . . . a jovial disdain for ugliness or deformity, and a luxuriant, infantilising celebration of the cute.'

Inevitably, there were countless projects that the well-resourced Disney studio developed but never came to fully realise often, it would seem, because of creative uncertainties and concomitant concerns about popular appeal. An entire book has been dedicated to this aspect of the studio and is titled *The Disney That Never Was: The Art of Five Decades of Unproduced Animation*.

Several intriguing projects that never went beyond conceptual art were adaptations of *Don Quixote* by Miguel Cervantes, *The Three Bears* and also adaptations of Hans Christian Andersen's tales for a biopic of the brilliant man. There was also *Chanticleer* and a project called *On the Trail* that would have focused on a Native American shepherd boy and his donkey in the deserts and canyons of the American southwest. One of the only female animators at the studio was Retta Scott and the project was hers as her beautiful concept art (of a little boy and his donkey against red rock and under blue skies) testifies.

Perhaps the most intriguing project that time and energy was spent on was an adaptation of Longfellow's epic American poem *The Song of Hiawatha*. This was a particular obsession of Walt Disney's and he saw in it some parallel with the Christ story. The adaptation introduced a villain into the narrative but ultimately the decision was made to abandon the project as it was considered not only too complex to animate so many human characters but also too heavy for the mass audience. It anticipates a similar sense around *The Lion King* during its development phase when there was concern the film was not light enough.

Of course, one pioneer builds on the achievements of their predecessors. In the decade before Disney really broke through, his 'soulmate' Winsor McCay was busy creating his fantastic comic-strip tales *Little Nemo in Slumberland* and *Gertie the Dinosaur*. In 1934, when Disney commenced work on *Snow White and the Seven Dwarfs*, Winsor McCay died and his spirit passed the torch of innovation and fantasy to the man from Missouri who openly claimed that 'I love the nostalgic myself. I hope we never lose some of the things of the past.'

Snow White and the Seven Dwarfs (1937)

(83 minutes)

Produced by Walt Disney
Screenplay by Ted Sears, Otto Englander, Earl Hurd, Dorothy Ann Blank, Richard Creedon, Dick Richard, Merrill de Marais, Webb Smith
Supervising Director: David Hand
Sequence Directors: Pierce Pearce, Larry Morey, William Cottrell, Wilfred Jackson, Ben Sharpsteen
Art Direction: Charles Philippi, Hugh Gennesy, Terrell Stap, McLaren Stewart, Harold Miles, Tom Codrick, Gustaf Tenngren, Kenneth Anderson, Kendall O'Connor, Hazel Sewell
Music: Frank Churchill, Leigh Harline, Paul Smith, Larry Morey
Character Designers: Albert Hunter, Joe Grant
Supervising Animators: Hamilton Luske, Vladimir Tytla, Fred Moore, Norman Ferguson
Animators: Frank Thomas, Dick Lundy, Arthur Babbitt, Eric Larson, Milton Kahl, Robert Stokes, James Algar, Al Engster, Cy Young, Joshua Meador, Ugo D'Orsi, George Rowley, Les Clark, Fred Spencer, Bill Roberts, Bernard Garbutt, Grim Natwick, Jack Campbell, Marvin Woodward, James Cullhane, Stan Quakenbush, Ward Kimball, Wolfgang Reitherman, Robert Martsch
Backgrounds: Samuel Armstrong, Mique Nelson, Merle Cox, Claude Coats, Phil Dike, Ray Lockrem, Maurice Noble
Produced at Walt Disney Studios

BUDGET: $480,000

BOX OFFICE: $8 million

RELEASE DATE: 21 December 1937 (general release 4 February 1938). Re-released 1943, 1952, 1958, 1967, 1975 and 1983

CERTIFICATE: U/G

VOICES: Adriana Caselotti (*Snow White*), Harry Stockwell (*Prince Charming*), Luolle La Vegne (*The Queen*), Moroni Olsen (*Magic Mirror*), Billy Gilbert (*Sneezy*), Pinto Colvig (*Sleepy and Grumpy*), Otis Harlan (*Happy*), Scotty Mattraw (*Bashful*), Roy Atwell (*Doc*), Stuart Buchanan (*Humbert the Queen's Huntsman*), Marion Dalrington (*Bird sounds and warbling*), The Fraunfelder Family (yodelling)

TAGLINE: Still the fairest of them all!

STORYLINE: A live-action image of a white book, inlaid with gold and the impression of the faces of the seven dwarfs folds open to reveal an illuminated manuscript establishing the relationship between the Queen and Snow White. The Queen wants to maintain her position as the most beautiful woman in the land. Her stepdaughter, Snow White, is made to live life as a scullery maid in order to keep her dowdy. Snow White dreams of falling in love with a prince and, sure enough, the Prince shows up and they sing together of their love. The Queen looks on jealously, eventually unable to look at all. She consults her Magic Mirror and it informs her that Snow White is now 'the fairest of them all'. In her anger, the Queen charges her huntsman, Humbert, with the task of killing Snow White. To ensure that he does this she gives him a wooden box into which he must put Snow White's heart as proof of her death.

Snow White is out on the edge of the forest picking flowers, unaware of the Queen's fiendish plan. Humbert watches and then moves in for the kill. As he approaches Snow White he is seized by guilt and a conscience. He cannot bring himself to commit the vile deed and he tells Snow White to flee into the forest so that the Queen will never find her. Snow White runs into the forest and is terrified. She falls asleep in a glade and the forest animals gather around and lead her to safety, showing her a little cottage in a clearing by a stream.

Snow White goes to the cottage, intrigued by who must live there. She sets about cleaning and tidying the home, with the help of the forest creatures. The job done, Snow White takes a nap upstairs on one of the seven beds.

Elsewhere in the forest seven dwarfs are happily at work. They mine diamonds and then seal them in a vault and head home. When they discover Snow White they are terrified and flee. They muster their courage and return to the cottage and soon enough Snow White has shown she is not a threat. Snow White and the dwarfs get along famously, singing and dancing and having a great time. How distant the perilous Queen now seems.

In her castle, the Queen consults the Mirror. She holds the box that Humber has returned and sure enough there is a heart in it. The Mirror informs the Queen it is a pig's heart. Furious, the Queen concocts a potion which transforms her into a hag. She will go and kill Snow White personally.

At the cottage, the Seven Dwarfs head off for work and Snow White stays behind and prepares a pie with the help of the animals. Suddenly, the hag appears at the window and convinces Snow White to eat the bright red apple she has with her. Snow White does so and dies, falling to the hag's feet. The hag flees. The forest animals alert the dwarfs to what has happened and they give chase. They arrive too late to save Snow White and head up into the rocks where the hag has run. The hag is cornered by the dwarfs and she finds she has no escape. With incredible strength she makes to send a boulder in the dwarfs' direction when a lightning bolt intervenes and the hag perishes.

Snow White is laid to rest in a glass coffin. The dwarfs keep vigil all through the winter and in the spring Prince Charming, who has heard of the death of Snow White, arrives at the vigil. He kisses Snow White and she awakens. She and the Prince ride off into the sunset.

THE DRAWING BOARD: *Snow White and the Seven Dwarfs* stands as a landmark in film history, as a technical accomplishment in the development of the animated feature film. Its technical achievements cannot be denied and the film also proved the Disney studio's affinity for the zeitgeist. The film was massively popular. Indeed, the Snow White story has variations worldwide.

By the mid-1930s, Walt Disney had established his studio as the pre-eminent animation producer, its work known worldwide. Recognising the appeal of the animated form, hungry to find new creative trails and with an affinity for fairy-tale traditions, Disney seized upon the widely know tale *Snow White*, as recorded by Jacob and

Wilhelm Grimm in Germany, and used it as the basis for a feature. Disney had a strong recollection of a silent live-action movie version of the story that he had enjoyed as a child in Kansas City. When Disney learnt there was a stage play of the story in copyright he bought the movie rights as a safeguard, having learnt his copyright lesson with the loss of the Oswald the Lucky Rabbit character to his distributor in the 1920s.

The beginnings of the *Snow White* film production have the quality of magic and a fireside story being told. One night in late 1934, Disney handed out some cash to his animators and told them to go and get some dinner and then come back to the studio. After the meal Disney took this team of lead animators on to a stage at the studio and began telling them his plan for a feature-length animated film. He began acting out the *Snow White* story to his mesmerised audience of colleagues. When the project was announced to the rest of the filmmaking community it was lambasted as 'Disney's Folly'. These filmmakers of little faith would be proved very wrong.

The original *Snow White* story explores concepts of origin, jealousy, expulsion, adoption, death and resuscitation; resonant themes that underpin the fancy. Disney expanded and detailed the basic Grimm story and also worked to take away some of the darkness. A small group began work on the project immediately in an office right next to Walt's so that he could monitor progress closely. To develop the necessary quality of their human character animation, Disney commissioned a *Silly Symphony* based on the Greek myth of Persephone. It was called *The Goddess of Spring* and would focus on a human character. The results were not considered as strong as had been hoped but, even though his brother, Roy, felt it was ill-advised, Disney still forged ahead with the *Snow White* project

Early in the film's development, perhaps the most exciting part of any creative endeavour, a key visual effort was contributed by Albert Hurter who supplied countless pencil sketches of key scenes and moments.

In part, the decision to move into producing features was dictated by economics. Although the cartoon shorts were very popular they were never the main theatrical attraction and costs were rising so there was a need to maximise profits.

So successful was the film that the profits from *Snow White* allowed Disney to purchase land in Burnbank and construct a new animation facility.

INSPIRATIONS: For *Snow White*, and indeed key to so many other Disney efforts beyond (and subsequently to other movies inspired by the Disney sensibility), was the influence of the work of the 'fantaissistes', a group of Late Romantic French illustrators from the 1850s. The most famous was Gustav Dore who developed a form of illustration that could compete with the vividly realised theatrical sets for melodramas.

The film is couched in the visual design of picture books and is supposedly set in Europe.

TOON TEAM: Disney pulled together a now-legendary team of animators and artists, many of whom became absolutely fundamental to the Disney animated feature over the next thirty years.

In his dedication to realism and authenticity, Disney even hired Frank Lloyd Wright, the legendary architect (of buildings such as Fallingwater), to lecture the staff on architecture. Artist Don Graham conducted a countrywide search for drawing talent and many artists were drawn from the Chouinard Institute in downtown Los Angeles.

Animators watched as many live-action films as they could and even attended the ballet to attune themselves to the intricacies and beauties of human movement. For the character movement of the seven dwarfs, vaudeville performers were used as references for the animators. This huge effort of accuracy was all in the pursuit of rendering human movement as it had never been seen before. Yes, the seven dwarfs could be a little more 'cartoony' but Snow White must be absolutely realistic in her gestures and stances.

Typically, on an animated feature an animator or a small team of animators are assigned work on a particular character. On *Snow White*, several of the great classic animators were at work. Norm Ferguson animated the Witch and Art Babbit animated the Queen. Norman Ferguson was regarded as especially gifted at broad staging of action. Hamilton Luske was known for his ability to analyse movement. Fred Moore was regarded as the most Disneyesque artist ever – his illustrations were the Disney feel. Animator Marc Davis said, 'Fred Moore *was* Disney drawing!' Finally, Vladimir Tytla was seen as being a genius at expressing emotion. In effect this was something of a Disney dream team.

The film's release was accompanied by a massive merchandising push that served to consolidate the importance of merchandising and built on what the studio had been refining since the early 1930s.

VOCAL TALENT: There was a huge casting call for the voice of Snow White. Unlike today, celebrity actors did not lend their voice skills to the cast, which enriches the story even more as the audience isn't waiting to hear the voice of a famous actor.

INK, PAINT AND HARD WORK: Amazingly, but not surprisingly for what was in many ways a grand experiment of artistry and organisation, the film's final budget was six times the originally proposed figure. The film's budget worked out at $200 per second. (The average short per second worked out at $50–75.)

The film comprised 2 million images of which about 250,000 were finally used.

In wanting to pursue such a vast and untested project, Disney trebled his workforce to 750 staff. There was even a special-effects crew dedicated to details such as lighting and other environmental illusions.

Inevitably, animation has a tendency to engage with new kinds of processes and *Snow White* was no exception. Unlike short animated pieces, the size of the painted cels (field size) had to be enlarged to contain more detail and as a result drawing boards were resized and animation cameras adjusted to photograph the larger image.

Disney had produced a short called *The Old Windmill* and it was notable for its use of the multiplane camera (see **The Disney Effect**). On *Snow White* the multiplane camera was used extensively. It was fourteen feet tall and had seven different levels, all of which were independently controlled.

The subtlety of the artwork on *Snow White* extended to tinting Snow White's pale face with rouge and applying a delicate airbrush technique to her black hair so as to soften its contrast with her skin.

Certain proposed sequences were cut, such as a scene where Snow White and the Prince dance in the clouds as she sings *Some Day My Prince Will Come*. A key scene where the Seven Dwarfs build Snow White a bed was also cut, a move which seemed unpopular with some of the animators, such as Ward Kimball who was on the verge of leaving. Walt reeled him back in with the offer to develop Jiminy Cricket for *Pinocchio*.

As his staff of animators worked away, one of Walt's tasks was to ensure the financing for the project continued. As they required a loan, the man who handled Disney business at the Bank of America came for an in progress screening. Some of the film was completed but rough storyboards remained in place and Walt narrated the story as necessary.

The man from the bank, Joseph Rosenberg, said nothing all through the screening. As he left to get in his car he told Disney the film would make a huge amount of money.

THEME: *Snow White and the Seven Dwarfs* dramatises classic fairy-tale concerns but it is also notable for a highly American take on the tradition. Disney, with this film, began, consciously or otherwise, to make his name synonymous with ancient European tales to the point where audiences might not even be aware of their origins beyond an animation studio in California.

In Norman Klein's fascinating study of the American cartoon, he pauses to consider *Snow White and the Seven Dwarfs*, noting that 'Walt was convinced, as if driven by a Kantian imperative, that he could feel what a true faerie interior needed.' Klein also talks about ' a Disney brand of architectural fantasy' present in Snow White that endured to form the basis for the Disneyland concept.

Disney's commitment to gentler, kinder emotions shines through in this film. This is a very pantheistic film that to some degree expresses Disney's fondness for the rural life of his childhood.

The film has a moral imperative: jealousy, anger and the pursuit of selfishness and disharmony can be people's undoing. True love and the spirit of community are presented as positive ways of behaving.

For all its eventual success the film was regarded as a retrograde step by some in its presentation and adaptation of a fairy tale. Disney's story emphasised true love – Snow White falls in love with the Prince before she ever sees him. Part of Disney's adaptation of the source material was that in the film version the evil stepmother falls to her death rather than being made to dance in painfully hot shoes at her stepdaughter's wedding as in the original text.

The film was significant in animation terms as it was the first time human beings had been represented so realistically.

STYLISH TOONS: The most obvious aspect of the overall design of *Snow White* is that it was in colour and made at a time when most features were still being made in black and white. It was not until *The Wizard of Oz* (Victor Fleming, 1939) and *Gone with the Wind* (Victor Fleming, 1939) were released that colour features really began to be part of Hollywood production. These two features were particularly lavishly produced pieces and the 1940s remained centred on black and white production.

In terms of its colour, *Snow White and the Seven Dwarfs* works from a restrained palette of soft browns and greens that feeds into a picture book sensibility. Certainly there are vivid colours involved in the film but they tend to be associated with the characters and key 'props', notably the bright red apple that the hag presents Snow White with.

The detail of the gorgeous watercolour backgrounds is a highlight of the film. Notice the owl face carvings on the end of each step in the cottage and the rabbits carved on the piano.

The colour of each dwarf's costume goes some way to expressing his temperament. The Queen dresses regally but her surroundings are bleak and cold and the chamber in which she conjures her potion of transformation is dark, lit only by candles.

Right across the film a great deal of attention was paid to creating a sense of texture in the castle, forest and cottage. One of the outstanding elements of the creation of environments is in the film's realisation of streams and rivers, which add to the prevailing tone of a pastoral dreamworld that the Queen threatens. When she transforms herself into a hag, she moves through mist, darkness and marshland to reach the bright and pristine forest glade where the sun always shines.

Details of texture were also applied to the costumes of the characters – for instance, a satin look was created for the Queen's collar. The look of velvet was given to her robe. For Snow White, the artists worked hard to give her dress the look of linen, while for the dwarfs a sense of their rounded bodies is achieved by rim shading so that the flesh tones are a little darker. Just check their cheeks and noses for this effect.

Fifty-one years later in *Who Framed Roger Rabbit?* this process of shading animated characters to boost their three-dimensional sense was vital for the illusion of integrating them into the live action. Even the poster and print advertising for animation of this kind never fails to include shading on characters to suggest something more corporeal.

Snow White took three years to make and was committed to a realist aesthetic. Walt even had a menagerie installed at the studio so that the animators could have real references for the forest animals and horses.

For the scene where the Huntsman goes to kill Snow White, the artists experimented to see how a man's shadow would fall at three o'clock in the afternoon. These details of realism were also part of the sound recording effort. For the scene where Grumpy falls into the stream after Snow White kisses him, a sound effects staffer sloshed around in a muddy bath for just the right sound. And for a scene where the dwarfs wash, the sound recordists indeed washed their faces and splashed water around for the right effect.

In terms of visual interest and dramatic involvement, an especially tough scene to animate had been the moment of the Queen's transformation into a hag. It was not so much her facial character change that was the challenge but the determination of what spectral forces would be shown accompanying her transformation. Certainly it is an intense moment that matches the intensity of Snow White's terror on entering the forest.

For all their association with happy-go-lucky action, the Disney animators were very adept at creating moments of real terror and sinister action. The 'Pink Elephants on Parade' song in *Dumbo*, prompted by Timothy Mouse and Dumbo's drunken stupor, is at points filled with frightening images.

Another storytelling challenge was to make as dynamic and emotionally intense as possible the moment when the Huntsman goes to kill Snow White. Disney encouraged the animators to draw on a montage technique to build tension. Even the detail of a shot highlighting the sun flashing on the Huntsman's blade contributed much.

For all the kinetic energy that is associated with animation it is sometimes, as in life itself, the moments of real stillness that are most potent. When the dwarfs kneel around Snow White's deathbed they barely move, yet the audience registers their grief and collective sorrow as much as their happiness in their endless movement and jollity during the time spent getting to know her. The film is brimming with witty visuals such as the crow's eyes peering out at the Queen through the skull's eye socket and the action with the Seven Dwarfs is packed with sight gags. Though a feature film, it still has much of its heart in the spirit of the short form.

Although the film draws the audience right into the drama, it is worth remembering that the film was also an experiment of sorts and a dazzlingly stylish display of what the Disney studio could produce. It advertised its human and hardware resources to the world. Just consider the opening scene where the Queen consults the Magic Mirror, which must have been really arresting to the 1937 audience with its multiplane camera shot of the castle and then the flames and effects accompanying the Magic Mirror.

An especially showy shot is that where the camera apparently looks up at Snow White from inside the well, through very realistic-looking water. The film's water effects are among its most effective flourishes. Just look at the fluidity of the stream as Snow White walks along picking flowers.

The studio's multiplane camera gets a lot of use throughout the film. At points in the film, foreground elements are thrown out of focus so that the audience can concentrate solely on a background action, such as a deer on the riverbank. The film also plays up its ability to convey atmospheric effects such as mist and moonlight. The scene when Snow White gets lost in the forest uses more abstract images such as big eyes looming at her in the darkness in a way that nicely breaks the overriding style of the film with its fast cuts and gauche colour scheme.

Less spectacular than the more obvious fantasy moments is the detail of human gesture mimicked in animation. Look at the scene where Snow White first appears, singing at the well, surrounded by attentive doves. The film is as confident in animating broad, vaudevillian humour (such as the brilliant Yodel Song scene) as it is the subtlety of Snow White's fingers tapping on the stone of the well, for example.

Foreground elements help enrich the action all through the story with atmospheric details. When the Queen descends to make her potion, rats scurry and watch her. When Snow White goes into the forest for the first time, the camera pans to follow as though behind the trees.

Enhancing the gentle, cosy feeling of the cottage, on a couple of occasions a scene ends with an exterior view of the cottage, the camera widening out as the soundtrack becomes very quiet.

The gentle pace of the film is interrupted at the climax in a fast-paced, quick-cut chase as the dwarfs race to capture the hag. The scene is enhanced by the storm.

For its climax the film follows the tradition laid down by silent film director, DW Griffith, by intercutting two pieces of simultaneous action for an effective and tense climax. Sound and image are of equal value in achieving the right effect. The film cuts back and forth between the dwarfs and animals noisily charging to Snow White's rescue and the silence of the cottage as Snow White is about to perish. The moment when Snow White dies is effectively handled by a shot of just her hand on the floor beside the apple with a bite taken out of it. Less is more in a film awash with visual spectacle and detail.

CHARACTER SKETCH: *Snow White and the Seven Dwarfs* confidently fuses the more obvious caricature characters from Disney's shorts in the often affecting dwarfs with the more subtle and realistic human characters.

Snow White began as a blonde. She is a classic American character at home with the natural world and well attuned to it, ably communicating with the animals. Grim Natwick, an animator on the film, commented that 'They didn't want her to look like a princess really. They wanted her to look like a cute little girl who could be a princess . . .' Snow White is a character who lives in harmony with everything around her, beginning with the doves, then the animals of the forest, then the dwarfs and finally the Prince.

Inevitably, the seven dwarfs remain the film's most memorable characters. In effect, the dwarfs are divided into major and minor players. The key dwarfs are Doc, Dopey and Grumpy. The 'minor' dwarfs are Happy, Sleepy, Sneezy and Bashful. Typically, character development saw different names come and go. Other names considered were Wheezy, Puffy, Stuffy, Biggo, Ego and Burpy, Jumpy, Baldy, Nifty. One name, Deefy, was axed immediately by Disney himself. Deefy was to have been a dwarf with hearing difficulties. Disney felt it was offensive to deaf people.

Originally, Dopey was not so merry, but something of an imbecile. The character of Grumpy was initially too tough and hard and so was softened slightly, though his aggressively crossed arms and arched eyebrows remind us of his wariness around women.

The figure of the Prince is not especially well rounded or memorable. He is really there simply as an archetype, serving a function. He is the only characterless character in the film. The Queen's crow has more personality.

Many critics praised Disney and his team for capturing the folkloric sense of these characters and giving them identities. Amusingly, the dwarfs, though inspired by European folklore, are very American in their expressions and language.

Such was the popularity of the dwarfs that they appeared in a few animated shorts in the form of information films to help the war effort. *The Standard Parade* (1939) showed them parading with other recognisable Disney characters. The Seven Wise Dwarfs, made for Canada, showed the dwarfs taking their hard-dug diamonds and investing them in war savings. Only Dopey is ill-informed enough to take the diamonds to the bank where he makes a loss. *All Together* (1942) was made for the National Film Board of Canada and the short encouraged people to invest in war savings bonds. A final short called *The Winged Scourge* (1943) featured the dwarfs.

The forest animals are all given personalities too, which really comes out during the 'Whistle While You Work' sequence. The squirrels make especially effective dish driers.

Walt Disney's description of the Witch was that she was a 'mixture of Lady Macbeth and the Big Bad Wolf'. It is very clearly her jealousy at the love of Snow White and the Prince that propels her evil and so her monstrousness is rooted in an emotion that is very believable. The Queen is very beautiful. The audience is also made to feel for her momentarily. When the Mirror tells her she is no longer the fairest of them all, the Queen's initial momentary reaction is a look of sadness, soon overtaken by anger. The Queen's rich, dark clothes contrast with the lighter costumes of the other characters.

When the old hag first appears she addresses the camera directly, unsettling the audience but making them complicit with her plan. When she arrives at the cottage she addresses the camera directly again, this time as she talks to Snow White through the window. Subtly, the audience is put in Snow White's position, confronted by this terrifying woman. A panning shot from Snow White at her window over to the Queen angrily and jealously looking down at her unites their conflict.

TOON TUNES: The film's opening credits begin with an orchestral fanfare and choir (this is an important movie, after all). The film contains several songs that have become globally known as part of popular culture. There is Snow White's winsome 'Some Day My Prince Will Come' and also 'Heigh Ho, Heigh Ho' and 'Whistle While You Work'. The Dwarfs' 'Yodel Song' is a comic highlight of the film as each dwarf plays an instrument. Dopey puts Charlie Watts to shame on the drums and Doc plucks a guitar so well, the Carter family would be astonished. Amusingly, the scene is far more American country than anything else.

The film's orchestral score moves easily between playful pieces and far more intense music, such as that accompanying the chase of the hag at the end.

Soundtrack listing: 'Overture', 'Magic Mirror', 'I'm Wishing / One Song', 'Queen Theme', 'Far into the Forest', 'Animal Friends / With a Smile and a Song', 'Just Like a Doll's House', 'Whistle While You Work', 'Heigh-Ho', 'Let's See What's Upstairs', 'There's Trouble A-Brewin', 'It's a Girl', 'Hooray! She Stays', 'Bluddle Uddle Um Dum', 'I've Been Tricked', 'Dwarfs Yodel Song', 'Some Day My Prince Will Come', 'Pleasant Dreams', 'Special Sort of Death', 'Why Grumpy You Do Care', 'Making Pies', 'Have a Bite', 'Chorale for Snow White', 'Love's First Kiss', 'You're Never Too Old To Be Young'.

TOON TALK:

The Dwarfs (in times of stress, such as when they come home from a hard day at work and see that someone is in the cottage): 'Jiminy Crickets!'

The Mirror to the Queen: 'Alas, she is more fair than thee.'

Doc: 'The whole place is clean.'
Grumpy: 'There's dirty work afoot.'

Queen/Hag: 'One bite and all your dreams come true.'

OTHER SIMILAR FILMS: *Snow White* of course opened up the new frontier of the fairy tale and children's story as a ripe source for animated features. Disney went on to adapt *Pinocchio, Dumbo, Bambi, Sleeping Beauty, Cinderella, Alice in Wonderland, Peter Pan, Beauty and the Beast, The Jungle Book, The Rescuers*, and *Aladdin*.

The realism of movement in *Snow White* laid a foundation for subsequent Disney studio animation that was then taken up by countless animated features in the years that followed.

For the Disney studio, its great classical animation experiment *Fantasia* (1940) combined subtly animated sequences based around pieces of classical music.

Leaping across the Pacific Ocean from California to Japan, check out the work of Hayao Miyazaki, a premiere fabulist working in the classical animation form. His films *Princess Mononoke* and *Spirited Away* are all-out fantasies with very human concerns at their heart.

RECOGNITION: 'The greatest moving picture ever made,' announced Westbrook Pegler of the *New York World Telegram*, while Frank Nugent of the *New York Times* agreed, saying 'If you miss *Snow White and the Seven Dwarfs* you'll be missing the ten best pictures of 1938.' The film received other good reviews, such as 'Motion picture miracle' stated the *LA Times*; 'A generally cute fantasy for American kids . . . Disney's adoption of Expressionist visual devices makes for genuinely powerful drama' stated *Time Out* and Munro Leaf's comment that 'He's just put all your dreams and my childhood fancies into life, where we can almost not-quite-touch them.'

Walt Disney also made the cover of issue 26 of *Time* magazine, photographed at a desk with seven models of seven dwarfs to hand.

AWARDS: The film won a Special Academy Award for such a pioneering project. At the Venice Film Festival of 1938 it won the Great Art Trophy and, in the same year, took the New York Critics Award.

COMMENT: 'I saw . . . (a movie of *Snow White*) when I was delivering papers in Kansas City, and the film made such an impression on me I'm sure it influenced my decision to use the Grimm fairy tale . . .' Walt Disney.

VERDICT: *Snow White and the Seven Dwarfs* at the least is important as a milestone in animated film history. It is also dazzling to watch. Where it is weaker perhaps is in the narrative (but it was the first of its kind). Subsequent Disney features really began to develop and tighten their stories (for a perfect example just watch *Dumbo*). This film feels a little too much like a series of sight-gag-based shorts wrapped around the fairy-tale narrative, which is very simple and concise indeed. The characterisations of the film are very strong and the technical marvels cannot be underestimated.

Pinocchio (1940)

(88 minutes)

Directed by Ben Sharpsteen and Hamilton Luske
Music and Song: Leigh Harline, Ned Washington, Paul J Smith
Story Adaptation: Ted Sears, Otto Englander, Webb Smith, William Cotterell, Joseph Sabo, Erdman Penner, Aurelius Battaglia
Backgrounds: Claude Coats, Merle Cox, Ed Starr, Roy Huffine
Art Directors: Charles Philippi, Hugh Hennessy, Kenneth Anderson, Dick Kelsey, Kendall O'Connor, Terrell Stapp, Thor Putnam, John Hubley, McLaren Stewart, Al Zinnen
Character Designers: Joe Grant, Al Hurter, John P Miller, Campbell Grant, Martin Provensen, John Waldbridge
Animation Direction: Fred Moore, Franklin Thomas, Milton Kahl, Vladimir Tytla, Ward Kimball, Arthur Babbit, Eric Larson, Wolfgang Reitherman

Animators: Jack Campbell, Oliver M Johnston, Benny Wolf, Don Lusk, John Lounsberry, Norman Tate, John Bradbury, Lynn Karp, Charles Nichols, Art Palmer, Joshua Meador, Don Tobin, Robert Martsch, George Rowley, John McManus, Dan Patterson, Preston Blair, Les Clark, Marvin Woodward, Hugh Fraser, John Elliotte
Sequence Directors: Bill Roberts, Norman Ferguson, Jack Kinney, Wilfred Jackson, T Hee

BUDGET: $2.6 million

BOX OFFICE: $18.864 million (factoring in 1992 re-release)

RELEASE DATE: 7 February 1940

CERTIFICATE: U/G

VOICES: Dickie Jones (*Pinocchio*), Cliff Edwards (*Jiminy Cricket*), Christian Rub (*Gepetto*), Walter Catlett (*J Worthington Foulfellow*), Mel Blanc (*Gideon*), Charles Judels (*Stromboli; Coachman*), Frankie Darro (*Lampwick*), Evelyn Venable (*Blue Fairy*), Don Brodie (*Barker on Pleasure Island*)

TAGLINE: For anyone who has ever wished upon a star.

STORYLINE: Jiminy Cricket sits on top of a book titled *Pinocchio* and sings 'When You Wish Upon a Star'. He begins narrating the story and tells of how he came to meet Pinocchio.
   A starry night and the workshop of ageing carpenter and toymaker Gepetto. He finishes up a wooden puppet and names it Pinocchio. Jiminy Cricket, on his travels, goes into the workshop for some warmth and shelter. Gepetto wishes he had a little boy. Unable to sleep, on account of the ticking clocks and snoring, Jiminy witnesses the arrival of the Blue Fairy to grant Gepetto his wish and Pinocchio comes alive.
   The Blue Fairy charges Jiminy with the job of being Pinocchio's conscience and Jiminy warns Pinocchio of the perils and pitfalls of temptation. Gepetto is elated when he discovers his wish has been granted and the next day sends Pinocchio to school. On his way, Pinocchio is waylaid by Honest John Foulfellow and his accomplice Gideon. They convince Pinocchio to leave home and become an actor as

part of a scheme on Foulfellow's part to sell Pinocchio to Stromboli the travelling puppeteer.

Pinocchio is a big hit in Stromboli's show but things turn sour when Stromboli's greed leads him to cage Pinocchio so that he will not run away. Stromboli even threatens to chop Pinocchio up when he runs out of audience appeal.

Not far away, Gepetto has been looking for his son without success. Jiminy Cricket tracks Pinocchio down. Jiminy returns to the workshop with Pinocchio but only after the Blue Fairy has intervened and reminded Pinocchio not to lie. At the Red Lobster Inn, Foulfellow cooks up a new money-making scheme with a sinister man called The Coachman. The Coachman is rounding up boys and is taking them to Pleasure Island. Foulfellow gets hold of Pinocchio, convincing him he is on the verge of a nervous breakdown and needs some rest and relaxation.

Soon enough, Pinocchio is bound for Pleasure Island where he befriends a boy called Lampwick. Jiminy Cricket finds Pinocchio and effects a rescue attempt after Jiminy learns what happens to the boys: once they have enjoyed Pleasure Island the boys are transformed into donkeys and are sent to work at salt mines and circuses, never to see their parents again.

Pinocchio and Jiminy return to the workshop but Gepetto is long gone, seeking his son. The Blue Fairy sends a bird down with a note informing them that Gepetto lives inside the belly of a whale, Monstro, having been swallowed in the course of his search for Pinocchio. Jiminy and Pinocchio track the whale down and Gepetto is reunited with his son. Pinocchio makes a plan to escape from inside the whale, which involves making Monstro sneeze. Pinocchio, Gepetto and Jiminy are chased on their raft by Monstro and eventually they ride to freedom.

Back home and safe, Pinocchio awakes and is a real human boy. Jiminy quietly sneaks away under the starry sky, no doubt heading off on more adventures with kids in need of help everywhere.

THE DRAWING BOARD: It is worth noting that *Pinocchio* is widely considered the best animated feature ever made in the classical style. It is not only dramatically compelling but also something of a Holy Grail of animation technique.

The film had a mammoth budget and was the follow-up to the mega-successful Disney production *Snow White and the Seven Dwarfs*. Financially *Pinocchio* was a risk with the outbreak of World War Two during its production. The war effectively cut off the European market, which was a problem because 45 per cent of the studio's income was generated overseas.

With Walt Disney supervising, the film was directed by Ben Sharpsteen and Hamilton Luske who had worked so successfully on *Snow White and the Seven Dwarfs*. Sharpsteen and Luske had the challenge of not simply adapting a well-known nineteenth-century novel but also of refining and expanding the Disney studio's technical palette. Furthermore, the film reinforces the singularity of Disney's adaptation of source material. For example, the film begins in Gepetto's workshop. The Collodi novel begins with a friend of Gepetto's called Dr Cherry (on account of his red nose) chopping into a log so that he can take it to Gepetto to furnish into a puppet. As Dr Cherry goes to axe the log the voice of the soon to be named Pinocchio calls out not to be hit.

The early sketches of Pinocchio were a little too close to the look of Doc in *Snow White and the Seven Dwarfs*. Initially he was given wooden hands and a stocking cap and looked very cocky, in keeping with the cockiness and brashness of the character in Collodi's book. It was Milt Kahl who suggested Pinocchio should wear the now famous Tyrolean cap.

In developing the narrative for the film version, the critical issue was not one of plot but of character. Early on Pinocchio was to have been confronted by another version of himself, a conscience, but this proved very clumsy storytelling. Walt Disney himself went back to the source material and was captivated by the brief moment where a cricket tries to illuminate Pinocchio about the perils of living just for fun, saying, 'Woe to those boys who turn against their parents . . . sooner or later they will repent bitterly.'

In the book, Pinocchio, annoyed by the insect's preachy interference, crushes the cricket. Disney resuscitated the little fellow and made him the conscience of the film and also instigated the role of the chirpy, upbeat sidekick in animated features that has lasted ever since. Think of Timon and Pumba's relationship with Simba in *The Lion King*, think of the Donkey's friendship with Shrek in *Shrek* and of course think of how Thumper relates to Bambi. The tradition is a strong one and goes back much further than even the nineteenth century. Don Quixote had his Sancho Panza as far back as 1605.

INSPIRATIONS: Originally published as a novel written by Italian author Carlo Collodi, *Pinocchio*, rather like the Grimm Fairy Tale iteration of *Snow White and the Seven Dwarfs* was boldly adapted to suit an American sensibility.

Collodi's source novel is of course the key starting point for the narrative and it is worth noting how potent this narrative has been to other filmmakers. Stanley Kubrick seized upon it in developing the film *AI: Artificial Intelligence* and Steven Spielberg in writing and directing the eventual film really found a way to make the motif rich and consistent with his own body of work.

In the 1990s Francis Coppola struggled to develop a version of the story, framed by a contemporary war story in eastern Europe. Italian actor and director Roberto Benigni made a live action version in 2002 that was very faithful to the original text but which was lambasted by critics.

To some degree the story has a connection to the classical story *Galataea* in which a statue of a woman of that name comes to life. Intriguingly, in Japan in the 1960s, the immensely popular *Astro Boy* cartoon series fused a kind of *Pinocchio* premise with a *Peter Pan* scenario, being about an artificial boy who fails to grow up.

TOON TEAM: For *Pinocchio*, Disney pulled together the team he had in germination on *Snow White*. Albert Hurter, who had provided so many powerful and imaginative concept sketches for the debut feature, served in the same capacity and director David Hand had been a long-time associate of the studio.

VOCAL TALENT: The most notable voice at work on *Pinocchio* was Cliff Edwards who was a radio star from Missouri where he was known as Ukelele Ike. Edwards had real warmth to his voice that completely suited the character of Jiminy Cricket, one of the most enduring Disney characters ever.

For Gepetto an actor named Spencer Charters was originally to have voiced the character but his voice was regarded as too harsh and so Christian Rub was hired in. He was from Vienna and so fitted the role that even his appearance and movement were drawn upon by the animators.

INK, PAINT AND HARD WORK: *Pinocchio* was directed by Ben Sharpsteen. Disney had been impressed by his work on *Snow White and the Seven Dwarfs* and so assigned him shared directorial duty on a film that required around 750 artists and technicians.

Pinocchio is replete with innovations and technical marvels. For example, the scene of Pinocchio in the birdcage comprises five different levels of animation all shot using the multiplane camera. The rearmost element of the shot was the moon, then light through the window of the carriage in which Pinocchio is imprisoned, then there are the rear bars of the cage and then those at the front. Towards the foreground are puppets hanging in the carriage and finally the light of the Blue Fairy illuminating all of the elements.

Another legendary technical development was the creation of glass with a ripple that would give the illusion of being under the sea where things are slightly distorted. To emphasise the whale Monstro's bulk by means of some shading, a frosted cel was created. Similarly, a fog effect is genuinely creepy for the establishing shot of The Red Lobster inn as the camera closes in on it.

The film's stand-out flourish though is the master shot of the town waking. This multiplane camera shot doesn't just move closer to subjects, but also across them. The image begins with birds high up in a tree before pushing in over rooftops and finally arriving on the doorstep of Gepetto's home as Pinocchio steps out for school. *ET: The Extra-Terrestrial* (Steven Spielberg, 1982) references this shot for the wide, high level shot of suburbia as the kids go out to play for Halloween.

THEME: The film dramatises the need for accepting responsibility and growing up in order to become a real person. The film is a classic fantasy about loneliness and friendship and in many ways has an affinity with *Dumbo*. In both films a child is separated from its loving parent and must venture into the world and discover its potential, finally returning home to the love it thought was lost.

There is a widely accepted notion that the fairy-tale tradition is a form of symbolism intended to acquaint children with the unavoidable pains and challenges of life. *Pinocchio* is an essential example of this process. It is about the growth of a character from ignorance to experience, going through all the key stages of a hero narrative, which in turn mirrors the stages of real emotional lives that real people go through. Family, loyalty, courage and honesty are all worked out in the film so that Pinocchio can awake as a real human, literally and figuratively, at the end of the tale.

STYLISH TOONS: The film's most painfully ironic moment is when Gepetto unwittingly passes by Stromboli's wagon looking for Pinocchio, who the viewers know is imprisoned within. At the moment when Gepetto calls out for his son, a thunderclap renders his call useless. The film's rain effects are even more subtle than those in *Snow White*. Late in the film, as Pinocchio leaps into the sea, the wide shot has an almost photographic realism to it of the water's surface, building supremely on the rendering of water effects in *Snow White and the Seven Dwarfs*.

Another subtle convention was refined further in *Pinocchio*. Previously the outline of characters and all their parts had been rendered in a uniform dark paint. This lessened the believability of them and so it was decided that whatever colour a costume or body part was would dictate the outline colour. For example, a flesh-coloured outline was given to Gepetto's arms and face, a white outline to his moustache.

For Pinocchio, a clever subtlety was applied: during his puppet time a black line was used to outline the place where his head joined his neck. However, when he becomes a boy then this line is replaced with a skin-toned line.

The combination of technical prowess and sure-fire narrative structure and characterisation led the noted Russian director Sergei Eisenstein to claim the film was among the greatest ever made. In this one comment, Eisenstein helped animation claim its own legitimate place alongside live-action cinema.

Certainly the film's closing sequence set at sea and under its surface is astonishing, easily alternating between the melancholy of Gepetto's loneliness and the thrilling action of the sea chase in which the immense weight of Monstro is so effectively rendered against the fragility of the raft. A shot of the camera apparently tracking ahead of Monstro as he thunders in on Gepetto and Pinocchio is astonishing and hugely dynamic.

As with *Snow White*, *Pinocchio*'s backgrounds are rich with detail, and the images of the workshop are especially beautiful and cheery with their reds, yellows and oranges. Late in the film the abandoned workshop has a bluer, greener pallor that chills.

In contrast to the warmth of the light in the workshop early on (check out the heat ripple over the fire as Jiminy approaches it) is the frightening world of Pleasure Island. In the establishing shot the huge circus and carnivalesque environment is a nightmarish kind of Coney Island and the terror is soon amplified by the drama that unfolds. Powerfully there is an eerie silence to the scene of Lampwick and Pinocchio playing pool and the scene is dominated by grey and green tones that conjure a very different feel to the bright colours of home and hearth. And just who are those white-eyed cowled henchmen of The Coachman? Are they human?

When the boys are transformed into donkeys the effect is very startling and painful. There is nothing funny about it.

CHARACTER SKETCH: Pinocchio is of course the subject of the film, undertaking an adventure of consciousness as he realises what it is to be human. As with many characters at the heart of an adventure story, Pinocchio is often not so much proactive as there to respond to the challenges and characters met along the way. Subsequently, the protagonist's sense of self and the world around them is developed and typically changed for the best.

Jiminy Cricket looks less like a cricket and more like a cute little fella with his smile and his big eyes. Animator Ward Kimball worked hard to eliminate the spikier aspects of a scientifically accurate cricket of many appendages and razor-sharp legs while still retaining some sense of a bug. He also appears in the films *Fun and Fancy Free* (1947) and *Mickey's Christmas Carol* (1983).

In the *Encyclopaedia of Disney Characters* it is noted how Jiminy Cricket has characteristics of both the American city slicker and the home-grown wisdom of rural America. He is a universal bug; a bug for all time. It seems that Ward Kimball suggested the name Jiminy Cricket. Jiminy is something of a ladies' man, and his feistiness, peppiness and compassion make him utterly winning. When Gepetto says how much he would like a son, Jiminy responds, 'a lovely thought, but not at all practical'.

Drawing on fairy-tale tones and forms, the film is able to take a short cut to our collective folk sensibility and association of certain animals with certain traits. So for the devious and cunning J Worthington Foulfellow (it's all in a name) a fox is chosen. He is a broadly comic and also immediately sinister character. His sidekick Gideon is too much of a buffoon to pose that much of a threat, ensuring that Foulfellow's efforts will come to naught. Their broad slapstick is hugely enjoyable and builds on the work of the animation of the dwarfs in *Snow White*.

In the characters of Gepetto and Stromboli the circus owner, there is a symmetry of fathers, Gepetto being very nurturing and associated with warm colours and firesides, Stromboli with night time and lightning and his behaviour veers wildly from smiles to physical violence. The most sinister character is The Coachman with his leering sneering visage and the work he does is especially disturbing. For all the film's happy-go-lucky surface fun it contains an inarguably dark plot twist that acknowledges the jeopardy that young people can unwittingly find themselves in.

In a very busy and energetic film, one of its most affecting sequences centres on something very still, namely Gepetto alone inside Monstro the whale, and the old man's sense of loss and hopelessness without relief. Consistent with Gepetto's homely nature, he even manages to make life inside the belly of a whale a warm and cosy place, living aboard a swallowed boat.

Contrasting with the obvious animation of the principal characters is the Blue Fairy who moves with almost invisible realism. The Blue Fairy was modelled on a woman named Marjorie Babbit (née Belcher) who had also been the model for Snow White. She is perfection with wings, and the grace with which she moves is echoed somewhat through computer animation in Steven Spielberg's future world Pinocchio story, *AI: Artificial Intelligence*. In the Disney film, the Blue Fairy is calm and something of a mother figure, her graceful movement matching her graceful character.

Figaro and Cleo, Gepetto's pet cat and fish respectively, are playful and enchanted characters who round out the happy-go-lucky tone of the film and who remain with their owner through good and bad times. Cleo also seems to have a crush on Figaro.

TOON TUNES: It is easy to forget how many well-known songs have come from animated films and *Pinocchio* is no exception in providing a tune that has become a household name. The film theme song is 'When You Wish Upon a Star', a piece that has become a Disney anthem and which Steven Spielberg references in his masterpiece *Close Encounters of the Third Kind* (1977) – also a story about a man with a boyish spirit being confronted by the pressures and responsibilities of life. The song endures, both melodically and in terms of its very accurate and poignant sense of how we yearn for wishes to be granted.

As the film shows, though, be careful what you wish for. 'When You Wish Upon a Star' sits neatly alongside 'Somewhere Over the Rainbow' (1939) which is no surprise as Leigh Harline, who worked on *Pinocchio*, also worked on *The Wizard of Oz* (1939).

The other standout musical number from *Pinocchio* is 'Give a Little Whistle', heard when Pinocchio and Jiminy sing and dance as Pinocchio learns how to move and talk. By contrast to these upbeat tunes there is a fantastic orchestral piece played out when Gepetto rues the loss of Pinocchio as he sits inside the belly of the whale, rather like Jonah, recalling the religiously themed work of Vaughan Williams. *Pinocchio* is a real hero's journey film for sure.

The *Pinocchio* soundtrack: 'When You Wish Upon a Star', 'Little Wooden Head', 'Clock Sequence', 'Kitten Theme', 'Blue Fairy', 'Give a

Little Whistle', 'Old Gepetto', 'Off to School', 'Hi-Diddle-Dee-Dee', 'So Sorry', 'I've Got No Strings', 'Sinister Stromboli', 'Sad Reunion', 'Lesson in Lies', 'Turn on the Old Music Box', 'Coach to Pleasure Island', 'Angry Cricket', 'Transformation', 'Message from the Blue Fairy', 'To the Rescue', 'Deep Ripples', 'Desolation Theme', 'Monstro Awakens', 'Whale Chase', 'Real Boy'.

TOON TALK:
Jiminy Cricket to Pinocchio: 'You've buttered your bread, now lie in it!'

Jiminy Cricket: 'He's a whale of a whale.'

OTHER SIMILAR FILMS: The most obvious comparison would have to be with *Dumbo*. In broader terms one can also turn to a couple of live action Steven Spielberg films to see the *Pinocchio* motif and theme present: *Close Encounters of the Third Kind* (1977) and *AI: Artificial Intelligence* (2001). Pinocchio also puts in a brief cameo appearance at the end of *Who Framed Roger Rabbit?* (Robert Zemeckis, 1988) when the citizens of Toon town come out to congratulate the victorious heroes, Eddie Valiant and Roger Rabbit.

RECOGNITION: Some critics and cultural commentators had a reservation about Pinocchio: that Disney had altered Collodi's tale too much and made the meaning and action of his film too obvious.

However, Roger Ebert on suntimes.com felt that 'The power of the film is generated because it is really about something.' Geoff Andrew in *Time Out* combined the two feelings about the film: 'Disney's second cartoon feature is a rum old mixture of the excellent and the awful ... *Pinocchio* ... probably shows Disney's virtues and vices more clearly than any other cartoon.'

AWARDS: In 1941 *Pinocchio* won the Oscar for Best Music, Original Score, for Leigh Harline, Ned Washington and Paul J Smith. The film also won an Oscar for Best Music, Song, *When You Wish Upon a Star*. 1989 won ASCAP award for Most Performed Feature Film Standards – Leigh Harline and Ned Washington for *When You Wish Upon a Star*.

In 1994, *Pinocchio* was included in the National Film Preservation Board's Film Registry of films of special cultural, historical and aesthetic value.

HOME VIEWING: *Pinocchio* is available on VHS and both Region 1 and Region 2 DVDs where it also includes a short behind the scenes look at the making of the film and also a storyboard to film comparison so that the film runs in one half of the screen with the corresponding storyboard parallel to it.

COMMENT: 'What I will be looking for in this production will be colour and dimension and wonderful effects of a kind that have never been seen in animated movies before.' Walt Disney.

VERDICT: *Pinocchio* is replete with a confidence in the animation that exceeds that of *Snow White*. The subtlety of gesture in that first endeavour is developed and refined. As with *Snow White*, *Pinocchio*'s essential and simple narrative lodges in the movie projector of memory and allows multiple opportunities for the audience to enjoy animation simply as movement and energy.

The film brilliantly balances the comic with the tragic and melancholy and the emotional and indeed moral focus of the story is never superseded by the rich visual design. Sometimes you might feel there are too many fussy, sight-gag moments and indeed the succinct running time of the similarly constructed *Dumbo* comes to mind. But, for all its brightness and warmth there is also a powerful darkness underscoring the second half of the film, never more so than in the sequence set around Pleasure Island. This segment is as arresting for its bleakness as the earlier sequences are for their energy and good humour.

As with *Snow White* and subsequent Disney studio literary adaptations, *Pinocchio* has a very American humour to it, so that when Jiminy climbs on the back of a seahorse it bucks like a bronco at a rodeo. The film is a classic adventure tale as fitting of celebration for proving the power of the genre as a range of live-action films. As with certain other 'classics', you might doubt people's all-out enthusiasm for them. However, once you have seen *Pinocchio* this stamp of approval is made evident and it is thrilling to see all those promises of the film's appeal coming true.

Dumbo (1941)

(63 minutes)

Directed by Ben Sharpsteen
Based on *Dumbo the Flying Elephant* by Helen Aberson and
Harold Pearl
Music: Oliver Wallace, Frank Churchill
Lyrics: Ned Washington
Orchestration: Edward Plumb
Story: Joe Grant, Dick Huemer
Story Development: Bill Peet, Aurie Battaglia, Joe Rinaldi,
George Stallings, Webb Smith
Story Direction: Otto Englander
Backgrounds: Claude Coats, Al Dempster, John Hench,
Gerald Nevius, Ray Lockrem, Joe Stahey
Art Direction: Herb Ryman, Ken O'Connor, Terrell Stapp,
Don DaGradi, Al Zinnen, Ernes Nordli, Dick Kelsey, Charles
Payzant
Character Designers: John P Miller, Martin Provensen, John
Walbridge, James Bodrero, Maurice Noble, Elmer Plummer
Directing Animators: Vladimir Tytla, Fred Moore, Ward
Kimball, John Lounsberry, Art Babbitt, Wolfgang Reitherman
Animators: Hugh Fraser, Howard Swift, Harve Toombs, Don
Towsley, Milt Neil, Les Clark, Hicks Lokey, Claude Smith,
Berny Wolf, Ray Patterson, Jack Campbell, Grant Simmons,
Walt Kelly, Josh Meador, Don Patterson, Bill Shull, Cy
Young, Art Palmer
Sequence Directors: Norman Ferguson, Wilfred Jackson,
Bill Roberts, Jack Kinney, Sam Armstrong
Supervising Director: Ben Sharpsteen

BUDGET: $812,000

RELEASE DATE: 23 October 1941

CERTIFICATE: U/G

VOICES: John McLeish (*Narrator*), Ed Brophy (*Timothy Mouse*),
Herman Bing (*Ringmaster*), Margaret Wright (*Casey Jr*), Sterling

Holloway (*Messenger Stork*), Verna Felton (*Elephant*), Norenn Gamill (*Elephant*), Billy Sheets (*Joe, Clown*), Billy Bletcher (*Clown*), Malcolm Hutton (*Skinny*), Cliff Edwards (*Crows*), Jim Carmichael (*Crows*), Hall Johnson Choir (*Crows*), Eddie Holden (*Clown*), The King's Men (*Roustabouts*), Harold Manley (*Boy*), Tony Neil (*Boy*), Charles Stubbs (*Boy*)

TAGLINE: The One. The Only. The Fabulous . . .

STORYLINE: A stormy night and a narrator tells how the storks never fail in their mission to deliver babies into the world. From behind the clouds emerges a flock of storks that fly gracefully across the moon, all with bundles hanging from their beaks. The storks fly in over Florida and drop the bundles over a circus site. The bundles are baby animals. A baby tiger lands next to a sleeping adult tiger, a baby kangaroo drops down next to a kangaroo mother. Mrs Jumbo, an elephant, watches expectantly but no such package arrives for her and she looks sad. The next day the circus train chugs along to the next venue. One of the storks, dressed in a postal worker uniform, returns with a bundle and drops in on the wagon holding the elephants. Mrs Jumbo finally has a new baby, with very large ears. The other elephants laugh but Mrs Jumbo can only love her new child. The other elephants name the elephant Dumbo. Dumbo is put into the circus parade but he clumsily falls over.

At night some boys tease Dumbo and Dumbo's mother is enraged. In her protective anger she is put in a cage and chained up. Dumbo is alone in the world. He is then befriended by Timothy Mouse who sets about improving Dumbo's morale. Dumbo is put into the circus show but is not a big success. Timothy and Dumbo accidentally get drunk one evening and awake high up on the branch of a tree. A gang of crows observe that Dumbo and Timothy must have got up there somehow. Dumbo flew up there surely. He tries to fly again and it works brilliantly.

Dumbo and Timothy return to the circus where Dumbo joyfully flies in the Big Top.

The circus train moves across country, Dumbo's mother back in the fold, Dumbo flying triumphantly above her, the star of the show.

THE DRAWING BOARD: *Dumbo* had begun as a cereal box cartoon strip which was then written up into a film storyline by Joe Grant and

Dick Huemer which Walt highly approved of. This original children's story comprised only eight drawings. Originally, the Dumbo film was to have been a featurette running around thirty minutes. That running time eventually doubled to 61 minutes, still about fifteen to twenty minutes shorter than most animated features. (Distributor RKO had wanted Disney to make a film nearer to seventy minutes long, but Disney felt he could stretch the story no more.) At the same time, and in the warm afterglow of the critical success of *Pinocchio*, the studio was also developing an adaptation of Felix Salten's novel, *Bambi*.

Dumbo was a cheap film to make, especially compared to the lavishly produced *Pinocchio*. *Fantasia* had not been a success at all: its segmented format and use of classical music, not known to the majority of people, diminished its commercial appeal. Atypically, Walt did not demand endless reworking of the *Dumbo* project and, according to one of the film's chief animators, Ward Kimball, 'the Disney cartoon reached its zenith with *Dumbo*'.

Dumbo became Disney's most profitable feature since *Snow White and the Seven Dwarfs*. At the time of *Dumbo*'s production, there was concern that it was dangerous to expose audiences to sustained brightly coloured moving pictures and so *Dumbo* alternates between the bright and garish and the dark and shadowy.

Unlike *Snow White, Pinocchio*, the later *Bambi* and *Fantasia* there was not the same pressure to create something that would stun audiences. This absence of pressure ironically produced something great. The film emerges as what many, for example the film historian and animation enthusiast Leonard Maltin, consider the best Disney animated film.

The film was produced using a relatively small unit of staff and a very simple story as its basis. As Leonard Maltin notes in the documentary *Celebrating Dumbo* on the 60th Anniversary DVD, perhaps this was the kind of film audiences longed for rather than a film like *Fantasia* which was far more experimental.

As has been noted many times, the visual design of *Dumbo* is very plain and unfussy and its running time is atypically short.

INSPIRATIONS: The rich track record of design for *Snow White and the Seven Dwarfs* and *Pinocchio* was the inverse of the work displayed in *Dumbo*, which is marked by its appealing simplicity. Given Disney's affinity for the fairy-tale medium and familiarity with Hans Christian Andersen's work, it is not too much of a leap to imagine that *The Ugly*

Duckling tale would have had its share of influence on the tone and heart of the *Dumbo* project. The film also owes a fair amount to the visual comedy of the Disney studio *Silly Symphony* shorts of the 1930s.

TOON TEAM: By the time of *Dumbo*'s production, the Disney studio had galvanised an astonishing team of animators from *Snow White and the Seven Dwarfs, Pinocchio* and *Fantasia*. Vladimir 'Bill' Tytla, who had animated so powerfully Stromboli for *Pinocchio* and the 'Night on Bald Mountain' sequence from *Fantasia*, worked hard to animate *Dumbo* – a very different challenge to the more abrasive and doom-laden characters of his other films.

VOCAL TALENT: *Dumbo* for its first half is virtually a silent film. Dumbo himself does not speak. Certainly there is humour in the exchanges between the silhouettes of the clowns as they ready for bed but it is when Timothy Mouse arrives in the story that the dialogue builds. The crow sequence in the last part of the film is verbally energetic.

INK, PAINT AND HARD WORK: The ease with which the narrative was developed and approved, remaining unchanged, was reflected too in the production of the film which ran for around a year. Indeed the story development phase lasted an unusually brief six months. Many of the studio's higher paid, lead animators had been put on to working on *Bambi*. The financial and time limitations imposed on *Dumbo* clearly worked in its favour. According to animation lore, more screentime had been occupied by the crows but this material was truncated to minimise its racist implications (see **CHARACTER SKETCH**).

THEME: The film centres on the themes of individuality and self-confidence, vital concerns for any viewer, especially children. As Timothy says, 'The very things that held you down are going to take you up and up!'

This is a hugely playful film that clearly sends its message home without preaching. The film's psychological richness is foregrounded because the visuals are so simple, thereby allowing the audience to really focus on the drama.

The film also expresses concern at animals kept in captivity. One of the principal narrative elements is the mistreatment of Mrs Jumbo and, during the parade scene, the animals in their cages are shown as tired and bored of the occasion.

STYLISH TOONS: *Dumbo* is celebrated for its simple visual style, an approach that is in real contrast to the intense naturalism and detail of the preceding animated features from the Disney studio such as *Snow White* and *Pinocchio*. Blocks and washes of colour dominate the landscapes and backgrounds of *Dumbo*. A prime example of the effectiveness of this is when Dumbo flies at the end of the film. A beautiful shot of his shadow across the fields is notable for the lack of detail in the landscape. The shadow is the focus of the image.

Another stylistic quality of the film is attributable to Ward Kimball who animated the crows at the end of the film. His design for their movement is in contrast to the house style that favoured naturalism even for the most fantastic premise, such as a talking mouse. Kimball and his team made the crows move in an accentuated manner that emphasises their liveliness.

To some degree the visual comedy in *Dumbo* keeps the kinship alive with the visual humour of the *Silly Symphonies*, in particular one called *Elmer Elephant*. In that short, Elmer goes to a birthday party for Tillie Tiger, the girl of his dreams. Elmer is mocked by all the other animals for his trunk. Subsequently, Elmer is kicked out of the party. Alone and exiled, Elmer befriends a wise old giraffe (wearing spectacles of course) who points out that the birds across the way have even bigger noses (beaks). Their conversation is cut short when Tillie's treehouse catches fire. It is Elmer who saves the day, extinguishing the fire with his hose-like trunk and then saving Tillie from falling. The very thing he had been mocked for is what saves and helps others. Tillie kisses her new-found hero.

The animation in *Dumbo* is largely playful, such as in the wonderfully economic shadow scenes with the clowns disrobing. Their vaudevillian high jinks are also hilarious. By contrast the film exhibits several moments of subtle tenderness, famously when Dumbo goes to see his mother chained up in the wagon.

In a showy opening for the film the studio's famed commitment to naturalism is writ large in the gorgeous and whimsical scene of the storks delivering the bundles of babies. Watch how the birds' necks retract and then extend in flight and rhythm with the beat of their wings.

In contrast to these subtle moments, look at the character of Casey the train engine, bursting with energy, its visual humour matched by its sonic amusement as its raspy voice riffs on the sound of a train puffing along. At one point, Casey's comic value is used to illustrate the message of the film. As it wheezes up a difficult mountain track Casey exhorts 'I think I can, I think I can' and then on the easy decline 'I thought I could, I thought I could.'

Set amidst the prevailing light-hearted, buoyant action is the stunningly abstract and modern sequence accompanying the song 'Pink Elephants on Parade'. The sequence marks a break from the rest of the film and manages to be funny and frightening all at once, as evidenced by an elephant marching towards camera composed entirely of elephants heads with black eye sockets. The sequence is a wonderful free association riff and builds to some degree on one of the highlight scenes in *Snow White* when she is lost in the forest and its menacing eyes seem to attack her.

The studio's affinity for sight and sound gags continues in *Dumbo*, such as when the kangaroo rocks its baby as though it were a rocking chair. The scene when Dumbo takes revenge on those who mocked him is handled through comedy as he hoovers up peanuts and then fires them like ammunition through his trunk. See also **Who Framed Roger Rabbit?**, in which Dumbo cameos early on hoovering up peanuts thrown up to him before roaring past the camera.

CHARACTER SKETCH: A lot of the inspiration for Dumbo the elephant came from Tytla's two-year-old son, Peter. Dumbo is endearing and his visual design has the quality of a baby in the shape of the head and especially the big blue eyes.

Mrs Jumbo might seem meek and humble but when she is provoked she rages.

The four elephants who comment on Dumbo and his mother are caricatured as gossips who finally get their comeuppance. They regard Dumbo as shameful to the elephant species because of his clumsiness and unique appearance.

Timothy Mouse is a real Brooklyn, streetwise mouse, part Mickey Mouse in his boundless energy and very much a cousin to Jiminy Cricket from *Pinocchio* in his capacity for big ideas and pep talks. For animator Andreas Deja, Timothy Mouse is 'just the ultimate buddy'.

Some objection was raised at the crows being given African–American voice characterisations, especially in addition to the fact that 'jim crow' is a slang, racist term. However, they are very upbeat crows and they help Dumbo realise his potential.

TOON TUNES: The song 'Baby Mine' is the heart of the film – tender and gentle and expressing the love of mothers for their children everywhere.

This buoyant film is all the brighter for the song about the train 'Casey' , 'Pink Elephants on Parade' and 'When I See an Elephant Fly'.

Dumbo soundtrack listing: Main Title, 'Look Out for Mister Stork', 'Loading the Train/Casey Junior/Stork', 'On a Cloud/Straight from Heaven', 'Song of the Roustabouts', 'Circus Parade', 'Bathtime/Hide and Seek', 'Ain't That the Funniest Thing/Berserk/Dumbo Shunned/A Mouse!', 'Pyramid of Pachyderms', 'No Longer an Elephant/Dumbo's Sadness/A Visit in the Night/Baby Mine', 'Clown Song', Hiccups/Firewater/Bubbles/Did You See That?/Pink Elephants on Parade', 'Up a Tree/The Fall/Timothy's Theory', 'When I See an Elephant Fly', 'You Oughta Be Ashamed', 'Flight Test/When I See an Elephant Fly', 'Save My Child/The Threshold of Success/Dumbo's Triumph/Making History/Flight Test/When I See an Elephant Fly', 'Spread Your Wings'.

TOON TALK:
Timothy Mouse about Dumbo: 'Socially, he's all washed up.'

Timothy Mouse: 'So you like to pick on little guys? Why don't you pick on me?'

Timothy: 'The world's mightiest midget mastodon!'

OTHER SIMILAR FILMS: *Dumbo* explores similar emotional territory to *Pinocchio* in its story of a lonely child, with a difference, struggling to find their place in the world.

In March 2002, the Disney studio were at work on a *Dumbo II* (following the adventures of Dumbo and his circus friends away from the circus) and tests were made to create Dumbo using computer-generated animation. Joe Grant, story supervisor on the original film and, by 2002, in his early 90s, was brought in to view the material and offer his opinion.

Dumbo's successor was *Bambi*, on which the studio lavished far more time and effort. Bambi is another of Disney's initial run of stunning animated features and work had begun on it in 1936, with extensive work being put into studying animal movement. It was directed by David Hand who also directed *Snow White and the Seven Dwarfs*. The source novel by Felix Salten had been published in 1943 in response to his wonder at the Alps wildlife on a visit there. Bambi is inspired by the Italian word for baby – 'bambino'. It was an animator at Disney, Maurice Day, who got Walt interested in the source material. The world premiere of the resulting film was held in Day's hometown of Damariscotta in Maine. The film was immensely popular and continues to be so today. The film was the first Disney feature with an exclusively animal cast, rather like *The Lion King*. The film was released in the UK before being released in America. The animators designed the characters along the lines of neighbourhood kids. Some unused footage from *Pinocchio* of woodland creatures and the forest fire was incorporated into *Bambi*. As with *Dumbo*, the studio has, more recently, considered a computer-generated sequel to the film called *Bambi and the Great Prince*. The follow-up has yet to see the light of day.

RECOGNITION: The *New York Times* was very complimentary about *Dumbo*: ' . . . the most genial, the most endearing, the most completely precious cartoon feature ever to emerge from the . . . brushes of Walt Disney's wonder-working artists!' as was W Stephen Gilbert in *Time Out*: 'One of the best animated features . . . The artwork . . . is magisterial.'

AWARDS: In 1942, *Dumbo* won the Oscar for Best Music Scoring of a Musical Picture, the award going to Frank Churchill and Oliver Wallace. The film was also nominated for an Oscar in the category of Best Music, Song for 'Baby Mine'. In 1947, the film won Best Animation Design at the Cannes Film Festival, the delay in recognition being explained by World War Two.

COMMENT: 'The first time I heard Walt outline the plot I knew that the picture had great simplicity and cartoon heart.' Ward Kimball.

VERDICT: *Dumbo* is a brilliantly compact film that balances laughs and melancholy with simple confidence. It is an airy and energetic film with several brilliant comic flourishes and beautiful images.

Dumbo combines the simple knockabout charm of the *Silly Symphonies* with the emotional appeal of *Pinocchio* but without any of the anxiously conceived eye candy of design that felt it had to prove itself. Its stylistic understatement is its strongest suit and represents a maturity in the creative spirit of the studio. The film's low budget allows for big emotions and so limitation becomes liberation, rather like Dumbo's very own ears.

Beauty and the Beast (1991)

(84 minutes – Special Edition 90 minutes)

Directed by Gary Trousdale and Kirk Wise
Produced by Don Hahn
Written by Roger Allers, Kelly Asbury, Brenda Chapman,
Tom Ellery, Kevin Harley, Robert Lence, Burny Mattinson,
Brian Pimental, Joe Ranft, Chris Sanders, Bruce Woodside,
Linda Woolverton, from the original story (author unknown)
Executive Producer: Howard Ashman
Associate Producer: Sarah McArthur
Music: Alan Menken
Editor: John Carnochan
Art Direction: Brian McFee
Special Effects: Dorse Lanpher
Animators: Anthony De Rosa, Glen Keane, Mark Henn,
James Baxter, Aaron Blaise, Geefwee Bedoe, Broose
Johnson, Rejean Bourdages, David Burgess, Tim Allen, Tony
Anselmo, Ruben A Aquino, Doug Krohn, Brad Kuha, Alex
Kuperschmidt, Lorna Cork, Michael Cedeno, Randy
Cartwright, Will Finn, Tony Bancroft

BUDGET: $30 million

BOX OFFICE: $145,863,363

RELEASE DATE: 13 November 1991 (Premiere), 22 November 1991 (general release) Special Edition – 2002

CERTIFICATE: U/G

VOICES: Paige O'Hara (*Belle*), Robby Benson (*Beast/Prince*), Richard White (*Gaston*), Jerry Orbach (*Lumiere the Candlestick*), David Ogden Stiers (*Cogsworth/Narrator*), Angela Lansbury (*Mrs Potts*), Bradley Pierce (*Chip the Tea Cup/Human Chip*), Rex Everhart (*Maurice, Belle's Father*), Jesse Corti (*Lefou, Gaston's Sidekick*), Hal Smith (*Philippe the Horse*), Jo Anne Worley (*Wardrobe*), Mary Kay Bergman (*Bimbette*), Brian Cummings (*Stove*), Mary Kay Bergman (*Bookseller*), Tony Jay (*Monsieur D'Arque*)

TAGLINE: The most beautiful love story ever told.

STORYLINE: Prologue: In a fairy-tale forest, there is a castle on a mountaintop and a prince whose arrogance is his undoing – a spell is cast that renders him beastlike.

In a nearby provincial town some years later Belle, an avid reader, goes to buy a new book. In town the villagers talk about her because she is a little different. Belle returns home where her inventor father is at work on a new project. Belle is the subject of Gaston, the hunter's, attention.

The next day, Belle's father rides away to a fair. En route he becomes lost in a dark and sinister forest and when wolves attack he is saved by a beast. The Beast takes Belle's father back to a fortress and imprisons him.

Belle soon realises that her father is in trouble and goes to find him. She reaches the castle and enters but the enraged Beast finds her. Belle offers to be held prisoner so that her father may go free. The Beast agrees. When Belle's father is gone the Beast tells Belle that she can go anywhere she likes in the castle and its grounds, with the exception of the West Wing.

In town, Belle's father tries to convince the villagers of what has happened but nobody believes him.

At the fortress, Belle is befriended by the walking, talking house furniture, all of whom think Belle is the one to break the spell that hangs over the Beast. Belle takes a tour of the fortress and, unnoticed, goes to the West Wing, the Beast's private chambers. As she walks through it she sees the upturned furniture and a portrait of him before the tragedy of transformation. The Beast banishes Belle from the room and she runs free of the castle. She is attacked by wolves in the forest and the Beast comes to the rescue but is badly injured. Belle returns to the fortress with him and she nurses him back to health.

In Belle's hometown, Gaston hatches a plan to assure that he will marry Belle. Unless she agrees to marry him, Belle's father will be taken into the asylum for his mad ravings. Belle's father prepares to set out to find his daughter.

In the fortress, the Beast seeks the romantic advice of his servant companions and the relationship between Belle and the Beast continues to grow. Belle and the Beast prepare for a special evening together and dance and talk the night away. Belle, though, wishes she could see her father again. The Beast says she should go to him.

Back home, Belle tells her father how changed the Beast is. A man from the asylum turns up to take her father away. Belle and her father are locked away in a cellar at their home by Gaston but they get free and race back to the fortress to prevent the mob, led by Gaston, from killing the Beast.

The mob enter the castle and are attacked by the furniture. Gaston goes to the Beast and confronts him. Belle arrives and watches as the Beast and Gaston fight. Gaston finally stabs the Beast and then Gaston plummets to his doom. The Beast lies dying, Belle at his side. She kisses him and a transformation takes place. The Beast is returned to his original youthful self. The ruined castle and dead flora return to life and all the servants become human again. They dance in celebration.

THE DRAWING BOARD: Incredibly, the Disney studio initially considered a version of the fairy tale as the follow up to *Pinocchio* but Walt Disney was not keen, feeling there was an unnecessary intensity to scenes that would show Belle imprisoned.

In 1984, Disney was put under the day-to-day supervision of ex-Paramount chiefs Michael Eisner and Jeffrey Katzenberg. One of their commitments was to reviving the animation output of the studio and Katzenberg made this his special focus. A notable, obvious change he made was the insistence that all animated features be scripted, existing as screenplays as for live-action films. This proved quite a contentious move initially. Previously, the convention had been story outlines that would then give way to eventual storyboards.

Beauty and the Beast was put into development at Disney in the late 1980s, having initially been considered as a live-action movie to be directed by the great Carroll Ballard, director of *The Black Stallion* (1979), *Never Cry Wolf* (1983) and *Fly Away Home* (1994), all wonderful movies about humans' relationships with the animal world.

When the challenge of realising the Beast in live action proved too much, the studio put the project into development as an animated feature. A series of screenplays between 1985 and 1988 failed to present a viable script to base a feature on. The studio's animated feature fortunes had been inconsistent since the death of Walt Disney in 1966, missing his direct supervision.

It was the screenwriter Linda Woolverton, the first woman to write a screenplay for a Disney studio animated feature, who finally provided the shape for an animated piece. The first version of the script had no musical numbers and when Jeffrey Katzenberg viewed the film after ten weeks' work on it he considered it too sombre and the production was put on hold for a rethink. It was at this point that the film's original director Richard Purdum left the project.

In 1989, the studio seemed to revive with *The Little Mermaid* (Musker and Clements). *The Rescuers* (1977) had been very popular (eventually getting a follow-up in *The Rescuers Down Under*) but *The Black Cauldron* (1985) a lavish dark, medieval fantasy had failed to ignite audience imaginations.

Smaller-scaled animation such as *The Fox and the Hound* and *Basil, The Great Mouse Detective* were relative successes, but what was really needed was something that would prove as eternally popular as *Snow White, Pinocchio, Dumbo* and *Bambi*. Something that would transcend its format and become a pop-culture reference point.

True to the Disney tradition, the studio looked to adapt a well-known fairy tale and, obviously, the *Beauty and the Beast* story was already well known. Film director Jean Cocteau had adapted the story to the live-action arena in 1946 in a seminal piece of fantasy filmmaking. Both spectacular and emotionally true, some of his visual motifs and elements inform the Disney version.

Of the Disney iteration, Marina Warner wrote at the time of its original release: 'The Disney film, of course, had abandoned the cynical combativeness of the tale's first interpreters and remained true to the romantic and idealist yearnings of later tellers.' For Marina Warner the film has been conceived in such a way as to maximise debates around sexual politics so that the story 'gives us a heroine of spirit who finds romance on her own terms'.

In 1987, a first draft script of *Beauty and the Beast* was completed and British director Richard Purdum and his wife Jill moved from London to Los Angeles to develop and direct *Beauty and the Beast*. However, the Purdums' take on the project was not in synch enough with Disney and a new directing team was found in Kirk Wise and Gary Trousdale. The film would mark their first directorial feature together, though they had found a way to make an EPCOT short called *Cranium Command* come together.

For Katzenberg the film was the closest to a live-action animated feature the studio had made. Animator of the Beast, Glen Keane, said at the time of the film's release, 'When Disney does a fairy tale, it's, like forever.'

INSPIRATIONS: The original tale serves as inspiration for the main narrative impulse. The *Beauty and the Beast* narrative reaches back as far as a second century AD piece of Latin called *Cupid and Psyche*, featuring in *The Golden Ass*. However, it is the version by Mme

Leprince de Beaumont that became fixed in the public consciousness in 1757, initially being published in her periodical *Magasin des Enfants*.

The Beaumont story begins with a rich merchant who has lost his fortune wandering into the gardens of an enchanted palace. The palace is the home of the Beast. The merchant takes a beautiful flower from the garden for his youngest daughter. The Beast is enraged and in retribution demands that the merchant surrenders one of his daughters to the Beast. The merchant promises to do so and his youngest daughter agrees. She goes to the castle and at this point her relationship with the Beast grows.

The Disney film is evidently inspired to some degree by the celebrated live-action film by director Jean Cocteau, *La Belle et la Bête*. There is also a wealth of visual material in it relating to various renditions of the story.

TOON TEAM: *Beauty and the Beast* was marked by the youthfulness of its core production team. The film's directors were untried in the feature format but they proved their facility. Working alongside them was animator Glen Keane, one of the most significant Disney animators of the last fifteen years, having worked on Disney animation since 1974. Keane had animated Bernard and Penny with Ollie Johnston on *The Rescuers* (1977), had animated the bear fight, Todd and Vixie in *The Fox and the Hound* and then gone on to work on *The Black Cauldron*. is material, however, was subsequently cut from the film.

It was with *The Little Mermaid* that Keane began making his most significant contributions to the studio's work. He animated Ariel for *The Little Mermaid* and then moved on to animating the Beast, Aladdin, Pocahontas and Tarzan, the eponymous stars of each film. Keane's self-acknowledged career highlight and defining moment, however, is the scene in which the Beast transforms back to his human self.

More intriguingly, Keane had collaborated with John Lasseter in the early 1980s on developing an early test run for computer animation which they titled *The Wild Things*. Taking a sequence from Maurice Sendak's *Where the Wild Things Are*, they created a short fusion of computer-generated background and hand-drawn animation showing the boy Max writing his name on the wall with the dog watching. Soon afterwards, Lasseter tried to develop the book *The Brave Little Toaster* into a computer-animated project at Disney but the reorganisation of the company did not allow for such a venture at the time.

VOCAL TALENT: Paige O'Hara, the voice of Belle, was a Broadway performer. So too was Richard White (Gaston) and Jerry Orbach

(Lumiere). Angela Lansbury who voiced Mrs Potts had starred in the Disney fantasy *Bedknobs and Broomsticks* and is probably most recognisable to audiences as the star of TV series *Murder She Wrote*. Tim Curry had tried out for the Beast, having been brilliantly beastly in the film *Legend* (Ridley Scott, 1985) and has also appeared in *The Hunt for Red October* (John McTiernan, 1990) and *The Three Musketeers* (Stephen Herek, 1993).

INK, PAINT AND HARD WORK: The film was made on a relatively low budget with largely inexperienced young animators. But *Beauty and the Beast* was the first time that each animator was credited for the character they worked on.

As was traditional a model was used to help guide the design of the female protagonist. Belle was modelled after a writer named Sherri Stoner who wrote scripts for the animated TV series *Tiny Toon Adventures* and the feature film *Casper* (Brad Silberling, 1995). She also modelled for Ariel in *The Little Mermaid*.

THEME: The story's preoccupation with love seeing through and beyond inadequacies of the heart underpins the fantasy.

The film also critiques the dangers of mob rule in the face of something or somebody they do not understand. Belle is the outsider in her community because she reads and possesses some wider sense of the world than her narrow-minded, small-town neighbours.

In contrast to the provincial stupor of her home life, Belle is taken into a world of imagination and transformation. The film's emphasis on humans under a spell that has turned them into house furniture clearly reminds audiences of animation's power to breathe life into the inanimate.

Throughout the film, shadow is used literally to keep the Beast out of the light but it also represents his emotional darkness. It is love that will pull him out of the shadows and into the light. Subsequently, alongside the more familiar jokes and light heartedness, the idea of true love growing from protection and faith is played out with a seriousness that satisfies both the young and adult viewer. The Beast is ultimately revived and saved by the healing power of love. His loneliness and isolation is destroyed in favour of belonging.

STYLISH TOONS: *Beauty and the Beast* is an unfussy, elegantly made feature. It revels in the fairy-tale traditions so evident in the source material. The prologue sequence recalls that of *Snow White*'s opening with the multiplane camera revealing a castle deep in a forest. The telling of the back story is strongly and clearly illustrated through the stained-glass windows of the castle.

The film as a whole adheres to the Disney tradition of highly detailed, realistically rendered environments. The village and countryside of Belle's hometown are warmly coloured and bright. By contrast the fortress interior is markedly cold with an emphasis on blues and greys. To establish the immense size of the hideaway, several establishing shots have a vertiginous quality to them showing walls dropping far, far away to the floor as Belle enters. In the later scene where the Beast takes her to the library, the immensity of the room is made clear by a low-height camera shot and pan revealing towering bookshelves. It is one of the most affecting moments in the film as the Beast's desire to be loved begins to shine through by making a dream come true for the girl he is falling in love with.

The film's musical numbers are zestful and amusing, choreographed as real dance and sparkling entertainments. The camera tracks along chorus lines of cutlery as in a Busby Berkeley musical number.

In its initial development phase the film was more sombre than the final version but this intensity shines through in places and suggests how compelling such a version would be. When the Beast watches the intruders in his castle he flits past the camera as a looming shadow. When he confronts Belle he enters the room like a predatory lion and when he ponders Belle's behaviour he paces like a lion in front of his fireplace.

Against the elegance of the main plot's animation, the subplot and surrounding story elements have a far more slapstick style, such as in the song Gaston sings in the pub. Similarly, the battle between the mob and the house furniture towards the end of the film is funny rather than dangerous, and even includes a diving diva of a closet.

At the time of its original release the film was noted for the integration of computer animation into the classical style. There is, for example, a computer-generated hall in which Belle and the Beast dance. The camera booms down past a chandelier and then down to meet their feet as they whirr gracefully past. The freedom of the computer's virtual camera allows for an impressive sweep to the movement that emphasises the perfect feeling of the moment for the characters.

The special-effects sequence that makes the film's intense ending and moment of transformation owes something to films such as *Raiders of the Lost Ark* (Steven Spielberg, 1981) and *Poltergeist* (Tobe Hooper, 1982), when the wind-enhanced blasts of light emanate for the changing beast.

Against the more obviously dazzling images there is also a sad delicacy to the motif of the dying rose, emanating a fairy dust glow as its petals drop like tears, symbolising death.

CHARACTER SKETCH: Belle announces herself as an outsider at the start of the main part of the film when she is introduced in the story singing her way through her town, acknowledging that she does not quite fit in and wants more from life.

The Beast is terrifying, tender and noble. His more monstrous gait has real force to it and he ultimately finds his soft side, the angles of his better nature (to borrow a phrase from Abraham Lincoln). The facial animation for the Beast takes him from anger and rage to confusion in a moment with a great deal of humanity. Watch how uncertain his look is when Belle says that she did not even get a chance to say goodbye to her father after the Beast sets him free.

Later in the film, the animation perfectly captures the uneasy, self-conscious silence between Belle and the Beast after they dance and when they have so much to say about one another and how they feel.

Gaston is the arrogant young man who wants to woo Belle but whose square jaw and broad shoulders cannot compare to the Beast's sensitivity, culture and strength. Gaston's case is not helped by his small, buffoonish sidekick, LeFeu, the most 'cartoony' of the film's characters. Gaston is easily and simply shown to be a vain fool with a fear born of ignorance, though he has an easy way that appeals to the mob.

Cogsworth, the fussy little clock is an amusing guide through the world of the film. Lumiere is Cogsworth's friend and rival and offers the Beast romantic advice. Mrs Potts is a warm, nurturing mother figure who is the most optimistic of the cutlery and condiments. One of the most nicely designed characters is the hat stand who at one point plays a violin.

Belle's father is quixotic and lovable and his love for his lost daughter endures. His search for her recalls Gepetto's search for Pinocchio.

Chip was originally only in the film for one line but the producers became endeared with the character and amplified his role.

TOON TUNES: Over the years the use of a musical idiom had been a staple of many Disney animated features and *Beauty and the Beast* continues that tradition. With *The Little Mermaid*, Disney had worked with Alan Menken and Howard Ashman to great success, winning an Oscar for their efforts. *Beauty and the Beast* consolidated their standing and also extended the legitimacy of the musical format for the Disney animated feature at least. The main theme for the film has become a staple of film theme CD compilations. Interestingly, however, Menken and Ashman were not that keen to work on the project straight after *The Little Mermaid*. They were far more interested in creating a road movie version of *Aladdin*. Unusually, but effectively, the music was recorded with all the cast and orchestra together as for the recording of an opera or stage show.

Such was the success of the film it was transferred to a live theatrical stage format. The Broadway show premiered on 27 November 1993 at the Music Hall Theatre in Houston, Texas and then opened in New York at the Palace Theatre on 18 April 1994. It is now the tenth-longest-running Broadway show in theatre history and the longest-running American musical.

Howard Ashman died six months before the release of *Beauty and the Beast* in November 1991.

Soundtrack listing: 'Prologue', 'Belle', 'Belle (Reprise)', 'Gaston', 'Gaston (Reprise)', 'Be Our Guest', 'Something There', 'Mob Song', 'Beauty and the Beast', 'To the Fair', 'West Wing', 'Beast Lets Belle Go', 'Battle on the Tower', 'Transformation', 'Beauty and the Beast (Duet)'.

TOON TALK:
Cogsworth: 'Who said anything about the castle being enchanted?'

Cogsworth: 'If it's not Baroque don't fix it.'

OTHER SIMILAR FILMS: A 1997 follow-up direct-to-video sequel was released called *The Enchanted Christmas*. An IMAX version of the film was released in 2002 with the tagline: 'The most beautiful love story ever told as it has never been seen before' with a poster showing Belle and the Beast in silhouette in front of a massive screen showing images from the film. Six minutes of footage was added to the original. This extra material includes the song and dance number 'Human Again' which centres on the household furnishings anticipating their return to human form. The song had been storyboarded for the original film but was considered too long. For the IMAX release the storyboards became new footage – the first time the Disney studio had added a new sequence to an existing movie.

RECOGNITION: Though *Sight and Sound* didn't feel that *Beauty and the Beast* was perfect, they were still complimentary: 'Fragmented as it is, this is the most stylish Disney animation in years', while the *Chicago Sun-Times* were even more so: 'The film is as good as any Disney animated feature ever made . . . And it's a reminder that animation is the ideal medium for fantasy, because all its fears and dreams can be made literal.' On the release of the Special Edition in 2002, the *Guardian* reviewed it from a different era in animation and felt it had stood the test of time: 'There's enough wit and ingenuity . . . to give the CGi whizzkids a run for their money.'

AWARDS: *Beauty and the Beast* was the first animated feature to be nominated in the category of Best Picture for 1991 at the Oscars. Since then a specialised Best Animated Feature Oscar has been established, first won by Shrek in 2001.

The recognition *Beauty and the Beast* received only enhanced the standing of animation as a potent cinematic format. At the 1991 Los Angeles Film Critics Association Awards the film won Best Animation and in the same year the National Board of Review gave the film a Special Award for Animation. In 1992, the film won the Oscar for Best Music, Original Score and Best Musical Song for 'Beauty and the Beast'. The film was also nominated for an Oscar for Best Musical Song, 'Be Our Guest' and 'Belle'. The film was nominated for an Oscar for Best Sound (Terry Porter, Mel Metcalfe, David J Hudson, Doc Kane). In 1993, the film won an ASCAP award for Most Performed Song from a Motion Picture, the award going to Howard Ashman and Alan Menken for their song 'Beauty and the Beast'.

The 1992 BMI Film and TV Awards awarded the film the BMI Film Music Award and at the 1992 Golden Globes the film won Golden Globes for Best Motion Picture (Comedy/Musical), Best Original Score, Best Original Song for 'Beauty and the Beast' and was nominated for Best Original Song for 'Be Our Guest'.

The film was nominated for a Hugo award in 1992 for Best Dramatic Presentation.

At the 1993 Grammy Awards the film was nominated for Best Instrumental Composition written for a Motion Picture or for Television. The film won the Grammy for Best Song written specifically for a Motion Picture or for Television for the song 'Beauty and the Beast'. At the 1993 BAFTAs the film was nominated for Best Original Film Score and Best Special Effects. In 2002, the National Film Registry included the film on its select list of culturally, historically and aesthetically important films. In 2003, the film was nominated for a Saturn Award for Best DVD Classic Film release.

HOME VIEWING: The film is available on VHS and Collector's Edition DVD that includes a director's commentary and documentary feature as well as conceptual artwork. It is a lavish set for a real fan of the movie.

COMMENT: 'This is the closest to a live-action movie . . . that I believe we have ever done.' Jeffrey Katzenberg.

VERDICT: Watching *Beauty and the Beast* in 2002, it seems astonishing how simple, quiet and unfussy it is compared to much animation produced more recently. As often with Disney animated narratives, the inclusion of musical and dance sequences expands a nicely tight main narrative. Knowing that this particular film began as a more low-key and intense film than the final product, those moments of more sombre action and intensity never fail to register and certainly prove the strongest parts of the film.

The elegance and naturalism of the design and animation sometimes jars with the lighter moments of comedy such as when the Beast is being readied for his big date with Belle. His funny, dried hair sticking out in all directions is at odds with the intensity established earlier in the film.

The film is ultimately very strong and affecting and its concern with hearts softening is nicely melancholy in such a family orientated feature.

Beauty and the Beast plays out far more as dramatic animation than animated comedy – though it has its share of laughs – and there is an underlying maturity that emerges over the more familiar Disney vaudevillian comedy. The film is not particularly sentimental and has a more adult approach to reaching the audience's emotions.

The finale of the film is powerful; if this film doesn't introduce young viewers to the power of a good fairy tale, then nothing will.

Stop-motion Miracles

As long as there has been cinema and animation there has been stop motion. As far back as 1906 stop motion has been an intriguing prospect, perhaps the most magical form of animation. A short film called *The Haunted Hotel* was made in 1906 by James Stuart Blackton in which food was served and a table set without human endeavour. Stop motion certainly seems invested with something eerie, as though the inanimate has truly been brought to life.

Away from the world of what we could call classical stop-motion animation (models specifically created for movement) there is Jan Svankmajer, a Czech filmmaker based in Prague. He animates found objects, frequently combining disparate objects and forms to create new characters and creatures in a frequently eerie and off-beat mode. Svankmajer has been working since the 1960s and in 1987 he made his feature debut with *Alice*, an adaptation of Lewis Carroll's story. More recently, Svankmajer has made *Little Otik* about a couple who adopt a log.

Key to the development of the stop-motion animated film is the work of Eastern Europeans. Jiri Trnka began in puppet theatre and transposed this affinity to film with work such as *Old Czech Legends* (1953) and *A Midsummer Night's Dream* (1955). His final film was a political allegory called *The Hand* in which a birdlike sculptor refuses to sculpt when a hand dictates that he must do so. The sculptor is imprisoned by the hand inside a cage where he does the work. On completion, the sculptor escapes but the hand pursues and destroys the sculptor who is then celebrated with a lavish funeral.

The work of Ladislaw Starewich is also noteworthy, including *The Magic Clock* (1925) and *The Beautiful Leukanida* in which the attentions of a very beautiful beetle are the source of rivalry between two insects. Like so many other animators in so many nations, Starewich recognised the potential of animation to bring fairy tales to life. He made *The Tale of the Fox* based on the La Fontaine story. Starewich's films are noted not only for the subtlety of their animation but for the way animal characters are presented in human clothes.

In Britain, Barry Purves's work has elevated and progressed the subtlety of the form with films such as *Screen Play*, set in Japan; an adaptation of the opera *Rigoletto* and an adaptation of the Achilles story.

In Japan, stop-motion animation built on the Japanese puppet tradition of bunraku, whereby rod puppets were moved by being connected to the legs of human performers. Kihachino Kawamoto studied animation with Trnka and went on to make *Demon* (1972), and *A Poet's Life* (1974).

Russian animation has also contributed more recently to stop-motion animation through the notable efforts of Moscow-based Christmas Films who have worked on *Shakespeare: The Animated Tales*, *Operavox* and *Testament* for British television.

Like all other areas of animation, the stop-motion world has its slew of heroes. Stop motion has existed in its own right but has also frequently been deployed as a way of creating the illusion of monsters and other creatures in a range of fantasy films, many of which have cult followings.

The names Willis O'Brien, Ray Harryhausen and Phil Tippett are legendary among film fans. It was Willis O'Brien who began the romance of Hollywood with stop motion. O'Brien's most famous work was animating King Kong in the 1933 film of the same name. It was this film that caught the attention of a movie fan called Ray Harryhausen and in turn Harryhausen's stop-motion work inspired the generation that yielded Phil Tippett, Dennis Muren, Ken Ralston, Will Vinton and Henry Selick, all of whom have contributed hugely to the cinema of fantasy.

It is, however, Ray Harryhausen's name that continues to stand like a titan, or more appropriately like Talos (the animated giant from *Jason and the Argonauts*) over the stop-motion world of fantasy filmmaking. Harryhausen no longer produces stop-motion material but his legacy is widely available and has a strong, ardent following. The name Harryhausen immediately conjures images of dinosaurs, monsters, winged horses and, most famously, sword-wielding skeletons. For Harryhausen, Willis O'Brien was a movie-making god but beyond cinema his main inspiration was the illustrator, Gustav Dore, whose images are notable for their dark foregrounds and very hazy backgrounds.

Harryhausen's legendary career began as an apprentice to his hero Willis O'Brien, working on features such as *Mighty Joe Young* (Ernest B. Shoedsack, 1949) before moving on to *The Beast from 20,000 Fathoms* (Eugene Lourie, 1953), *It Came from Beneath the Sea* (Robert Gordon, 1955), *Earth vs The Flying Saucers* (Fred F Sears, 1956), *The Seventh Voyage of Sinbad* (Nathan Juran, 1956), *Mysterious Island* (Cy Endfield,

1961), *Jason and the Argonauts* (Don Chaffey, 1963), *Valley of Gwangi* (James O'Connolly, 1969), *One Million Years BC* (Don Chaffey, 1966), *Golden Voyage of Sinbad* (Gordon Hessler, 1974), *Sinbad and the Eye of the Tiger* (Sam Wanamaker, 1977) and *Clash of the Titans* (Desmond Davis, 1981).

Harryhausen's particular stop-motion process was labelled DynaMation. This technique involved a split-screen rear-projection process to insert stop-motion characters into specifically choreographed background live-action plates that had been shot on location or on full-size sets. For the famous skeleton army scene in *Jason and the Argonauts*, Harryhausen spent four months animating the models for what amounted to five minutes of some of the most dazzling effects work ever seen. For the figure of Talos, the stone giant, Harryhausen made an 18-inch high model that in its motion had to look mechanical even though Harryhausen had committed his career to fluid movement. Talos is regarded as a high-water mark of stop-motion animation. For the moment when Talos crumbles, Harryhausen had to animate each piece falling away in synch with the overall fall of the creature.

On *Clash of the Titans* one of the great achievements was the character of Calibos, inspired by Caliban in *The Tempest* (William Shakespeare, 1611). Harryhausen's stop-motion work intercut almost seamlessly with the live-action footage of the actor as the character had an amount of dialogue. For the Gorgon sequence Harryhausen's animation matched the effect of live-action flames on the body of his stop-motion model so that it integrated with the live-action plates.

Inevitably, Harryhausen had a host of projects that never got made such as *Evolution*. He produced some material for the film but it was never completed. *Evolution* would have told the story of the dawn of life on Earth. Harryhausen's other unrealised visions were *The Hare and the Tortoise*, *Skin and Bones*, *David and Goliath*, *Baron Munchausen*, *The Hobbit*, *Food of the Gods*, *Valley of the Mist* (originally developed by Willis O'Brien), *Force of the Trojans*, *People of the Mist* and the brilliantly and unambiguously titled *Sinbad Goes to Mars*.

Ironically, *Clash of the Titans* was released in the aftermath of the success of the George Lucas-produced film *Star Wars: The Empire Strikes Back* (Irvin Kershner, 1980) which was replete with its own dazzling stop motion for the beast of burden at the start of the film and the snow battle. Harryhausen acolyte, Phil Tippett, was working on this film. Tippett's major contribution to *Empire* was the stop-motion sequences.

* * *

Phil Tippett found a mentor in Harryhausen and then went on to have his own dazzling career, contributing much to the development of stop-motion animation in fantasy films. Tippett now works in the digital animation era. Tippett's credits include image-making for some of the most iconic effects movies of the last thirty years: *Star Wars* (George Lucas, 1977) *The Empire Strikes Back* (Irvin Kershner, 1980), *Dragonslayer* (Matthew Robbins, 1981) *Return of the Jedi* (Richard Marquand, 1983), *RoboCop* (Paul Verhoeven, 1987), *Willow* (Ron Howard, 1988), *Jurassic Park* (Steven Spielberg, 1993) and *Starship Troopers* (Paul Verhoeven, 1997).

Tippett was self-taught, inspired especially by *King Kong* and *The Seventh Voyage of Sinbad*. He started his professional career at Cascade Pictures in Los Angeles where seemingly all the other 1970s animated special-effects hot-shots also began. Tippett was hired along with his friend Jon Berg to supply stop-motion chess characters for *Star Wars* when another film showed a similar effect with people in suits. The chess game is a fondly remembered moment from a film with far larger and brassier effects and animation.

Another Lucas production, *Indiana Jones and the Temple of Doom* (Steven Spielberg, 1984) was another chance for a classic display of stop-motion animation (the original version of *ET: The Extra-Terrestrial* features stop motion for the boys flying past the setting sun on bikes) in the creation of the mine car chase where live action and animation are intercut ferociously. Tippett also contributed to the advance of animation effects with the little-seen fantasy adventure *Dragonslayer* (Matthew Robbins, 1981) which developed the go-motion form.

In 1983, Tippett left ILM and set up his own studio in Berkeley. He began work on *Prehistoric Beast*, which ran to ten minutes, and formed the basis for the TV series, *Dinosaur*. Tippett won an Emmy for the effects on the show. Tippett's skills still were required at ILM and he worked freelance for them designing the stop-motion characters for *Howard the Duck* (Willard Huyck, 1986), *The Golden Child* (Michael Ritchie, 1986) and *Willow* (Ron Howard, 1988).

Tippett's sense of animating movement and animal behaviour in the creation of movie monsters also informed the design of the dragon for the film *Dragonheart* (Rob Cohen, 1996). On *RoboCop* (Paul Verhoeven, 1987) he animated the bipedal, armed robot ED209. For the scene where it tumbles down a stairway, the camera ran at 72 frames per second (rendering very slow images) and the model was simply thrown down the stairs, its joints loosened so they would move of their own volition.

Jurassic Park was considered the end of the era of stop motion being integrated with live action. Originally Phil Tippett and his team, notably Tom St Amand, whom Tippett has called 'king of the armature makers', were to have supplied stop-motion dinosaurs intercut with the full-size animatronic ones created by Stan Winston. However, when Steven Spielberg saw Dennis Muren and ILM's computer test of a T-Rex running through a live-action field, the plan changed. Initially perturbed, Tippett then realised he and his crew still had a very viable role. They continued to provide animatics (moving storyboards) using stop motion and then later created the Dinosaur Input Device which hooked up a stop-motion armature to the computer to assist animators in achieving a realistic, animal-like movement rather than cliché monster moves.

Another key player in the field of stop motion was the late David Allen who had long been a hero to stop-motion fans. He died in August 1999 during work on his lifelong labour of love, *The Primevals*. It had been backed as a low-budget independent movie by Charles Band, a leading light of low-budget horror and fantasy for whom Allen had created numerous stop-motion sequences. Allen began *The Primevals* in 1968 and virtually all the greats of special effects had lent their skills to it at one time or another.

The film was originally called *Raiders of the Stone Ring*. The roster of helping hands on the film will be familiar to many fans of animation and visual effects: Jim Danforth, Dennis Muren, Ken Ralston, Phil Tippett, Randy Cook, Tom St Amand, Dave Carson, Jon Berg, Chris Endicott and Kent Burton. Allen also contributed to **batteries not included* (Matthew Robbins, 1987) making the little spaceships walk and move. A real highlight was animating the ant in *Honey, I Shrunk the Kids* (Joe Johnston, 1989). Allen received an Academy Award nomination for his stop-motion work on *Young Sherlock Homes* (Barry Levinson, 1985).

Not to be overlooked is the form of stop motion called claymation of which the oldest surviving example is a film called *The Sculptor's Nightmare*. Perhaps the most famous practitioner of the claymation form is The Will Vinton Studio based in Portland, Oregon. The studio most well known for their California Raisins commercial has also produced narrative animation as well as claymation sequences for live-action films, including for the Francis Ford Coppola short *Captain Eo* (1986). The Vinton studio also supplied the excellent claymation effects for the undervalued, virtually unknown and worthy of rediscovery, live-action fantasy *Return to Oz* (Walter Murch, 1985).

Claymation is well named, essentially being animated clay rather than the more typical stop-motion approach whereby foam is laid over an armature that can be easily manipulated. A creative success for the Will Vinton Studio was *The Adventures of Mark Twain* (1986) in which the great author tells Huck, Tom and Beck stories from his own work. The film begins with a book opening on Twain's roll top desk and the Mississippi River gushing forth. A pen becomes a fish, an inkwell a tree stump. Will Vinton is currently working with Tim Burton on *The Corpse Bride* for Halloween 2005.

In Britain, the stop-motion tradition has been most widely exemplified by the work and output of Aardman Animation, such as *Creature Comforts* (see **Britoons**). With Nick Park, Peter Lord and David Sproxton have produced hugely popular and recognisable stop motion since the 1970s (Park joining the company in the late 1980s).

For most people, though, there are two recently produced stop-motion features. In both cases, technique and expansive resources are justified by smart and engaging storytelling. The films are *The Nightmare Before Christmas* (Henry Selick, 1993) and *James and the Giant Peach* (Henry Selick, 1996).

The Nightmare Before Christmas (1993)

(76 minutes)

Directed by Henry Selick

Story and Characters: Tim Burton

Screenplay by Michael McDowell and Caroline Thompson

Producer: Denise DiNovi

Executive Producer: Tim Burton

Co-producer: Kathleen Gavin

Associate Producer: Jill Jacobs, Diane Minter, Phillip Lofaro

Cinematography: Pete Kozachik

Editor: Stan Webb

Assistant Art Director: Kelly Asbury

Storyboard Artist: Mike Cachuela

Supervising Sound Editor: Richard L Anderson

Music and Songs: Danny Elfman
Armature Supervisor: Tom St Amand

BUDGET: $18 million

BOX OFFICE: $50,003,043

RELEASE DATE: 13 October 1993 (limited), 29 October (wide)

CERTIFICATE: PG

VOICES: Chris Sarandon (*Jack Skellington the Pumpkin King*), Danny Elfman (*Jack Skellington, singing voice; Clown with the Tearaway Face*), Catherine O'Hara (*Sally, Shock*), William Hickey (*Dr Finkelstein*), Glenn Shadix (*The Mayor of Halloweentown*), Paul Reubens (*Lock*), Ken Page (*Oogie Boogie*), Ed Ivory (*Santa*), Susan McBride (*Big Witch*), Debi Durst (*Corpse Kid, Corpse Mother, Small Witch*), Greg Proops (*Harlequin Demon, Devil, Sax Player*), Kerry Katz (*Man Under the Stairs, Vampire, Corpse Father*), Randy Crenshaw (*Mr Hyde, Behemoth, Vampire*), Sherwood Ball (*Mummy, Vampire*), Carmen Twillie (*Undersea Gal, Man Under the Stairs*), Glenn Waters (*Wolfman*)

TAGLINE: A ghoulish tale with wicked humour and stunning animation.

STORYLINE: A forest in the pale autumn light. A ring of trees stand distinct, their bark painted with images signifying the key American holidays: Easter, Halloween, Thanksgiving and Christmas. A narrator's voice says this wood contains the 'holiday worlds of old' and prompts the question about where holidays come from.

In Halloweentown, another Halloween celebration unfolds, led by Jack Skellington, the Pumpkin King, the most popular resident of Halloweentown. After the celebrations, Jack makes a quick exit and goes out alone beyond Halloweentown. He is bored of the Halloween holiday. He walks on through the night.

Also living in Halloweentown is Sally, a stitched-together girl who is in love with Jack. She longs to escape the mad scientist who created her.

The next day, the Mayor goes to discuss plans for the following Halloween with Jack but he is not at home. Jack has found himself in the wood where the holiday season trees are. Jack is entranced by the trunk with a bright green Christmas tree painted on it. He opens the door and falls inside the tree and finds himself in Christmastown. Jack is intrigued by this new place and investigates. After immersing himself in Christmastown, Jack returns home and tells the townsfolk what a marvellous place it is.

Vexed by what Christmas is and how it is put together, Jack conducts a range of experiments and calculations to try and work it out, but it proves difficult. Jack announces that Halloweentown will do Christmas and everybody and every creature and ghoul sets about making decorations and preparations.

Three Halloweentown children, Lock, Shock and Barrel, have the mission of kidnapping Santa Claus and bringing him to Halloweentown. But, against Jack's wishes, they take Santa to the mysterious Oogie Boogie man.

Concerned for Jack, Sally tells him that she has had a premonition that he will be hurt if he continues with his plans for Christmas. Jack is unconvinced and the countdown to Christmas continues. Jack is going to dress up like Santa Claus and ride a reindeer-driven sleigh over the world. Sally tries to stop Jack's flight but is unsuccessful.

Jack rides out over suburbia on Christmas Eve. News soon spreads about the Santa Claus impostor and Jack is shot down by the military. Jack returns to Halloweentown and rescues Santa and Sally from the Oogie Boogie man who is destroyed. Jack apologises to Santa who returns to Christmastown. Halloweentown gets back to business and everyone is happy that Jack is back.

THE DRAWING BOARD: Having made a splash with his shorts *Frankenweenie* and *Vincent,* Tim Burton moved into mainstream features with his feature directorial debut *Pee-Wee's Big Adventure* (1986), a quirky fantasy comedy about a man-boy and his search for his stolen bicycle. Burton followed this up with the black comic fantasia of *Beetlejuice* (1988), a movie about the afterlife writ in bold cartoonlike terms. A year later he directed one of the quintessential blockbusters, *Batman* (1989) and since then has gone on, like several other directors, to become something of a brand name, so identifiable is his kind of fantasy cinema.

Like other directors whose names have real marquee value (Lucas, Spielberg, Cameron, Coppola, Scott), Burton found himself in the position to be able to executive produce one of his ideas as a film and have his name above the title as a testament to its narrative quality and tone.

Burton initially considered *The Nightmare Before Christmas* as a possible TV special. He'd always been a fan of Christmas-themed TV specials such as Chuck Jones's rendition of the Dr Seuss story, *How the Grinch Stole Christmas* (which was eventually made as a live-action movie starring Jim Carrey in 2000 and directed by the underrated Ron Howard). Burton suggested *The Nightmare Before Christmas* to Disney but they felt it was too off-beat for their image in the 1980s.

By the early 1990s, though, with Burton apparently the heir to the intelligent blockbuster cinema of Steven Spielberg, Disney listened to him again, with renewed interest. At the time the studio were beginning to experience an animation renaissance on the back of the success of *The Little Mermaid* (John Musker and Ron Clements, 1989) and in 1991 they had experienced a smash success with *Beauty and the Beast*. Though *The Nightmare Before Christmas* was only modestly successful in its theatrical release it has developed a healthy cult following, in large part because of it being a stop-motion feature film.

Chosen to direct the film was Burton's old animation friend Henry Selick whom he regarded as the best stop-motion director working. The film set up its production base in San Francisco under the name Skellington Productions, after the name of the hero of the film, Jack Skellington. (After the assured cult success of *Nightmare Before Christmas*, Selick went on to direct *James and the Giant Peach* as a stop-motion feature and then the live-action–stop-motion mix *Monkeybone (2000)* in which a comic book artist's creation, Monkeybone, exists in the real world as a stop-motion character.) At about the same time, across the Atlantic, Nick Park was establishing his credentials as a top flight stop-motion animator of a very different kind with his *Wallace and Gromit* stories. In both instances though, fantasy and reality fuse to compelling effect where comedy (dark and light) is evident in every frame.

It is difficult to say whether *The Nightmare Before Christmas* is more a Tim Burton film than a Henry Selick film. Burton established the story, tone and character template that Selick and his army of animators then detailed and embellished.

Before Disney committed wholeheartedly to the project Selick and his team produced a twenty-second proof of concept sequence to show they could do what they claimed. It was to be the most complex stop-motion film ever made.

Burton reunited with screenwriter Caroline Thompson who had written *Edward Scissorhands* for him. Thompson gives both films a very believable human truth.

The original script for *The Nightmare Before Christmas* was written by Burton's *Beetlejuice* collaborator, Michael McDowell, but it didn't quite fulfil the concept although it did offer up many valid moments and pointers. Caroline Thompson revised the material, engaging in a productive dialogue with the animators and designer as she refined her version of the script. Words informed pictures and pictures informed words. One of the key elements in this process was the availability of the songs and musical sketches that Danny Elfman had already prepared ahead of Thompson joining the project (see also **TOON TUNES**).

INSPIRATIONS: *The Nightmare Before Christmas* is informed not just by Tim Burton's aesthetic but also by his affinity for horror movies, Dr Seuss and German Expressionism in films such as *The Cabinet of Dr Caligari* (Robert Wiene, 1919). Parts of the film, such as those set in Christmastown are very Seussian in their curves, brightness and colour, whereas the sequences set in Halloweenland are very morbid, shadowy and angular.

A further inspiration for the project was the animated TV specials from the Rankin-Bass animation studio in the 1960s, notably their two Christmas-themed pieces, *The Year without Santa Claus* and *Rudolph the Rednosed Reindeer*. Of course, the most obvious inspiration, other than the Halloween and Christmas seasons, is the title of one of the essential American Christmas stories, Clement C Moore's rhyming tale *The Night Before Christmas*.

Burton is currently involved in a new claymation project by Will Vinton Studios for release in Halloween 2005 called *The Corpse Bride* (based on a European folktale about a man who accidentally marries a corpse).

TOON TEAM: *The Nightmare Before Christmas* represents a collaboration between old animator friends, Tim Burton and Henry Selick. The film had been a pet idea of Burton's since his days in the early 1980s working as an animator at the Disney studio on *The Fox and the Hound* (1981). As anybody who has seen *The Fox and the Hound* can testify, it is a long way from Burton's nice kind of nasty and American Gothic. One of Burton's compadres at Disney back then was Henry Selick who went on to specialise in stop-motion animation. A noted short of his is called *Slow Bob in the Lower Dimensions*.

Selick had proved his worth with several shorts, notably one called *Seepage* about a conversation between two people by a swimming pool.

This was made using stop motion and watercolours. Selick also directed *Slow Bob in the Lower Dimension*, a combination of live action, stop motion and cut-out animation. *Slow Bob* won first prize at the Ottawa Animation Festival and second prize at the Chicago Animation Festival.

The crew for *The Nightmare Before Christmas* were assembled from across the United States and included collaborators of Selick's from earlier years. Harley Jessup and Tom St Amand had worked on a range of high-profile visual-effects movies. The film's armature maker, St Amand, is a special effects legend, who has contributed to some of the biggest fantasy movies ever. He built the armatures for *ET: The Extra-Terrestrial* (Steven Spielberg, 1982) and was involved in animating the mine car chase in *Indiana Jones and the Temple of Doom* (Steven Spielberg, 1984) as well as the dinosaur models used as references for the computer animators on *Jurassic Park* (Steven Spielberg, 1993).

VOCAL TALENT: Chris Sarandon, the speaking voice of Jack Skellington, had appeared on screen previously in *Dog Day Afternoon* (Sydney Lumet, 1974), *Fright Night* (Tom Holland, 1985) and *The Princess Bride* (Rob Reiner, 1987). Catherine O'Hara as Sally had starred in *After Hours* (Martin Scorsese, 1985), *Home Alone* (Chris Columbus, 1990). Paul Reubens as the voice of Lock had appeared in Tim Burton's live-action feature debut *Pee Wee's Big Adventure* (1986) and went on to appear in *Batman Returns* (Tim Burton, 1992), *Matilda* (Danny DeVito, 1996) and *Blow* (Ted Demme, 2001).

INK, PAINT AND HARD WORK: Animated films follow certain strict procedures and in stop motion the rules of detailed planning are even more intense. One of the key things about this film is that, where most animation tends to hold one shot for an average of four seconds, *The Nightmare Before Christmas* averaged shots lasting between five and six seconds. Given that there are 24 frames of film running per second and each frame requires an animated move, that is a significant cumulative difference in workload.

Once character designs were approved they would be converted into sculpted reference models from which moulds would be taken. Armatures were made allowing the eventual models to be subtly articulated. The sculpted and fabricated bodies of the characters would be placed on the armatures, after which their costumes or paint jobs would be added.

Sally's dress, for example, was a silkscreen pattern laid on to foam. Her hair was made of foam latex lined with lead to allow for precise animation. She also had countless replacement eyelashes. Once set designs had been approved they were constructed, textured and painted.

Because a stop-motion animation set is going to be given some serious knocks by animators moving about, it is fixed very firmly to the ground. If a set moved it would throw the illusion being captured in the camera. Such was the detail of the film that a set had to be built just for a few-seconds' long shot of Jack reflected in a doorknob.

An interesting design quirk on the project was initiated by Kelly Asbury who discovered that a more skewed design sense could be effected in the work by illustrating with the wrong hand. Soon other animators had adopted the approach and found that it really worked.

Once the dialogue had been laid down in a temp track the storyboards were matched to it to give a rough flow of the pace of the eventual film.

THEME: The film contains Tim Burton's highly recognisable concerns and thematic preoccupations. The melancholy and joyful morbidity of his live-action features are all in place as are a collection of protagonists who feel isolated from society. Edward Scissorhands, Batman and Ed Wood would all feel at home in this film. More than anything, though, the film reminds its audience to be who they are, to be individuals, as playing someone else's game only ends in sadness.

STYLISH TOONS: In the 1950s American TV and fantasy cinema had a director star called George Pal. He produced a series called *Puppetoons* where the puppets were made of wood, each facial expression being individually carved. For this film, the same principle was applied in plastic, so that Jack Skellington and Sally and other main characters had numerous changeable heads that fitted expression and verbal articulation from one frame to the next.

The film pulses with comic energy and also finds spaces for very affecting emotional expressions, notably during Jack's walk early on as he mulls over his future, Sally's lament for Jack and also the stunning image of Jack lying across the outstretched arms of a stone angel in a graveyard. The film doesn't only do downbeat very well, but it also has a great comic invention. Jack's song 'What's This' is a real highlight of the film as he dances wondrously across Christmastown like a kid discovering a new toy.

Halloweentown is marked by its permanently grey skies and a foetid, rusty patina which contrasts with the moonlit snow of Christmastown with all its bright lights.

There are many visual jokes throughout the film including a chorus of vampires, a mad scientist who flips the lid of his skull open to scratch his brains and who later reanimates the skeletons of long-gone reindeer. Watch too for the skeletal cockerel that crows at sunrise over Halloweentown. A set-piece scene is Jack's Christmas Eve visits to houses in suburbia where the kids creep downstairs only to be terrified by shrunken heads and a candy-striped snake that swallows an entire Christmas tree.

For all its manic energy, the film benefits too from quieter passages such as when Jack and Sally unite in an embrace at the end of the film, the camera pulling away to reveal them framed by the moonlight.

CHARACTER SKETCH: Tim Burton's visual style of emaciated caricatures with large eyes and winsome expressions defines all of the characters, notably Jack Skellington and Sally.

Jack is an innocent whose imagination is stirred by the novelty of Christmastown. He is a well-read and articulate character, who dances as gracefully as Fred Astaire, and whose wish to please prompts a degree of pain for him. Ultimately, he takes a much needed holiday from Halloweentown and returns the better for it.

Sally is hopelessly in love with Jack and hopes that he will notice. She is devoted to him and also wants a real life away from the mad inventor who made her. She is a stitched-together being, somewhere between Frankenstein's monster and Snow White.

The Mayor of Halloweentown is a buffoonish character who is literally two-faced as the situation demands.

Zero the dead dog is Jack's constant companion who late in the film sees his bright red nose used to great effect.

Santa Claus is classically round and cheery. Jack Skellington mistakes his name for Sandy Claws. When Santa is brought to Halloweentown he is referred to as 'the big red lobster man'.

The Oogie Boogie man is the essence of terror, living below ground in a menacing carnivalesque world. He is a Hessian-covered monster comprised of worms and bugs. His world recalls something of the manic menace to be found in Burton's film *Beetlejuice* (1988).

TOON TUNES: A key collaborator of Tim Burton's has been composer Danny Elfman. Their collaboration has been as singular and definitive as the Spielberg–John Williams combination, the Zemeckis–Silvestri team-up and the Bernard Herrmann–Alfred Hitchcock effort. Elfman's work with Burton to date has been *Pee-Wee's Big Adventure* (1986), *Beetlejuice* (1988), *Batman* (1989), *Edward Scissorhands* (1990), *Batman Returns* (1992), *Ed Wood* (1993), *Mars Attacks!* (1996), *Sleepy Hollow* (1999), *Planet of the Apes* (2001) and *Big Fish* (2003). Elfman's music, swirling and melodramatic and often immensely playful, works on its own merit and immediately conjures Tim Burton movies to mind, the music swooping and looping around Burton's skewed reality.

For *The Nightmare Before Christmas*, Elfman wrote not only the underscore but also ten songs that formed the lynchpin of the narrative. Elfman worked from character sketches at first. Originally Tim Burton and Michael McDowell were going to write the songs together but Elfman was so enthusiastic that they handed over the task to him. Elfman regarded the project as nothing less than an animated musical. Of the music, Elfman said, 'I wanted a very punchy, old-fashioned sound on this.' The song 'What's This?' is the film's showstopper.

The Nightmare Before Christmas soundtrack: 'Overture', 'Opening', 'This Is Halloween', 'Jack's Lament', 'Doctor Finkelstein/In the Forest', 'What's This?', 'Town Meeting Song', 'Jack and Sally Montage', 'Jack's Obsession', 'Kidnap the Sandy Claws', 'Making Christmas', 'Nabbed', 'Oogie Boogie Song', 'Christmas Eve Montage', 'Poor Jack', 'To the Rescue', 'Finale/Reprise', 'Closing', 'End Title'.

TOON TALK:

A swooning witch to Jack: 'You're a witch's fondest dream.' 'Life's no fun without a scare.'

Jack: 'I, the Pumpkin King, have grown tired of the same old thing.'

Jack: 'I'm the master of fright, the demon of light.'

The Mayor: 'I'm only the elected official here. I can't make decisions by myself.'

OTHER SIMILAR FILMS: *The Nightmare Before Christmas* leads the way to *James and the Giant Peach*, again a story about fantasy opening up a character's sense of self. The Pixar film *Monsters, Inc.* deals with similar ideas. As Burton said himself, the Chuck Jones adaptation of *The Grinch Who Stole Christmas* is a cousin to *The Nightmare Before Christmas*, especially in two sequences: the opening one in which the citizens of Whoville sing about Christmas and second in the sequence of the Grinch sneaking around houses on Christmas Eve. Both films have the same kind of energy and combination of a nice kind of darkness and something a little cuter.

As the time of writing, Tim Burton is collaborating with the claymation studio Will Vinton based in Portland, Oregon on an adaptation of an Eastern European tale, *The Corpse Bride* in which a man inadvertently marries a corpse. Selick had originally worked on the concept with Burton and then left the project. The film is being produced in England under the direction of Mike Johnson who had worked as an assistant animator on *The Nightmare Before Christmas* and as an animator on *James and the Giant Peach*. Carolyn Thompson who wrote *The Nightmare Before Christmas* is writing the screenplay and Pamela Pettler has since done a rewrite.

RECOGNITION: According to Peter Travers in *Rolling Stone*, *The Nightmare Before Christmas* 'Restores originality and daring to the Halloween genre. This dazzling mix of fun and fright also explodes the notion that animation is kids' stuff.' *Time Out* agreed: 'This beautifully realised confection will delight grown ups of all ages.'

HOME VIEWING: The film is available on VHS and also as a special-edition DVD. Alongside the film, the disc contains several scenes cut from the final version of the film. These are an extended version of Jack's experiments to determine what Christmas is (with a temporary track that uses John Williams's 'Dance of the Witches' theme from *The Witches of Eastwick*); a scene with vampire hockey players using a model of Tim Burton's head for a puck; Lock, Shock and Barrel in a scene where they go and look at Oogie Boogie's lair and finally a short scene of Oogie Boogie's silhouette dancing.

The disc also includes Tim Burton's short films from the early 1980s, *Vincent* and *Frankenweenie*, both of them in black and white. *Vincent* is a stop-motion piece about a boy called Vincent Molloy who is obsessed with morbidity and wanting to be like his hero, Vincent Price. Price narrates the film in rhyme, anticipating the rhyme in *The Nightmare Before Christmas*. This must be the only film where a dog is named 'Abercrombie' to rhyme with the word 'zombie'.

Frankenweenie is a live-action short in which a boy's dead dog is reanimated rather like Frankenstein's monster. There is a melancholy edge to the black and white action that anticipates *Ed Wood* and much of *The Nightmare Before Christmas*.

AWARDS: *The Nightmare Before Christmas* was nominated for an Oscar in 1994 for Best Visual Effects. In the same year the film won the Saturn Award for Best Fantasy Film and Best Music and was nominated for a Golden Globe for Best Original Score. The film was also nominated for a Hugo award for Best Dramatic Presentation.

COMMENT: 'I see *Nightmare Before Christmas* as a positive story, without any truly bad characters.' Burton.

VERDICT: *The Nightmare Before Christmas* is a terrific Christmas movie, taking the essence of the festivities and brilliantly fusing it with its morbid opposite Halloween. The film is a genuinely American take on its own folklore. The use of songs energises the story boundlessly.

To the credit of the filmmakers, the fantasy and spectacle never overwhelm the characters who are part of that fantasy world. What the film leaves its audience with is a celebration of Halloween, Christmas, individuality and the thrills of animation.

James and the Giant Peach (1996)

(79 minutes)

Directed by Henry Selick
Screenplay by Karey Kirkpatrick, Jonathan Roberts, Steven Bloom
Produced by Tim Burton, Denise DiNovi
Executive Producer: Jake Eberts
Co-producer: John Engel, Brian Rosen, Henry Selick
Music: Randy Newman
Cinematography: Pete Kozachik (animation), Hiro Narita (live action)
Editor: Stan Webb
Production Design: Harley Jessup
Art Direction: Kendal Cronkhite, Blake Russell, Lane Smith
Set Decoration: Kris Boxell
Costume Design: Julie Slinger
Visual Effects Supervisor: Scott E Anderson

BUDGET: $38 million

BOX OFFICE: $28,900,101

RELEASE DATE: 12 April 1996

CERTIFICATE: U

VOICES: Simon Callow (*Grasshopper, voice*), Richard Dreyfuss (*Centipede, voice*), Jane Leeves (*Ladybug, voice*), Joanna Lumley (*Aunt Spiker*), Miriam Margoyles (*Aunt Sponge, The Glow-worm, voice*), Pete Postlethwaite (*The Old Man*), Susan Sarandon (*Spider, voice*), Paul Terry (*James*), David Thewlis (*Earthworm, voice*), J Stephen Coyle (*Reporter No. 2*), Steven Culp (*James's Father*), Cirocco Dunlap (*Girl with Telescope*), Michael Girardin (*Reporter No. 1*), Tony Haney (*Reporter No. 3*), Kathryn Howell (*Woman in Bathrobe*), Chae Kirby (*Newsboy*), Jeff Mosely (*Hard Hat Man*), Al Nalbandian (*Cabby*), Emily Rosen (*Innocent Girl*), Mike Starr (*Beat Cop*), Susan Turner-Cray (*James' Mother*), Mario Yedidia (*Street Kid*)

TAGLINE: Adventures this big don't grow on trees.

STORYLINE: James is on the beach on a perfect sunny day with his parents. James's father shows him where they are soon to travel to as a family: New York. The dreamlike moment is cut short when an angry rhino appears in the sky and gobbles up James's parents.

Sometime later and James lives with his cruel aunts, Sponge and Spiker in a crooked house on a crooked rocky outcrop on the coastline. James is treated badly and yearns to escape. He makes a lantern out of paper and sets it out like a balloon from his bedroom window.

James is met by a stranger who hands him back his lantern. Inside the lantern are tiny glowing sprites that are apparently crocodile tongues. The man tells James that they are magic then vanishes. James returns home and trips accidentally, setting the sprites free.

Soon, a peach is spotted on the barren tree outside the house and as the aunts berate James they are cut short as the peach begins to grow to an enormous size. The aunts decide to charge people to come and look at the giant peach. James is made to clear up the mess left by the visitors. Soon afterwards he finds that he can push a hole into the peach and he climbs up inside. James is befriended by equally big insects.

Soon the peach, with James in it, breaks free of the tree, when the centipede feels compelled to spook the interfering aunts. The peach bounces across the country and into the sea. James looks at his leaflet about New York and sees that it now includes an image of the peach headed for New York. They need to fly the peach to New York. James and the insects tether a flock of seagulls to the peach and it becomes airborne. The peach then drops back to sea as a huge mechanical shark charges at it. At the last minute the peach is airborne again.

Squabbles break out between the insects, especially between the streetwise centipede and the genteel grasshopper. James holds the gang together. James and the spider talk about being alone and the joy of friendship. James has a dream and in it sees himself being pursued by his aunts. The dream ends with the intrusion into it of the rhino.

James wakes to find the peach has drifted off course and is over arctic waters. Centipede is captured by pirate skeletons and monsters and James and the spider effect a rescue. The journey continues.

A storm gathers and the rhino rushes at James and he defeats it. The peach approaches New York where it lands on top of the Empire State Building, skewered by its mast. A crowd gathers and James tries to explain what has happened. His aunts show up and attempt to kill James and gain possession of the peach again. James says he will not go back with them. The insects intervene and tie the aunts up. The crowd cheers James.

Sometime later James has a new home in New York, living in a house made from the stone of the peach. James spends his days telling other children about his adventures.

THE DRAWING BOARD: Based on the Roald Dahl novel of the same name, *James and the Giant Peach* had initially been considered by the Disney studio in the 1980s. After the success of *The Nightmare Before Christmas* and proof that stop motion really worked as a feature form, Henry Selick found himself heading up the new project, with many of the same crew joining him from *The Nightmare Before Christmas*.

In summer 1993, Disney chief Michael Eisner became aware of talk about adapting the Dahl novel but he was not so sure about its prospects. Selick pushed the studio, reminding them that Dahl's novel had been a children's bestseller since its first publication in 1961. Eisner was convinced and a screenplay was set in motion, of which Roald Dahl's daughter Lucy would have approval.

The first draft was written by Dennis Potter but his take was deemed to stray too far from the original text. Potter had chosen to set the story during World War Two. By early summer 1994, the project was put on hold in order that concerns about the screenplay could be addressed. By this time a budget had been prepared and design and model work was in progress. In late July 1994 the project was officially green lighted.

INSPIRATIONS: The first inspiration was the source text and, most importantly, its tone. Also important was the very immediate legacy of *The Nightmare Before Christmas*.

TOON TEAM: For *James and the Giant Peach*, Henry Selick went with the tried and tested. He reteamed with many of the Skellington Productions (fourteen out of twenty) crew from *The Nightmare Before Christmas*. Tom St Amand reprised his role as armature builder and production design was handled by Harley Jessup, a key player in visual effects through his work at Industrial Light and Magic in the 1980s. Jessup had worked with Selick back in the early 1980s when they were involved with the George Lucas/Alan Ladd Jr-produced animated feature, *Twice Upon a Time* (John Korty, 1982) which was made using 'lumage' – illuminated cut-out figures.

After *James and the Giant Peach*, Henry Selick went on to direct the live-action–stop-motion combo *Monkeybone* which was poorly marketed by 20th Century Fox. At the time of writing he is developing an animated adaptation of Neil Gaiman's *Coraline*.

VOCAL TALENT: The film's graceful and vivid animation is matched by a range of British and American voices. Paul Terry (James; see **INK, PAINT AND HARD WORK**) voices the animated version of his live-action self while Simon Callow voices The Grasshopper. Callow's other credits include *Amadeus* (Milos Forman, 1984), *A Room with a View* (James Ivory, 1985), *Postcards from the Edge* (Mike Nichols, 1990), *Four Weddings and a Funeral* (Mike Newell, 1994), *Jefferson in Paris* (James Ivory, 1995), *Ace Ventura: When Nature Calls* (Tom Shadyac, 1995), *Shakespeare in Love* (John Madden, 1996).

Susan Sarandon's long-running film career includes starring roles in *Atlantic City* (Louis Malle, 1980), *The Witches of Eastwick* (George Miller, 1987) *Bull Durham* (Ron Shelton, 1988), *Thelma & Louise* (Ridley Scott, 1991), *Lorenzo's Oil* (George Miller, 1992), *Dead Man Walking* (Tim Robbins, 1995) and *Stepmom* (Chris Columbus, 1998).

Richard Dreyfuss as The Centipede has starred in *American Graffiti* (George Lucas, 1973), *The Goodbye Girl* (Herbert Ross, 1977), *Jaws* (Steven Spielberg, 1975), *Close Encounters of the Third Kind* (Steven Spielberg, 1977), *Down and Out in Beverly Hills* (Paul Mazursky, 1984), *Tin Men* (Barry Levinson, 1987), *Stakeout* (John Badham, 1987), *Always* (Steven Spielberg, 1989), *What About Bob?* (Frank Oz, 1991) and *Mr Holland's Opus* (Stephen Herek, 1995).

David Thewlis as the hapless Worm has appeared in *Naked* (Mike Leigh, 1994) and *Dragonheart* (Rob Cohen, 1995).

Pete Postlethwaite, who appears briefly as the stranger at the start and conclusion of the adventure, broke through into films with *Distant Voices, Still Lives* (Terrence Davies, 1988), *In the Name of the Father* (Jim Sheridan, 1993), *The Usual Suspects* (Bryan Singer, 1995), *Dragonheart* (Rob Cohen, 1996), *Jurassic Park: The Lost World* (Steven Spielberg, 1997), *Amistad* (Steven Spielberg, 1997) and *Brassed Off* (Mark Herman, 1996).

INK, PAINT AND HARD WORK: Film journalist Mark Cotta Vaz accurately wrote of the film that it represented 'a landmark fusion of the physical reality of stop motion and the virtual reality of the digital realm.'

A key collaborator on the project was children's book illustrator, Lane Smith, who joined the project to design the characters. About the choice of Smith, Henry Selick commented that 'My own natural design style is a little harsh for most family films. Lane Smith's work looks like a cousin to what I do. It is still wild stuff, but a little sweeter.' Lane Smith's biggest contributions were to the design of the Grasshopper, the Centipede and the Glow-worm. The toughest assignments were designing a look for the animated James puppet that matched the young actor Paul Terry (coincidentally also the name of one of animation's pioneers). Four different styles of James puppet faces were created for specific emotions such as happiness, sadness and panic. The other challenge was Miss Spider. Smith and Selick worked through over a hundred images and at one point Smith even suggested they lose the character.

Building a full-scale peach for the animation work would have been unfeasible so it was eventually constructed in different sections made of plaster and fibreglass covered with coloured industrial felt.

In stark contrast to the stop-motion images that comprise almost all of the film, one scene that stands out shows James dreaming of the peach, hanging in space like a mobile. The image has more in common with digital imaging than stop motion.

For the charging rhino cloud, the rhino puppet was filmed against a green screen in the cloud tank and lightning animation was added.

After all these challenges, one more remained which was when stop motion met live action at the climax of the story. The difficulty here was ensuring the eye lines of actors and stop-motion characters matched one another so that they were unified in the same sense of space.

After designs were approved, sculptures were made and moulds taken. Armatures were built and covered with foam skins that were painted. Each layer of oil paint was thinned with turpentine to give a texture to the characters.

The animators worked harder than even on *The Nightmare Before Christmas* to make the animation subtle and compelling as the sets were more minimal. The Arctic surface set was 24 feet wide and 30 feet deep and the moving ice-floe element comprised a flexible base that was sculpted from foam simulating the icy surface.

THEME: The film very simply animates the idea of family, love and the overcoming of fear to realise a dream. This is an incredibly wistful, generous film.

STYLISH TOONS: Unlike *The Nightmare Before Christmas, James and the Giant Peach* would be bookended by live-action segments. The live-action sets were built in forced perspective on a set at Treasure Island in San Francisco. Treasure Island is a man-made island that was once a naval base in the San Francisco Bay.

The film, for all its animation, also included 350 separate special effects shots which involved cel animation and even cloud tank effects. Buena Vista Visual Effects provided 240 digital composites, 180 blue-screen shots, 20 cg shots and 35 rod removals.

A significant computer-generated element of the film was the ocean which was made to look as though it had somehow been animated through stop motion. Robert Minsk, a software developer at Sony Imageworks, prepared a program based on ocean physics so that each wave had a hand-animated curve.

In Dahl's book, a school of sharks attacks James and his peachy friends but Selick felt it would be more movie-friendly and dynamic to create just one sea monster. Selick's decision was inspired partly by the Imperial AT walkers in *Star Wars: The Empire Strikes Back* (Irvin

Kershner, 1980), a film which George Lucas always called his stop-motion movie.

The film's panoply of visual effects also involved the creation of an aurora borealis effect. In such a high-tech movie the illusion was achieved with real simplicity: three overlapping layers of bridal veil were lit separately and then combined together. In a nod to animation history the film's underwater sequences were inspired by the Disney animated feature *Pinocchio* where just a few slow-moving elements suggested an underwater environment.

The film is marked by a real sense of beauty and delicacy. The scene where the peach drifts across a sky of clouds shaped like teapots is dazzling as is the dreamy beginning that encapsulates much of the film. James and his mother and father lie on the beach looking up at the ever-changing shape of the clouds.

The night-time sequence that begins with James listening to the Grasshopper play violin is emotionally true, culminating as it does in a song sung by all the insects to remind James of the love they have for him.

The rhino is a powerful image of the film and the mechanical shark is comically menacing.

Unsurprisingly, there is much visual humour derived from the inventive action such as the insects and James making peach juice.

Perhaps one of the most beautiful images is of James and the Grasshopper standing on the top of the peach silhouetted by the white disc of the full moon. There is a lot to enjoy simply in the film's colour palette.

The film's primary action takes place in the daylight – the bright peach and the blue sea. The film also manages to look suitably cold when the adventurers reach icy waters, and New York, as the clouds part above it, looks jewel-like with its pretty coloured lights.

The rich colour scheme of the film reflects the emotional colour James experiences once he's left the monochromatic misery of life with his aunts, and he anticipates this himself when he draws his colour picture of New York early on. James is the source of the realisation of his dream.

The film's closing image reminds us of the power of storytelling and the way that fantasy and reality can come together for the better.

CHARACTER SKETCH: James is the classic misunderstood, displaced hero character whose journey reveals to himself and those around him his potential and strengths. For the early part of the film, James is portrayed by young actor Paul Terry. But from the moment he enters the peach to the moment he exits it the live-action actor is represented by a stop-motion puppet voiced by the actor. James is a nervous, quiet and thoughtful child and this thoughtfulness is his greatest asset.

Centipede is a cocky, streetwise New York bug whose confidence sometimes gets the better of him.

Spider is an enigmatic, misunderstood character who has a special bond with James as he showed her great care before he met the other insects, protecting her from the aunts.

The Grasshopper is the wise old soul of the adventure and his quiet night-time chat with James and subsequent violin playing is a highlight of the film.

The Worm is comically anxious and the Ladybird is a bustling, nurturing mother figure.

The aunts, Spiker and Sponge, though only seen as live-action characters, are so brilliantly caricatured and monstrous they have the aura of animated ghouls.

In essence, the insects become James's surrogate family, offering him all the emotional support and encouragement his aunts never have done. They help James realise his dream.

The stranger character who appears just twice in the film is presented as a magic character who is perhaps the spirit of Roald Dahl.

The Rhino is of course symbolic of death and a wider fear of the world and the climax of James's journey is destroying the Rhino by denying it any fearfulness.

TOON TUNES: The film's music and songs were written by Randy Newman, the man synonymous with the scores for the first four Pixar films: *Toy Story, A Bug's Life* (John Lasseter and Andrew Stanton, 1998), *Toy Story 2* (John Lasseter, 2000) and *Monsters, Inc.* (Pete Docter, 2001). Newman's other credits include *The Natural* (Barry Levinson, 1984), *Avalon* (Barry Levinson, 1990), *Awakenings* (Penny Marshall, 1990), *Pleasantville* (Gary Ross, 1999) and *Seabiscuit* (Gary Ross, 2003). Newman's main theme for *James and the Giant Peach* is what can be dubbed James's theme, a really wistful and sad piece played on violin which is then heard in the action of the film being played by the Grasshopper under the moonlight.

The film's soundtrack: 'My Name is James', 'That's the Life', 'Eating the Peach', 'Family', 'Main Title', 'Clouds', 'Spiker', 'Sponge and a

Rhino', 'Magic Man', 'Giant Peach', 'Into the Peach', 'James Makes Some Friends', 'Peach Rolls', 'All at Sea', '100 Seagulls and One Shark', 'Lullaby', 'James' Dream', 'Way Off Course', 'Rhino Attacks', 'Empire State Building', 'New York City', 'Spiker and Sponge Come to America', 'Place Where Dreams Come True', 'Good News'.

TOON TALK:
The Worm (on Centipede's heroic dive into the sea): 'Good heavens! He's committed pesticide!'

The Stranger's promise to James: 'Marvellous things will happen!'

OTHER SIMILAR FILMS: In contrast to the all-out sweetness and gentility of *James and the Giant Peach*, there is the manic energy and fun spookiness of Selick's previous stop-motion feature, *The Nightmare Before Christmas*. Indeed the protagonist from that film, Jack Skellington, makes a cameo in *James and the Giant Peach* as a long-dead pirate.

RECOGNITION: *Box Office* magazine found *James and the Giant Peach* '. . . an imaginative combination of live action and stop-motion animation, all coloured with Selick's uniquely dramatic, preternatural aesthetics' while Wally Hammond in *Time Out* felt it had ' . . . an enchanting, at times ghoulish appeal . . . it most beautifully captures the book's free floating, fantastic sense of adventure and wonder.'

AWARDS: The film was nominated for an Oscar for Best Music, Original Musical or Comedy Score and in 1997 was nominated for a Golden Satellite award for Best Motion Picture, Animation or Mixed Media.

HOME VIEWING: The film is available on VHS and DVD. The DVD also contains a brief behind the scenes piece and the trailer.

COMMENT: 'I like to do outlandish designs for characters because then it is more of a miracle when they come to life.' Henry Selick.

VERDICT: This is a charming film and one of the best fantasy movies for young people you could hope to find, centring as it does on the growth of a child's self-confidence and finding his place in the world.

What is also so admirable is how the action sequences are rooted in the distinct personalities, strengths and weaknesses of the characters.

The animation is graceful and elegant and the film is happy not to be a non-stop assault of action.

Britoons

British animation has a long tradition going back to cinema's earliest days and the work of James Stuart Blackton in the early twentieth century. More recently, one of the stand-out features has been *Animal Farm*, directed by John Halas and Joy Bachelor from the novel by George Orwell. Another key figure in British animation is Richard Williams, once based in England for thirty years, now back in his home country of Canada, and responsible for training up many animators through his *Thief and the Cobbler* project. One of the stand-out British animation directors in the classical style was Simon Wells who worked for Steven Spielberg's short-lived Amblimation studio in London. Wells had worked on *Who Framed Roger Rabbit?* for which Richard Williams had provided the animation direction. Wells went on to co-direct *An American Tail: Fievel Goes West* (1991), and *Balto* (1995), both made in London.

In the 1970s the most successful British animated feature was *Watership Down*, based on the novel of the same name by Richard Adams.

In contrast to the American animation industry, one of the sources and opportunities that opened up for more experimental work was a series of information films commissioned by the GPO. A series of short information films in the 1930s gave the perfect opportunity for fresh and arresting animated-image-making. Chief among these artists was Len Lye. From New Zealand, Lye came to London in 1926 and in the 1930s was commissioned to make several information films about the benefits of the Post Office. In the 1950s and 1960s he became a leading figure of the kinetic art movement. His interest was in movement and making films without a camera, by making impressions and painting directly on to film negative. His films for the Post Office that are still available today were *Colour Box* (1935) which ran for four and a half minutes promoting cheaper postal rates; *Rainbow Dance* (four minutes) which was all about Post Office savings accounts, and used solarised images of people and abstract shapes; *Trade Tattoo* (six minutes) which reminded people to post items early in order to keep Britain running smoothly. His films are playful and economical and foreshadow the work of filmmakers like Stan Brakhage, whose work certainly feeds into the spirit of animation.

In turn Brakhage's work has informed contemporary, blockbuster directors such as David Fincher, whose *Se7en* (1995) opening credits owe a debt to the spirit of both Lye and Brakhage. Lotte Reiniger was another filmmaker who made inventive, abstract animation such as *The Tocher*, a short film ballet using silhouettes, again for the Post Office.

In the 1930s and 1940s there was no animation feature industry in Britain. By the 1950s, though, with the country recovering from World War Two, animated features began to trickle through, notably the Halas and Bachelor adaptation of George Orwell's satirical novel *Animal Farm* which was the first British animated feature made. The film represented a moment of apotheosis for the studio that had established itself as one of the major animation producers in western Europe.

John Halas and Joy Bachelor were a husband-and-wife team who had made their name during World War Two with a series of inventive and memorable pieces of animation made as government-funded propaganda. In all, seventy shorts of this kind were made between 1941 and 1945, potentially dull subjects often being given witty treatments. Enhancing the work of the studio's visuals were the musical contributions of two celebrated composers – Francis Chagrin and Matya Sieber.

After the war the Halas and Bachelor studio produced the Poet and Painter series which saw them collaborating with Henry Moore, Ronald Searle and Mervyn Peake (the author of the fantasy *Gormenghast* trilogy). This endeavour culminated in the production of *Animal Farm*. Incredibly, all the voices for the characters in this classically animated film were voiced by one actor, Maurice Denham.

The film was well received, despite some negativity over its ending. In Orwell's 1945 novel on which the film was based, there is no hope held out for the survival of democracy. In the film version it is suggested that the farm animals will not tolerate the police state (represented by pigs). Among the studio's animators were Bob Privett, Digby Turpin, Vic Bevis, Tony Guy and Brian Borthwick. *Animal Farm* is notable for the seriousness of its tone given the usual association of animals in animation with laughs and chuckles.

The Halas and Bachelor studio funded much of its own more personal work through commissions to animate commercials. In the 1950s the studio made a series of experimental pieces of work for screening at the 1951 Festival of Britain, some with Len Lye. The studio also produced several animated TV shows, notably *Foo Foo* and *Snip and Snap*.

John Halas went on to write several books about animation: *The Technique of Film Animation*, *Design in Motion* and *Art in Movement*. In the 1960s he began investigating the possibility of allying the computer with the animated form and the potential of holograms and laser technology intrigued him. In 1967 he produced a computer-animated short about mathematics.

At a time when audiences justly celebrate the achievements of the Aardman Animation studio in Bristol it's important to remember those who came before with an equivalent surfeit of energy and storytelling excellence. In the 1960s there was *The Yellow Submarine* and in the late 1960s animated shorts got a fresh wind courtesy of 'one-man band' Bob Godfrey who came on the scene making shorts. Television certainly proved a haven for short form work, typically made for young people. Perhaps only now in the early twenty-first century is animation's appeal and appropriateness for adults really beginning to shine through.

In the 1970s, a British animation studio produced an adaptation of Richard Adam's iconic novel *Watership Down* that proved popular. This was then followed by the film *Plague Dogs* by the same company, again working from a Richard Adams novel.

The 1980s British animation scene in terms of one-off projects is perhaps best recalled by two adaptations: the first was the John Coates animated version of Raymond Briggs's storybook *The Snowman* (Dianne Jackson, 1982). The film retained the book's crayon images and certainly lends it a distinct visual quality. It was narrated by David Bowie.

The success of this short piece (it continues to air most Christmases on British television) was followed by an adaptation of Briggs's picture book *When the Wind Blows* (1986). Directed by Jimmy T Murakami, the book and film tell the story of an elderly couple, Jim and Hilda Bloggs, as they follow government instructions in preparing for nuclear war. When the bomb falls and the wind blows, Jim and Hilda suffer the nuclear winter. Bowie's collaboration continued as he supplied the film's title song.

Two other key animated features were produced in Britain in the 1980s for television audiences. They were adaptations of classic children's literature, produced by the same studio – Cosgrove Hall in Manchester. The first was the completely charming stop-motion adaptation of Kenneth Grahame's *The Wind in the Willows* which had such incredible detail to character and set design that was matched by fantastic vocal characterisations from David Jason as Toad, Ian Carmichael as Rat and Michael Hordern as Badger. The film captured Toad's manic energy and Mole's sweetness and presented a brilliantly idealised picture-book countryside filled with super-cute mice and weasels. The film was first broadcast over Christmas 1983. Production costs were around £400,000 with around £5,000 being spent on the creation of each richly designed character.

A little later in the decade the studio adapted Roald Dahl's novel *The BFG* to full ink and paint animation. Originally, the project was to have been a theatrical release. Again it starred David Jason as the voice of the gangly, big-eared Big Friendly Giant and the film has become something of a staple of many Christmas TV schedules.

For many audiences, British animation is now synonymous with Aardman Animation who were notably successful in the 1990s. It was via television that animation flourished, notably in the work of the Aardman studio, established by Peter Lord and David Sproxton in the 1970s. In the 1980s a couple of commissions from Channel 4 allowed the company to flex its wings. They were commissioned to make *Conversation Pieces*, which led to *Creature Comforts* which anthropomorphised animals with such inventive wit.

It was the *Wallace and Gromit* thirty-minute specials that further enhanced the reputation of the studio. The first of these was *A Grand Day Out* which Nick Park had begun at film school many years before. The film introduced audiences to Wallace and his dog Gromit. The film saw Wallace, a whimsical inventor, take his dog to the moon in a home-made rocket. Nick Park has called himself a frustrated inventor and fan of Heath Robinson. That kind of clunky, convoluted but charming kind of invention pervades the Wallace and Gromit shorts. These films also echo the work of Chuck Jones in their energy and characterisation. Of course, the other significant feature of Wallace and Gromit is that they are clay animated characters.

A Grand Day Out was successful enough to warrant a follow-up called *The Wrong Trousers*. Costing £800,000 at Aardman, this film sees Wallace invent a pair of mechanical trousers with a life of their own. *The Wrong Trousers* is a very satisfying Hitchockian-style mystery and it confirmed Nick Park's facility for both pastiche and parody that would be so abundant later in the *Chicken Run* feature. For the realism of the sets, art director Yvonne Fox even went to Manchester to study the architecture there.

There was a follow-up called *A Close Shave*, which was commissioned by the BBC, with a broadcast slot of Christmas 1995. The eighteen-month schedule for scripting, storyboarding, shooting and completing the half-hour film was tight and called for a greater number of animators (but the budget was £1.3 million). In part, though, the concept was to see how a larger team would work as already thoughts were turning to producing an animated feature (which did come to pass in 2000 as *Chicken Run*).

In *A Close Shave*, Nick Park directed more than he actually animated and for him the concern was 'how you manage to keep that consistency of style and quality when there are many different hands at work'.

As usual, Park worked with his writing partner Bob Baker from the very start. Previously, Park had created the story outline and then Baker had started his involvement. Park's long-standing affinity for genre and old British cinema shines through *A Close Shave* with allusions to *Brief Encounter* and *The Terminator*. Enhancing the mood of the film was Julian Nott's musical score which used a 65-piece orchestra.

One of the enduring reasons for the popularity of the Wallace and Gromit characters and the world they are living in is that it is so recognisably British. Park's movie history savvy also enriches the storytelling, appealing to a shared popular knowledge of film. Simon Louvish, in *Sight and Sound*, has written that 'Park and company are great plunderers of our Glorious Movie Past.'

Watership Down (1978)

(92 minutes)

Directed by Martin Rosen
Written by Martin Rosen from Richard Adams's novel
Watership Down
Animation Director: Tony Guy
Music Prologue and Main Title by Malcolm Williamson, all
other tracks by Angela Morley
'Bright Eyes' written by Mike Batt and sung by Art
Garfunkel

BUDGET: $4.8 million

BOX OFFICE: $30 million

RELEASE DATE: 1 January 1978

CERTIFICATE: U/G

VOICES: John Hurt (*Hazel*), Richard Briers (*Fiver*), Michael Graham Cox (*Bigwig*), Harry Andrews (*General Woundwort*), Ralph Richardson (*Chief Rabbit*), Zero Mostel (*Keehar*), Roy Kinnear (*Pipkin*), Denholm Elliot (*Cowslip*), John Bennett (*Captain Holly*), Simon Cadell (*Blackberry*), Richard O'Callaghan (*Dandelion*), Terence Rigby (*Silver*), Nigel Hawthorne (*Captain Campion*), Hannah Gordon (*Hyzenthlay*), Mary Maddox (*Clover*), Lyn Farleigh (*Cat*), Michael Hordern (V*oice of Frith*), Joss Ackland (*Black Rabbit*), Michelle Price (*Lucy*), Derek Griffiths (*Vermin*), Clifton Jones (*Blackavar*)

TAGLINE: 'All the world will be your enemy, Prince with a thousand enemies and when they catch you they will kill you.'

STORYLINE: A prologue shows an ancient time and the creation of the animals and specifically the rabbit who is cursed with being the enemy, it seems, of all other animals.

The present day. Sunset over a country field. Hazel and his younger brother Fiver move out into the evening light. Fiver is agitated and is convinced something terrible is going to happen to the warren. He is sure they need to head to a safer place. Hazel tries to speak to the Chief Rabbit but is ignored. Hazel, Fiver and several other rabbits make the break for freedom and their adventure begins.

The brave rabbits reach a stream and are confronted by a dog from whom they escape across the water. Their journey takes them as far as a road and then way beyond. One of the rabbits, Bigwig, gets caught in a snare and almost dies. The rabbits have begun to question Hazel's wisdom in undertaking the journey. Seeking shelter, the rabbits are offered the chance to stay in a warren by a rabbit called Cowslip. The warren is an eerie place run by the tyrannical General Woundwort. Their travels take them to a farm where Hazel sees several does in a hutch.

An injured rabbit called Captain Holly reaches Hazel and the others. Holly is battered and bloody and has escaped the warren run by the tyrannical Woundwort where no rabbits are allowed to go free and roam.

Hazel, Fiver and the others venture on to the high ground they have been trekking towards. Once there they realise they have a problem: there are no does in their group. The rabbits meet a seagull called Keehar and ask if he will go and scout for does.

Hazel and Pipkin venture to a nearby farm where they see and liberate does. Hazel is shot by the farmer and discovered by Fiver just in time.

Keehar alerts the rabbits to a patrol of Woundwort's guards and Bigwig is captured and taken to Woundwort's warren. Hazel sends Keehar to go and tell the captured Bigwig that they are concocting a rescue plan. Woundwort is highly suspicious of Bigwig who talks with the doe Hyzenthlay who had tried to get Woundwort to let the rabbits find a new warren before. Bigwig says he will liberate the rabbits. Bigwig tells Keehar that there are many rabbits ready to leave and the news is relayed to Hazel.

Bigwig leads the exodus from Woundwort's warren. The rabbits cross the river with Hazel's help and head for Watership Down. Woundwort confronts Hazel and says the deserters should be handed back. Hazel suggests they should all live peacefully.

In his anger, Woundwort and his troops come to the warren at Watership Down to find Bigwig and kill him.

Hazel returns to the farm and lures the dog up to the warren where it confronts Woundwort. The rabbits are finally free. Summer passes to autumn and then winter and Hazel dies, leaving behind a thriving community up on safe ground.

THE DRAWING BOARD: *Watership Down* is a seminal moment in British animation, building on the tradition set by Halas and Bachelor with *Animal Farm* as well as in more general terms showing that full, classical animation could be produced in Britain. At this time the Disney studio, so synonymous with lushly produced animation, was in a state of flux.

Inevitably there are anomalies and changes in the process of adapting any novel to film format and *Watership Down* has certain scenes that are reframed slightly or excised. The film amplifies the Newtown sequence where the rats attack Bigwig in graveyard outbuildings; the novel only refers to this moment. By contrast, the Cowslip's Warren sequence from the novel is truncated as it is more about internal emotional life as opposed to the exterior world that animation can represent best.

In the book, the rabbits' fight with rats occurs in a barn. In the film this confrontation occurs in a cemetery workshop. The film creates a rabbit called Violet. Other rabbits are not included in the film version, namely Hawkbit, Acorn and Speedwell. In the film it is Hyzenthlay who leads the dog to Watership Down but in the book it is Blackberry and Dandelion.

INSPIRATIONS: The film is an adaptation of Richard Adams's classic novel of the same name, based around a rabbit warren on the South Downs. This search for a new home relates to the Don Bluth animated feature *The Secret of Nimh* (1982). Disney's adaptation of the Felix Salten novel *Bambi* can also be regarded as a key influence.

TOON TEAM: Noted American animator John Hubley, who had worked in the animation world since the 1940s at Disney, had originally been involved in this adaptation. His tenure did not last but traces of his creative input can be seen. Hubley had always been committed to animation's capacity to present social issues and there are moments in the film where this shines through, such as Hazel's plea to Woundwort for all the rabbits to live peacefully together rather than in conflict.

After the success of *Watership Down*, director Martin Rosen continued in adapting the work of Richard Adams (such as *Plague Dogs* – see **OTHER SIMILAR FILMS**) and kept with him some of the same animation team.

VOCAL TALENT: John Hurt is one of the great British actors of the past thirty years. He has appeared in *Alien* (Ridley Scott, 1979), *1984* (Michael Radford, 1984), *Harry Potter and the Philosopher's Stone* (Chris Columbus, 2001). Hurt also voiced one of the main characters in *Plague Dogs* (Martin Rosen, 1982), the successor to *Watership Down*.

Ralph Richardson is familiar to fans of fantasy films from his role in *Time Bandits* (Terry Gilliam, 1982) and *Greystoke The Legend of Tarzan, Lord of the Apes* (Hugh Hudson, 1984).

Richard Briers can be seen in *Much Ado About Nothing* (Kenneth Branagh, 1993) and *Frankenstein* (Kenneth Branagh, 1994) and the TV series *The Good Life*. More recently, Briers has starred as Smee in *Peter Pan* (PJ Hogan, 2003).

INK, PAINT AND HARD WORK: Critical to the success of the film was balancing realism with a level of dynamism appropriate for animation. Martin Rosen noted that if the rabbits were too realistically rendered they would vanish into the background, but if they looked too cartoony they would be at odds with the backgrounds.

The background artists based their backgrounds on the actual locations of the film so that The River Test, The Enbourne, Nuthanger Farm and other spaces were geographically and seasonally accurate.

THEME: The film communicates a sense of nature under threat from man's thoughtlessness but also the violence inherent in nature. The film is a pastoral piece and the loving depictions of the English countryside are idyllic but are shown to contain tensions and uncertainties.

STYLISH TOONS: A commitment to naturalism defines the aesthetic of this film. There are sweeping vistas but the English countryside scenes also go into terrific detail, such as a grasshopper hopping from one blade of grass to another. Look too at the ghostly sculptures in the graveyard workshops.

The most engaging sequences though are the more abstractly designed prologue (inspired it would seem by aboriginal tribal art) and also the dark visions of doom that Fiver experiences. The first of these shows blood like a wave across a field, the trees merging with it in a nightmarish scene.

Believing Hazel dead, Fiver is distraught and has a vision of his brother's soul flying across the landscape.

For the sequence early on where the rabbits find themselves in the wood at night, low-key images are used, playing up the hostility and threat of the branches and the darkness in a way that recalls Snow White's experience when lost in the woods in *Snow White and the Seven Dwarfs*.

A key strength of the film is its depiction of violence towards and among the rabbits. The scene of Bigwig's near death when caught in a snare has a documentary-like atmosphere to it and his final battle with Woundwort, while more subjectively presented, does not shirk from the wounds inflicted.

CHARACTER SKETCH: Hazel is the assured, calmly confident leader of the rabbits on their quest to safer ground. His heroic status is assured by the sacrifices he makes, as well as his encounter with the great rabbit spirit Frith at the end of the story.

Fiver is Hazel's nervy, younger brother who has visions of danger for all rabbits. His love for his brother is his defining trait.

Woundwort is a genuinely arresting-looking tyrant, his one eye milky white, his face scarred.

Keehar the seagull is naturalistically drawn but certainly offers the most comic effect and relief in the film. In some way Keehar anticipates the actions of Jeremy the crow in *The Secret of Nimh* (see **INSPIRATIONS**).

Over all the action is the spirit of Frith, the rabbit's creator who is both challenging and ultimately compassionate.

TOON TUNES: Like many animated feature films, *Watership Down* includes a song that went on to become a popular hit, the song 'Bright Eyes' written by Mike Batt and sung by Art Garfunkel. Angela Morley's orchestral score tracks much of the action and is imbued with the spirit of English composer Ralph Vaughan Williams.

TOON TALK:
Fiver: 'They'll never rest until they've spoiled the earth.'

OTHER SIMILAR FILMS: The follow-up to *Watership Down* by director Martin Rosen was *Plague Dogs* (1982) based on another Richard Adams novel. *Plague Dogs* had animals at its centre and dramatised the relationship between the animal and human worlds. In 2001, a TV series produced by Nepenthe (the production company of *Watership Down*) continued the world of *Watership Down*.

Plague Dogs follows the adventures of two lab dogs, Snitter and Rowf, who escape from a Lake District research centre and are pursued by the authorities who think the dogs have anthrax. *Plague Dogs* is an anti-vivisectionist story, featuring the same realist commitment as *Watership Down*. *Plague Dogs* was in production for two years in both London and Los Angeles and focuses almost exclusively on the dogs, unlike the novel, which is more able to explore the human pursuers. The film was budgeted at $5 million and has the same muted watercolour tones as *Watership Down*. *Plague Dogs* was not popular though, most likely because of the seriousness of its story rather than the accomplishment of its animation. The film's distributor was so concerned about the material that they pulled out so Rosen distributed the film himself.

For American video release, several of the more violent pieces of action and language have been edited out. The film again featured John Hurt in a leading vocal role – as the dog Snitter. Christopher Benjamin provided the voice for Rowf and James Bolam for Tod, the fox the dogs befriend.

RECOGNITION: *Watership Down* was not a blockbuster but was successful and endures as a firm favourite today.

AWARDS: The film won a Saturn Award in 1979 for Best Animated Feature.

HOME VIEWING: The film is available on both VHS and DVD and continues to screen on the occasional Christmas film schedule.

COMMENT: 'Certain demands are made on the audience which they have not been used to in animation before.' Martin Rosen.

VERDICT: *Watership Down* is certainly lush to look at and is commendable for its naturalism. From time to time it becomes rather monotonous in its pace but this is compensated for by its serious tone and commitment to its issues (in some ways it has much in common with Japanese animation such as *Princess Mononoke* (Hayao Miyazaki, 1997)). *Watership Down*'s strongest visual moments are the several sequences based around Fiver's visions of death, and the inventive prologue sequence.

Chicken Run (2000)

(81 minutes approx.)

Directed by Nick Park and Peter Lord
Written by Nick Park, Peter Lord, Karey Kirkpatrick
Executive Producer: Jake Eberts, Jeffrey Katzenberg, Michael Rose
Producer: Peter Lord, Nick Park, David Sproxton
Line Producer: Carla Shelley
Associate Producer: Lenny Young
Music: Harry Gregson-Williams and John Powell
Editor: Mark Solomon
Production Design: Phil Lewis
Art Direction: Tim Farrington, Rosalind Shingleton
Costume Design: Sally Taylor
Key Animators: Merlin Crossingham, Sergio Delfino, Suzy Fagan, Jay Grace, Guionne Leroy, Seamus Malone, Dave Osmand, Darren Robbie, Jason Spencer-Galsworthy, Ian Whitlock

BUDGET: $42 million

BOX OFFICE: $214 million

RELEASE DATE: 21 June 2000

CERTIFICATE: U/G

VOICES: Mel Gibson (*Rocky*), Phil Daniels (*Fetcher*), Lynn Ferguson (*Mac*), Tony Haygarth (*Mr Tweedy*), Jane Horrocks (*Babs*), Miranda Richardson (*Mrs Tweedy*), Julia Sawalha (*Ginger*), Timothy Spall (*Nick*), Imelda Staunton (*Bunty*), Benjamin Whitrow (*Fowler*), John Shannon (*Circus Man*), Jo Allen (*Chicken*), Lisa Kay (*Chicken*), Laura Strachan (*Chicken*)

TAGLINE: This ain't no chick flick!

STORYLINE: A farm. It is night time and a chicken named Ginger rushes to the perimeter fence of the chicken yard. She begins digging her way to freedom with a spoon. On the other side of the fence, the farmer Mr Tweedy patrols with his two dogs. Ginger goes unnoticed until some of the other chickens attempt to escape but get stuck. Mr Tweedy sees what is happening and takes Ginger and locks her away. When Ginger returns to the sheds the chicken's plan to dig their way out to freedom is in full swing with an underground tunnel in progress and plans all over the walls. Meanwhile, Mrs Tweedy recognises that she needs to be running a more productive farm and because egg yields are low she decides to invest in a machine that will make chicken pies.

In the huts, Ginger attempts to rally the chickens to begin preparing for their escape but many of the chickens think they will fail in their mission. Ginger remains ever hopeful but when she steps outside she feels completely hopeless. At that moment, from out of the sky, drops Rocky the Flying Rooster. He has escaped from the circus although he likes to think he is an independent rover. Rocky's landing inspires a new thought in Ginger – the chickens will fly over the fence to escape, not dig out from under it.

Soon, Rocky is charming all the chickens. But his easygoing manner disappears when a man from the circus turns up looking for him. Ginger helps Rocky avoid detection and in return Rocky begins rallying the chickens and boosting morale. Two rats, always running a scam, befriend Rocky and supply him with goods to help prepare for the escape.

Ginger realises that something is wrong when the chickens are being fattened up by Mr and Mrs Tweedy, ready for the pie machine. Sure enough, Ginger is the first chicken to experience the pie machine when

Mrs Tweedy uses her to show Mr Tweedy how the machine works. Rocky rides to Ginger's rescue in a tense, white-knuckle race through the machine. Rocky and Ginger escape and the machine breaks down. Rocky is recognised as a hero and the plans to get out of the farm once and for all begin. The chickens design and construct a flying machine with the help of the rats who steal whatever they need from Mr Tweedy's toolbox.

At night the chickens pilot the flying machine across the yard. Mr Tweedy attempts to stop them but fails. Mrs Tweedy sees the commotion and the 'plane' launches into the air, taking Mrs Tweedy with them as she holds on to a string of fairy lights that has become ensnared in the vehicle on take off. Mrs Tweedy battles with Ginger and falls to her doom, landing in the pie machine which explodes. The plane, with all the chickens aboard, flies to freedom. The chickens live happily ever after on a little grassy island on a lake. Rocky and Ginger are a couple.

THE DRAWING BOARD: Aardman Animation had been established in 1972 by Peter Lord and David Sproxton and had famously – in the UK at least – provided the character of claymation tyke Morph for *Take Hart*, a children's TV show about making art with the great, cravat-wearing Tony Hart. In the mid-1980s the Bristol-based studio were commissioned to provide animation for a music video for Peter Gabriel's song 'Sledgehammer'. Not long after this Aardman were producing material for the Penny segment of American TV's *Pee-Wee's Playhouse*.

In 1989, young animator Nick Park directed *Creature Comforts* for the studio. It proved highly popular, winning an Academy Award as Best Animated Short, beating Park's *A Grand Day Out*. These were followed over the next few years by *A Close Shave* and *The Wrong Trousers*. American studios became interested in the immensely popular shorts and the prospect of financing for a feature was soon in the air.

However, Aardman elected to be patient until just the right concept was realised. It was Jake Eberts, the executive producer behind *Dances with Wolves* and the stop-motion animated *James and the Giant Peach* who was instrumental in setting what would become *Chicken Run* in motion. He had read about the studio's interest in developing a feature. Having enjoyed their shorts he contacted them, met with them and soon enough Aardman were in talks with various possible financiers.

Aardman initially went into discussions with Disney but eventually they signed with new studio, DreamWorks SKG, established by Steven Spielberg, Jeffrey Katzenberg and David Geffen in 1994. Katzenberg's main focus at SKG has been animation. Prior to SKG he had guided several massively successful animated features through production, for example, *The Little Mermaid*, *Beauty and the Beast* and *The Lion King*.

The first of Aardman's projects was *Chicken Run*. They then embarked on *The Hare and the Tortoise* that has since been put on hold. Work has been shifted to a Wallace and Gromit feature simply called *The Wallace and Gromit Movie*.

Chicken Run represented the occasional big-budget investment in stop motion also evidenced by the production of *The Nightmare Before Christmas* and *James and the Giant Peach*, both made for Disney and both of which generated keen followings. In an age of computer effects and computer animation, there was an element of nostalgia for something as apparently old-fashioned as stop motion.

The basic concept for *Chicken Run*, a kind of *Great Escape* with chickens, was in keeping with the elements of live-action movie parody present in Nick Park's Wallace and Gromit projects. As with those shorts, the feature contained generic backgrounds and moments in that it was not set in a specific time period – it could be the 1940s; it could be the present day.

Charmingly, it had been a sketch of Nick Park's that had sparked the concept. It showed a chicken digging under a wire fence with a spoon. When writer Karey Kirkpatrick came on board as screenwriter to embellish and refine the Nick Park–Peter Lord storyline, it was suggested the character of Rocky be American in order to enrich the drama with a culture clash evocative of the American soldiers based in Britain during World War Two.

INSPIRATIONS: These include *The Great Escape* (John Sturges, 1963) and *Star Wars*, *Raiders of the Lost Ark* (Steven Spielberg, 1981) and *The Flight of the Phoenix* (Robert Aldrich, 1965). When Rocky and Ginger journey through Tweedy's chicken pie machine there are even references to *Star Wars* and *Indiana Jones*. Indeed, maybe Lucas repays the homage in *Attack of the Clones* with the clone trooper factory.

TOON TEAM: Nick Park and Peter Lord split the directing duties on *Chicken Run*. Kirkpatrick had been a writer on *James and the Giant Peach*.

VOCAL TALENT: *Chicken Run* was Hollywood star Mel Gibson's first animated feature project and he starred as the hapless but heroic Rocky. Mel Gibson has starred in *Mad Max* (George Miller, 1979), *The Bounty*

(Roger Donaldson, 1984), *Lethal Weapon* (Richard Donner, 1987), *Braveheart* (Mel Gibson, 1995), and *Signs* (M. Night Shymalan, 2002).

Several of the other main characters were voiced by actors very familiar to British audiences. Julia Sawalha and Jane Horrocks are best known for their roles in the TV sitcom *Absolutely Fabulous*. Miranda Richardson has appeared in many feature films including *Dance with a Stranger* (Mike Newell, 1985), *Empire of the Sun* (Steven Spielberg, 1987) and *Spider* (David Cronenberg, 2002).

INK, PAINT AND HARD WORK: Aardman's regular set-building collaborators Farrington Lewis and Co. built the sets for the film and used the computer to design set layouts, allowing them also to establish the best lens options for shooting the action. All the sets had removable walls and rooftops.

There were ten main animated chicken characters. Park and Lord discovered that anything resembling a real chicken was not very friendly to the animation format.

Once a design had been approved it would be rendered as a plasticine maquette that would then be approved and models made from it. These models were then the basis for steel armatures and finally 'skin'. Some clay and latex chicken body parts were replaced every day. Replacement eyes were also created for various expressions and over 900 separate eyes were manufactured.

Aardman puppets usually tended to be about ten inches high but with *Chicken Run* there was an issue of scale because chickens would be seen in the same frame as animated human figures. The human figures were made a foot tall and there were three- and ten-inch-high models for the chickens. Sometimes a frame was split into two separately shot elements that were then merged to get the figures scaled correctly.

Some video footage of human movement was made to use as reference, including Mel Gibson reading his lines. Gibson's film *Maverick* (Richard Donner, 1994) was also referenced a lot for expression and gesture.

For Peter Lord, 'smoothness is rather low on our list of priorities. Animating with strength and simplicity, and with directness and energy, are things we regard as being of much greater importance than smoothness.'

THEME: Very simply, the film's comedy drama expresses the value in communal action and also the need for a healthy dose of self-belief.

STYLISH TOONS: *Chicken Run*'s expansive budget allowed for hugely detailed animation and set design. Some of the sky backdrops were achieved practically on set while others were created through computer imaging. The film was extensively refined and images 'cleaned up' by the Computer Film Company who had also been involved in *A Close Shave*. On *Chicken Run* their job was to scan every film frame into the computer, allowing for the maximum range of fine tuning.

Motion blur was used for fast-falling objects and point-of-view shots. Motion blur and unblurred action were not combined. It was one or the other.

The film's focus pulls, booming camera shots and tracking shots all invest the animated action with a very cinematic spirit and the film has a constant energy to it.

Almost every image contains some amusing detail or bit of business and no character or creature is without personality – even the Tweedy's dogs.

There are several instances where the film delights purely in the set-piece movements, notably in the keep-fit scene, the dance scene, the pie machine adventure and the escape scene. The pie machine rescue scene and escape scene are presented vividly like live-action adventure movie sequences. Of course, these dynamically staged and animated pieces of action are massive developments on the miniature versions of action found in the Wallace and Gromit half-hour films.

CHARACTER SKETCH: *Chicken Run* centres on the relationship between Ginger and the newcomer Rocky and the film charmingly shapes their situation in the style of romantic comedies of old. Ginger is a pragmatic and strong-willed girl and Rocky's confidence soon reveals his inadequacies. Once in Ginger's company he finds he cannot hide much for long. Ginger is the driving force of the story and she believes that she and the other chickens on the Tweedy farm can get to freedom and a much better life. At times, Ginger's optimism is challenged by events and the doubts of the other chickens, but she prevails.

Rocky's commitment to himself ultimately undergoes a change and he realises the value of committing to others, taking on the challenge of helping the chickens escape. His reluctant-hero status makes him something of a feathered version of Han Solo from the *Star Wars* movies.

In a film brimming with comedy it is unsurprising that around the two relatively non-comic heroes are a clutch of amusing supporting characters. Notable among these is Babs, always late to catch on, and the inventor and brains, Mac. The film's funniest character, though, must be Fowler, who assumes the veneer of a war veteran but who, it emerges, has never flown a plane in his life. As the chickens undertake their mission to escape, comic support is lent by two wheeler-dealer rats.

The film's two human characters are Mr and Mrs Tweedy, the farmers. Mr Tweedy is, appropriately enough, a hen-pecked husband, bumbling and dim-witted. Mrs Tweedy, in contrast, is monstrous and pure evil. Her grand plan to create chicken pies gives her an air of old-time movie villain megalomania. Mrs Tweedy is also the source of the film's darkest moment when she wields an axe over a chicken in doom-laden silhouette.

As with Nick Park's Wallace and Gromit characters, all of the chickens have been given a similar facial design that emphasises an ever-present anxiety. The film gets a lot of strong comedy out of the group hysteria of the chickens and a moment of silence typically arises in the moment before a collective shriek.

Much of the film's humour is created around Mr Tweedy being convinced he has seen chickens acting intelligently. This is nowhere better shown than when he looks in on the chickens and finds them all asleep. Moments previously they have been talking and planning their escape in a hive of activity. When the chickens hear footsteps they rapidly return their hut to its usual state, recalling various POW films.

TOON TUNES: *Chicken Run* is atypical of much of mainstream animation as it does not feature any musical numbers. What is does feature is a nicely parodic orchestral score by Harry Gregson-Williams, which echoes very closely the spirit of Elmer Bernstein's score for *The Great Escape*.

Harry Gregson-Williams is a British composer relatively new to the film-scoring scene. For *The Borrowers* he complemented the screen action with a fully blown orchestral score, while for *The Replacement Killers,* a thriller, he utilised an electronic palette.

Gregson-Williams is a graduate of the Guildhall School of Music and Drama in London. His film music career began working alongside Stanley Myers and he also contributed to Hans Zimmer's London-based soundtrack recordings, such as *The Lion King* (1994), *Crimson Tide* (Tony Scott, 1995), *Beyond Rangoon* (John Boorman, 1995) and *Two Deaths* (Nic Roeg, 1995). Gregson-Williams also collaborated with

Zimmer on *Broken Arrow* (John Woo, 1996), *The Fan* (Tony Scott, 1994), *The Rock* (Michael Bay, 1996) and the classically animated feature *The Prince of Egypt* (Simon Wells, 1998). Gregson-Williams scored DreamWorks' first computer-animated feature, *Antz* (Eric Darnell, Tim Johnson, 1995).

The *Chicken Run* soundtrack: 'Opening Escape', 'Main Titles', 'Evil Mrs Tweedy', 'Rats!', 'Chickens are not Organised', 'We Need a Miracle', 'Rocky and the Circus', 'Flight Training', 'Really Big Truck Arrives', 'Cocktails and Flighty Thoughts', 'Babs' Big Break', 'Flip, Flop and Fly', 'Up on the Roof', 'Into the Pie Machine', 'Rocky a Fake All Along', 'Building the Crate', 'Wanderer', 'Chickens are Revolting', 'Lift Off', 'Escape to Paradise'.

TOON TALK:
Ginger (on trying to rally her fellow chickens into an escape plan): 'The fences aren't just round the farm, they're up here in your heads.'

Rocky: 'Keep thinking those flighty thoughts.'

OTHER SIMILAR FILMS: *Chicken Run* relates, of course, to the Wallace and Gromit shorts, to which it is very close in general spirit and execution. The battle for freedom also echoes in the computer-animated feature *A Bug's Life* (John Lasseter, 1998).

RECOGNITION: BBC online felt that the strength of the film was that 'You come to care greatly for these chickens' while the *Village Voice* was pleasantly surprised: 'This upmarket production is jollier than its premise . . . a combination of *Barnyard Follies* and *Schindler's List*.' On the subject of the animation, 'You realise just how much physical and emotional texture Park and Lord have worked into crafting their film's seemingly effortless charm,' said *Sight and Sound*.

AWARDS: *Chicken Run* enjoyed not just commercial success but also recognition in a range of awards, nominated for many and winning some. At the 2000 Annie Awards, the film was nominated for Outstanding Achievement in an Animated Theatrical Feature. At the 2000 Los Angles Film Critics Association Awards it won Best Animation. In the same year, the film won Best Animated Film from The National Board of Review and from the New York Film Critics Circle Award it won Best Animated Film.

Its score won the ASCAP Film and Television Award for Top Box Office film. At the Academy of Science Fiction, Fantasy and Horror the film was nominated for a Saturn award in the category of Best Fantasy Film and Best Writing (Karey Kirkpatrick).

The *Evening Standard* awarded the film the Peter Sellers Award for Comedy. At the Empire movie magazine awards the film was nominated for Best British Director, Best British Film and Best Directorial Debut. At the 2001 BAFTA awards, it was nominated for the Alexander Korda Award for Best British Film and also in the categories of Best Achievement in Special Visual Effects. At the 2001, Golden Globes the film was nominated for Best Motion Picture, Comedy or Musical and at the Hugo awards it was nominated in the category of Best Dramatic Presentation.

HOME VIEWING: *Chicken Run* is available on VHS and DVD. The DVD contains a behind-the-scenes featurette and other Aardman material.

COMMENT: 'It had to be chickens. Scientific study proved that they are the silliest animals in creation.' Nick Park and Peter Lord.

VERDICT: *Chicken Run* is highly entertaining and has a good balance between the British humour established in the Wallace and Gromit films and American pace and sensibility. The film manages to find quieter moments for just enough character development.

Certainly, the film comes into its own with the action sequences. In many ways it shares an outlook and tone with the computer-animated *A Bug's Life* in its story of a community having to evade a bully. In both films the building of a mechanical contraption is part of the plan. With its all-animal main cast, *Chicken Run* brings British animation full circle in a way to the first British feature *Animal Farm*.

Japanimation

While American and European animation dominates the mainstream sensibility towards the form there is another region whose output has run for as many years and which is currently experiencing its highest profile yet with Western audiences. This distinction between East and West is useful up to a point. The universal concerns and implications of drama reach way beyond ethnicity and history.

As in so many other aspects of cinema, Japan offers up its genius practitioners and great works. Its vitality in live action with directors such as Kenji Mizoguchi, Akira Kurosawa and Yasujiro Ozu is matched by its animation directors and in 2003 none rides with a higher profile than Hayao Miyazaki, regarded on an artistic and commercial par with Steven Spielberg and JK Rowling.

Anime is the Japanese word for animation. In Japan it references all animation regardless of style and country of origin. Ironically it is only in the West that the word is used specifically to denote Japanese animated films.

At about the same time that America was beginning to understand the magic and possibility of animation with the efforts of Winsor McCay and others in the early twentieth century, Japan was developing its animation tradition and aesthetic. In 1917, the earliest animation in Japan was re-telling Japanese folk stories – a choice again attesting to animation's affinity for the fantastic and the fanciful. At one point, paper silhouette animation was especially popular.

As the years passed the Japanese idiom found richness in fusing the past and the future.

As in America, it was during the 1920s and 1930s that Japanese animation production ramped up with animators working from home studios, single-handedly producing material that they would then sell to distributors. By the close of the 1930s the emphasis in Japan on the folk tale and the allure of the past had morphed into more modern, sometimes militaristic material that to some degree reflected Japan's growing military might. One of the most popular cartoon short characters (an equivalent to Mickey Mouse) was *Private Second Class Norakuro*, literally a dog soldier who starred in a series of short animated pieces. Japanese animators, like those in the West, recognised the appeal of cute animal characters.

It was in the 1940s that the first Japanese feature was produced, commissioned by the government, and ultimately used as a piece of propaganda. The piece was black and white and ran about sixty minutes. It showed the animal sailors of the Imperial Navy fighting in Malaysia and freeing people from Western oppression.

In 1956, the first true Japanese animation studio, Toei Animation Company, was established. Its first production was *Doodling Kitty*. The popularity of the format was swiftly proven and every year, in tandem with the Disney production model, a new animated feature was released.

However, it was the early 1960s when the Japanese idiom began to break through in the West, particularly in America. The same was happening with the work of live-action directors such as Akira Kurosawa with his films *The Seven Samurai* (Akira Kurosawa, 1954) and *Yojimbo* (Akira Kurosawa, 1961). What paved the way for the late 1980s' and 1990s' affinity for Japanese feature animation was the wildly successful run of animated TV series, notably *Astro Boy* which began in 1963. It told the story of a robot boy who tried to be like a real boy. It is hardly surprising that *AI: Artificial Intelligence* (Steven Spielberg) was such a hit in Japan when released in 2001.

Other Japan-produced animation shows aired in America such as *Mazinger Z* in which giant robots protect the Earth, *Space Battleship Yamato* and *Captain Harlock*. These programmes were animated quickly and cheaply. In the late 1980s some of these series were renamed so that *Space Battleship Yamato* became *Star Blazers* and *Macross* became *Robotech*. In the late 1980s the epic animated adventure *Akira* received its Western release. This film was so popular that it generated a new and enduring wave of interest in the form.

Interestingly, the seriousness of much Japanese feature animation and also its willingness to engage with social matters has long played its part and extends to more documentary forms of animation such as the Japanese piece *Pika Don* (1978) by Renzo Kinoshita which attempts to recreate and hence remind audiences of the bombing of Hiroshima on 6 August 1945. Many of his films are noted for the satire on contemporary life.

In 2003, there was only one animation director's name on everybody's lips in Europe and North America.

As with any field of expression, Japanese feature animation has its 'auteurs' such as Isao Takahata and Hayao Miyazaki, the latter of whom is currently experiencing huge popular attention in the glow of his two most recent features: *Princess Mononoke* (1997) and *Spirited Away* (2003). Miyazaki is enjoyed for fusing a Western focus on emotional involvement with the dynamism of Japanese visuals (movement in frame, colour, atmosphere) and his own particular brand of fantasy. Miyazaki's pop-culture kudos and standing puts him on a level with a filmmaker like Spielberg.

Miyazaki's most recent film *Spirited Away*, the most popular film in Japanese film history, is regarded as his masterpiece. In a review of the film at www. filmjournal.com the reviewer wrote 'at times it seems as if the director is funnelling his dreams directly into the screen'. Similar enthusiasm shepherded the film on to select screens in the UK in late summer 2003.

Hayao Miyazaki was born in 1941 and grew up during the atomic age, which is arguably a massive influence on much Japanese animation of the last twenty years. He began his career at Toei Douga working on many classic Japanese animated features.

In 1971 he began working with Isao Takahata at A Pro and then Nippon Animation. Miyazaki directed his first TV series, *Conan, The Boy in Future* and in 1979 his first feature for Tokyo Movie Shinsha, *Lupin III: The Castle of Cagliostro*. It was in the 1980s that he really began to establish his credentials and legacy. In 1984 he made *Nausicaa of the Valley of Wind* which was based on the manga of the same name that he had drawn. Studio Ghibli (pronounced jee-blee) was begun on the success of this movie.

Miyazaki's most recent success had been *Princess Mononoke*, which earned the Japan Academy Award for Best Film and was the highest-grossing Japanese film ever (US$150 million) until Miyazaki trumped himself with the follow-up *Spirited Away*, very much in the vein of an *Alice in Wonderland* narrative.

In an article in the *Guardian* on 1 August 2003, British animator Nick Park wrote glowingly of Miyazaki that he has 'a style that is pure and rich . . . Miyazaki is as concerned with atmosphere as he is with action.'

Miyazaki's influences have included the live-action cinema of Vittorio de Sica, Yasujiro Ozu and Robert Bresson (all of which possess that lyric rather than epic quality) alongside the animators Lev Atamanov who made *Snow Queen* (1957) and Paul Grimault whose film *The Shepherdess and the Chimney Sweep* proved to Miyazaki that animation could and should have adult appeal. Yuri Norstein and Frederic Back were other influential animators.

As a director and writer Miyazaki has always been more hands-on than an animation director might usually be, even redrawing frames if necessary. In 1998, he announced that he was no longer going to make films the way he had been. This was widely taken to mean he was retiring, but in fact he just intended to be essentially less hands-on.

In his treatment for *Princess Mononoke*, Miyazaki's warmth and sincerity of feeling about what animation can do is apparent when he writes in a section called Purpose of the Project: 'To depict what constructs the unchanged basis of humanity throughout time . . . The main characters will be the people who don't appear in the centre stage of history . . .' His notes go on to talk about presenting 'deep nature' prior to big populations and agriculture.

Miyazaki is committed to a refreshing humanism in his animation. It is more than monsters and fantasy and to read interviews with him is to sense a man who truly and encouragingly believes that popular cinema, storytelling in its broadest sense, can be life-affirming.

A key distinguishing feature of Japanese narratives is that they derive from the lyric rather than the epic tradition. The epic tradition essentially tells a story of sequential events. Intriguingly, the lyric tradition is less busy, instead focusing on the expression of a feeling and the crystallising of a perception. As such it is more singular, passive even, with not a lot happening on the surface but much occurring just below. This emphasis on feeling is especially pertinent to an anime subgenre called shoujo (Japanese for young girl). Shoujo is aimed very much at young girls and tells stories that have less interest in action and sprawling narratives and much more in relationships. They are not necessarily soft stories, though, simply less genre-biased and some way from the science fiction and fantasy leanings of so much anime. Famous titles include *Fancy Lala* (Tomomichi Mochizuki, Takahiro Omori, 1998) and *Fushigi Yogi* (Yu Watase, 1995–6). *Fushigi Yogi* is a fantasy soap opera of sorts in which a young girl is transported into an ancient world where she must rise to a series of challenges that will summon a being who can grant the girl three wishes.

There is a series of key aesthetic points worth mentioning here to get some idea of the differences between the design of animation in Japan and the Western animated format.

Where in Western animation bodies often emphasise the meaning and import of dialogue (growing out of the theatrical animated short which was well financed and allowed for detail of gesture), in Japan, animation's roots are in the economics of television. This situation calls for the most effect for the least expenditure of energy and hence money. In Japanese animation, movement does not tend to accompany dialogue but instead body movements are directed towards goals, such as walking, picking things up, or very specific poses that express a state of mind.

On the technical side, dialogue in the West is recorded first and the animation typically matches it, like lip synch. In Japan, dialogue tends to be recorded after the animation so that, while the audience is aware who is speaking, there is less of a strong match between mouth movement and the words spoken.

One of the most appealing aspects of Japanese animation (and let us not forget its relationship to manga of the Japanese comic books) is the expressive use of background. What we are venturing into here is the *mise en scène* of animation, which is fundamentally based on the form's ability to be very elastic in its presentation of space.

In the Japanese idiom, realism is secondary to emotional accuracy and import and so backgrounds are used to express inner emotional and psychological states. Rather like in manga, realistic backgrounds are not the driving impulse. Often abstract lines replace a detailed sense of environment and often natural phenomena are seen to have no effect on the human characters. Certainly, backgrounds can even overemphasise emotion. This is a device also present in numerous live-action movies, though a good example is *Kagemusha* (Akira Kurosawa, 1980), in which a highlight sequence is a very theatrically, overartificial dream scene.

The often vivid, melodramatic narratives of Japanese animation have some root in Kabuki theatre, originated by women who were banned by the Japanese government from the stage in 1629. The form reached its zenith in the 1660s and 1970s and uses high action scenarios where men fight valiantly to overcome evil. Supernatural revenge often informs the stories and strange creatures abound.

In 1983 a term that has become a household word was coined in science fiction. The word was 'cyberpunk'. It was used as the title of a short story published in a 1983 edition of *Amazing Stories*. Writer and editor Gardner Dozois used the term to describe a burgeoning literary movement that arguably reached back into the 1940s and 1950s (in the works of writers such as Samuel R Delaney, Vernor Vinge's *True Names* and John Brunner's 1975 novel *The Shockwave Rider*).

In 1984, the term and concept of cyberpunk took a quantum leap with William Gibson's novel *Neuromancer*. The cyberpunk subgenre refers to a world where people are being increasingly engaged (controlled) by computers, subsequently with a loss of their essential humanity and interaction. Thus cyber (from original Greek for steering) and the punk term refer to the kind of countercultural heroes at the centre of such stories. In the cyberpunk world, technology is rampant and urban space sprawls; rather like the urban Japanese matrix. Anime richly expresses the cyberpunk spirit in films such as *Akira, Ghost in the Shell* and *Appleseed.* They are in stark contrast to the more romantically inclined stories of *Princess Mononoke* and *Spirited Away,* which reach into the past for their creative heartbeat.

In considering the Japanese animated form that has become so well established it is useful to recall post-nuclear trauma (the impact and value, or otherwise, of technology and industry) and also the rise of Japanese Fascism, Imperial Expansion in Asia and the Japanese economic miracle of the 1980s.

The film *Akira* explicitly explores the impact of technology in its story of a teenage boy subjected to experiments by the military that unleash destructive psychic powers. The 2001 film *Metropolis* also articulates similar concerns. There is also the notion of the floating world developed by well-to-do merchants in the seventeenth century; the notion that all was OK, and that in their wealth and comfort they lived in a state of happiness. The word is ukiyo, which in its original meaning breaks down into sadness (uki) and life (yo).

One of the notable features of Japanese characters is their large eyes and simple noses, a style that seems to hark back in part to the Japanese representational style of hikime-kagihan which translates as 'dash for the eyes, hook for the nose'.

Finally, the other key thematic concern that can be seen to canopy much of Japanese animation is the interplay between the ancient and traditional and the modern and futuristic. This preoccupation was articulated greatly during the Edo period (1615–1687) and is vividly expressed in films like *Akira, Ghost in the Shell* and *Princess Mononoke* where the dialogue focuses on the eternally compelling tensions and conflicts that go to the heart of being alive and the growth of cultures.

There are countless animated features that are available to the newcomer to Japanese animation: *The Ghost in the Shell, Akira, Laputa: Castle in the Sky* (Hayao Miyazaki, 1986), *Tenchi: The Movie* (Hiroshi Negishi, 1996), *Grave of the Fireflies* (Isao Takahata, 1988) and *Barefoot Gen* (Mamoru Shinzaki, 1983).

Akira (1988)

(124 minutes – original edition)

Directed by Katsuhiro Otomo
Written by Katsuhiro Otomo and Izo Hashimoto
Produced by Shunzo Katoand and Ryokei Suzuki
Associate Producer: Yoshimasa Mizuo
Executive Producer: Sawako Noma
Music: Shoji Yamashiro
Cinematography: Katsuji Misawa
Editor: Takeshi Seyama
Production Design: Kuzuo Ebisawa, Yuji Ikehata, Koji Ono
Art Direction: Toshiharu Mizutani
Sound Recording: Director Susuma Akitagawa

BUDGET: 1,100,000,000 yen

BOX OFFICE: 6,346,343,871 yen (In North America the film grossed $439,162)

RELEASE DATE: 1988 (Special Edition 2001)

CERTIFICATE: USA: R, UK: 12

VOICES: Mitsuo Iwata (*Kaneda*), Nozomu Sasaki (*Tetsuo*), Mami Koyama (*Kei*), Tessho Genoa (*Ryusaku*), Hiroshi Otake (*Nezu*), Yuriko Fuchizaki (*Kaori*), Masaaki Okura (*Yamagata*), Kazuhiro Kaifuji (*Masaru*), Tatsuhiko (*Takashi*), Fukue Ito (*Kiyoko*), Taro Ishida (*Colonel Shikishama*)
English language version: Joshua Seth (*Tetsuo*), Johnny Yong Bosch (*Kaneda*), Wendee Lee (*Kei*), Sandy Fox (*Kiyoko*), Emily Brown (*Kaori*)

TAGLINE: Neo Tokyo is about to explode.

STORYLINE: A prologue set in 1988 shows the immense sprawl of Tokyo. There is a flash of light: a huge nuclear explosion.

It is the year 2019 and Neo Tokyo is a densely populated mega city in the aftermath of World War Three. Biker gangs thunder around the city.

Corruption defines the administration where army, police and government are in an unholy alliance.

Two teenage boys named Kaneda and Tetsuo are hardcore bikers, tearing up the city. One night, as a riot ensues, they race a rival gang. Tetsuo nearly kills a very sick-looking, grey-faced boy. Tetsuo is injured. A huge army helicopter descends. The grey-faced boy goes aboard. Tetsuo is also taken.

Kaneda and friends wonder where he is. Tetsuo is taken to a military base in the city overseen by the Colonel. Tetsuo undergoes intensive medical and psychological tests. He breaks free of the centre and reunites with his friends but is taken away again.

The military science test centre houses a power called Akira. Religious sects daub the name Akira on the streets and chant his name, saying that one day he will come.

It emerges that Tetsuo has strong telekinetic powers and he begins destroying everything, including his own friendships. Trapped in the centre, Kaneda and Kei (a terrorist, anti-government), attempt a rescue mission. Tetsuo's situation worsens.

Meanwhile the Colonel wants to maintain the military programme. The three ill children under his supervision are precognitive. Tetsuo is also psychologically strong.

Kei and Kaneda are imprisoned and Kei tells Kaneda what Akira is: a power that reaches back to primordial times. If harnessed it can be all-powerful. Kei and Kaneda are freed. Tetsuo experiences terrible visions and has a psychokinetic showdown with the other kids and the Colonel. Kei and Kaneda attempt to intervene. Tetsuo makes his way to the Olympic stadium beneath which the mighty Akira is stored. Tetsuo breaks in, destroying countless army and tanks, and discovers Akira is no more than a cluster of vials and containers holding Akira's organs.

Tetsuo's power becomes ever more explosive and he becomes an immense and grotesque monster in a thunderous showdown with the Colonel and Kaneda in the ruins of the Olympic stadium. The Colonel tries to stop Tetsuo as does Kei. Finally Kaneda confronts Tetsuo and the showdown culminates in a vast explosion that utterly ravages Neo Tokyo. Tetsuo has gone. Kei and Kaneda watch a new day begin.

THE DRAWING BOARD: *Akira* began life as a very popular manga series by Katsuhiro Otomo in the Japanese publication *Young Magazine* in December 1982. The manga was never designed with a film in mind but it was suggested to Otomo that it might make a good film.

Interestingly, 1982 was the year that the live-action film *Blade Runner* (Ridley Scott) was released. This can be considered something of a cinematic cousin to the film version of *Akira* (see **INSPIRATIONS**).

In the manga version, each issue allowed Otomo to explore the identity of the city. In the film he felt he could make it more convincing still; he could 'just let the characters go'.

INSPIRATIONS: The Japanese engagement with nuclear power in the shadow of Hiroshima and Nagasaki seems to form an undercurrent to the science fiction surface of the story. The influence of *Blade Runner* also appears to play its part in the film. In turn, *Blade Runner* had images suffused with references to Japan and the East.

TOON TEAM: Otomo's crew was large. Otomo himself had, by the time of *Akira*, generated a keen following. As a manga artist his breakthrough had been with *Short Piece*. His films as a director have included *Robot Carnival* (1987). Since *Akira*, Otomo has been involved in a range of projects, such as *Ash* (2000). His latest project – due for a 2004 release – has elicited much excitement. Budgeted as the most expensive Japanese animated feature, *Steamboy* is a fantasy piece set in Victorian England. The film is notable for extensive use of computer-generated animation, the Japanese idiom still being largely animated through drawn characters.

VOCAL TALENT: In a break from the traditional Japanese anime production process, the dialogue for *Akira* was recorded prior to work on the animation beginning.

INK, PAINT AND HARD WORK: One hundred and fifty thousand cels were generated for the film and the film was divided into 783 scenes. Significantly, and unusually, the film was shot on 70 mm to accommodate its visual scope and the detail of character and environment. There were five different colour schemes for each character. One of Otomo's aims was to experiment with colour. The film is dominated by dark blues and greens and greys against which the bright red bike and Kaneda's bright red outfit are striking. Late in the film, the colour red assumes a metaphorical value when Tetsuo wraps himself in a red cloak.

THEME: The film dramatises a range of issues from the personal to the political so that the story embraces individual responsibility, the spectre of the ancient and unknown and, more obviously, the corruption of government and the hardness and aggression that cities at their worst can nurture.

In its visuals alone the film presents the urban sprawl as a dangerous and negative space that harbours violence and secrecy. The closing image of the film shows a ravaged Neo Tokyo but it is also the first time real sunbeams have shone through – suggesting hopeful, better times ahead. The way the discs of sunlight strike the city echoes the way the discs of light from helicopter searchlights swept the city earlier in the film.

There is a powerful sense of rebirth and the metaphor of Akira (life energy) is key to the meaning of the film. Energy is one thing, harnessing it appropriately is another. This is a classic science-fiction motif that reaches back to Mary Shelley's novel *Frankenstein*. The more compelling aspect of the story at this level is its idea of an almost genetic memory in all of humanity that relates to the idea of a life force.

The film is drenched in a dark fairy-tale quality that is most powerfully unleashed in the nightmarish visions of the toys come to life. Not even the innocence of childhood is a very valid notion in this film.

STYLISH TOONS: For all its violence and urban edginess, the film has a naturalistic, tech-noir feel right down to the enchanting light trails made by the bikes as they speed through the city at night.

Its most forceful moment is when this style gives way to something more surreal and openly fanciful. The film's highlight sequence is when Tetsuo's visions in the facility show him besieged and attacked by nightmarish dreams of oversized toys and then ventures into the toy room. These moving toys recall the robo toys of *Blade Runner*, especially when he imagines miniature versions of them marching across his pillow towards him.

The other stand-out stylistic device is the multiplane image-making of the city as the camera tracks between the shifting perspectives of the skyscrapers and roadways. This approach immerses the audience in the environment so that they become ever closer to the characters.

CHARACTER SKETCH: *Akira* is comprised of a core group of teenage characters, defined by their frustration at the world and in some cases a desire to change it however they can. Their faces break into laughter sometimes but most of the energy is put into raging at the world and their furrowed brows and clenched jaws typify this. For all their anger, though, the film finally presents young people as the best hope any culture has for the future – see also the end of **Princess Mononoke**.

The character of Kaneda is a cocky, punk teen whose adventure in trying to rescue Tetsuo from himself permits Kaneda the chance to grow up and act responsibly. By the end of the film his endless joking seems far removed from his committed gaze amidst the ruins of destroyed Neo Tokyo.

Kei, like many female anime characters, is a strong-willed, politically motivated young woman whose understanding of the past and knowledge of what Akira represents and contains makes her the wisest character in the story.

Tetsuo regards himself as the runt of his biker friends and so the powers he discovers are exploited by him. Finally, he is the one that nobody can mess with. He is never really likeable and even in his most intense moments, where his mindset is besieged by terrifying visions, he does not really inspire the audience's sympathy.

Kiyoko, Taksahi and Masaru are the aged children (because of the medication they are on to control their energy) who consult with the Colonel about the fate of Tetsuo. These children are defined by their wisdom, gentility and compassion. The world outside is too strong for them.

The character of Akira, the spirit, is defined by Kei in the film as being the knowledge and energy of the world that allowed evolution to take place. Akira is shown as a young boy in one sequence giving the film an opportunity to reinforce the idea that power is not marked by size alone.

TOON TUNES: The film is supported by a driving and thunderous score for much of its action, perfectly fitting the abrasive drama and the expansive scale of so many of the images.

The *Akira* soundtrack: 'Kaneda', 'Battle Against Clown', 'Winds Over Neo Tokyo', 'Tetsuo', 'Dolls Polyphony', 'Shohmyeh', 'Mutation', 'Exodus from the Underground Fortress', 'Illusion', 'Requiem'.

TOON TALK:

Colonel: 'Maybe we weren't meant to meddle with that ultimate power.'

Kei: 'Akira is ultimate energy.'

Kiyoko: 'There ought to be a future we can choose. It's up to us to find it.'

OTHER SIMILAR FILMS: *Ghost in the Shell* is a notable film in the context of *Akira*'s apocalyptic visions and engagement with both the good and the bad of technology.

RECOGNITION: 'In the manner of contemporary Japanese comics, it is supercolourful, explicitly violent, intellectually provocative and emotionally engaging with its Perils-of-Pauline pace' said the *Washington Post* while *Time Out* also felt it 'Features some of the most mind blowing animation ever seen . . . suggesting a weird expressionist blend of *The Warriors, Blade Runner* and *Forbidden Planet.*'

AWARDS: The film won the Silver Screen Award for Best Direction at the Amsterdam Fantastic Film Festival in 1992.

HOME VIEWING: Available on both VHS and DVD, *Akira* is best enjoyed in its Special Edition DVD format. With a digitally remastered image the package is enhanced by a production featurette, interviews with the film's restorers and an interview with Otomo. Also, the disc contains around 4,500 images of production art and even a translation facility for all the Japanese graffiti seen throughout the film.

COMMENT: 'Akira seems to have attempted too much . . . Being overly intellectual is a flaw almost unknown in American animation.' Anime expert and commentator Fred Patten.

VERDICT: *Akira* is a dazzling and quite exhausting film that demands to be watched more than once. Its density of environments engulfs you in its world and its dense, rich story demands a second viewing. For all the thunderous, hugely scaled action (a live action-film version could surely never be made) it is the film's expression on faces and detail in its creation of environments that is most absorbing. The film's commitment to a serious, adult engagement with science, the military and personal responsibility is admirable.

Contrasting with the overall superseriousness of the film there is a nice element of broad, black humour, notably in the bombed-out, lawless high school. The film is not afraid to show violence and as such it is a long way from the comic violence of other pieces of animation. This film is far more bound by the rules of live action.

Like *Princess Mononoke*, the film carries a strongly spiritual quality that underpins the expected kinetic energy and wild and sometimes grotesque fantasy. It is well worth watching in tandem with the live-action film *Blade Runner* (Ridley Scott, 1982) and also *The Matrix* and its sequels (The Wachowski Brothers, 1999–2003).

Ghost in the Shell (1995)

(82 minutes)

Original story and manga: Masamune Shirow
Director: Mamoru Oshii
Screenplay: Kazunori Ito
Music: Kenji Kawai
Art Director: Hiromasa Ogura
Animation Director: Toshihiko Nishibuko
Producers: Yoshimasa Mizuo, Ken Iyadomi, Mitsuhisa Ishikawa, Ken Matsumoto
Executive Producers: Teruo Miyahara, Shigeru Watanabe, Andy Frain
Character Designer: Hiroyuki Okiura
Production Designer: Takashi Watabe
Editor: Shuichi Kakesu

BUDGET: $4 million

BOX OFFICE: $515,905

RELEASE DATE: 1998

CERTIFICATE: 15

VOICES: Akio Otsuka (*Bateau*), Atsuko Tanaka (*Motomo*), Steve Buten (*Section 9 Staff Cyberneticist*), Tom Carlton (*Garbage Collector*), George Celik (*Old Man*), Richard Epcar (*Bateau*), William Frederick (*Section 9 Department Chief Aramaki*), Christopher Joyce (*Togusa*), Abe Lasser (*Project 2051/ The Puppetmaster*), Michael Sorich (*Ishikawa*), Mimi Woods (*Motomo Kusanagi*)

TAGLINE: It found a voice – now it needs a body.

STORYLINE: Taking place in the near future, Section 9 is a group that combats technological terrorism. In this age of computers, virtual technology and cybernetics many 'people' are in fact cyborgs – more machine than human. Their thoughts can even be hacked into.

Dominating this illegal activity is the Puppetmaster who can control lives through computer power.

Major Motomo Kusanagi is charged with the mission of tracking down and stopping the Puppetmaster. Motomo is first seen perched high above the city. She listens in on a conversation and then balletically launches into the gunfire below, shielding herself in an invisibility coat. She was created as a cyborg, her brain encased in a titanium shell.

Motomo is shown in a van travelling through the city to execute a mission. She puts on her protective armour and readies her gun. She is in pursuit of a hacker being controlled by the Puppetmaster. A tense chase and shoot-out ensues and the young hacker named Corgi is brought in for questioning where it emerges he has no memory and no identity.

At the Section 9 facility the torso and head of a cyborg are under surveillance. The cyborg's consciousness awakes and the Puppetmaster speaks through it. There is an explosion and the body is stolen. Motomo and her partner Bateau go in pursuit. A tank is put out to defend the body and Motomo battles it. Bateau destroys the tank before it finally destroys Motomo. They retrieve the cyborg torso and Motomo is then connected to it so she can dive into the Puppetmaster's mind. The Puppetmaster wants to merge with Motomo to create a new identity. In the moment after connecting with Motomo the Puppetmaster-controlled cyborg explodes, destroyed by a military attack from above.

The film's epilogue shows Motomo at Bateau's hideaway. She is hooked up to medication. She then leaves and walks out into the world.

THE DRAWING BOARD: *Ghost in the Shell* is a touchstone anime and certainly considered by many to be a masterpiece, ranking alongside *Princess Mononoke* and *Akira*.

Ghost in the Shell began as a manga, serialised every three months in Kodansha's '*Young*' magazine, Pirate Edition, through 1989–1990. In America the title was reprinted by Dark Horse comics, though they had to censor certain more explicit sex scenes. On 28 June 2001, *Ghost in the Shell 2: Man/Machine Interface* (*Ghost in the Shell: Koukaku Kidoutai 2*) was published.

The basic *Ghost in the Shell* concept explores the relationship between artificial intelligence and human beings. Human brains are fitted out with interfaces that allow them to hook up to and learn from computers. The human soul is known as the ghost and the most successful hackers are those who can hack into a ghost. For doing this there is the severest penalty.

INSPIRATIONS: Undoubtedly, the influence of *Blade Runner* is visible in much of the film. Like *Ghost in the Shell*, the Ridley Scott film dramatises a story about artificial beings in search of home and their memories.

TOON TEAM: The team brought together for *Ghost in the Shell* featured several major names in Japanese manga and anime. Producer Yoshimasa Mizuo had also been a producer on *Akira*.

VOCAL TALENT: Unlike a Japanese animated feature such as *Princess Mononoke*, released in North America through the Disney company, the voices for the film are not those of familiar stars.

INK, PAINT AND HARD WORK: *Ghost in the Shell* used Digital Generate Animation, a non-linear process that allowed the film to work on animation, music and dialogue simultaneously rather than in a linear production. The film combines cel animation with computer-generated images.

Alongside the traditional 2-D animation, the film also incorporates a number of computer-generated images in terms of surveillance and mapping sequences.

THEME: The film overflows with intelligence and a real seriousness about its theme. Riffing on technology, morality and memory it is the film's engagement with this issue that gives the material its resonance.

Ghost in the Shell grapples with what it is to be human in terms of the power and necessity of memory. The film's main character is a cyborg and she ponders endlessly about this. Indeed, most of the characters in the film are to some degree not completely human.

The film presents the future as even more immersed in computer and virtual technology than at present and this is regarded sceptically. As *Akira* showed, technology can be harnessed for positive effect but it is when it is harnessed and exploited negatively that crises ensue.

Also similar to *Akira* is the film's reservation about corporations and authority. The pervading sense is that the world is not necessarily being protected. The film opens with a piece of text that reads: 'In the near future – corporate networks reach out to the stars, electrons and light flow throughout the universe. The advance of computerisation, however, has not yet wiped out nations and ethnic groups.' Identity is going to be at the heart of this high-tech movie about what it is to have a soul, an issue dealt with in a very different tonal way in the American animated feature, *The Iron Giant* (Brad Bird, 1999).

The familiar Japanese interest in how the past interacts with the present is apparent in the film through its exploration of what an identity is. Memory and genetics are presented as roots back into something more ancient. This whole exploration of memory and thought and how one's mind could be hacked into like a computer gives the film a real affinity with *Strange Days* (Kathryn Bigelow, 1995).

The film's core 'philosophical' scene is when Motomo and Bateau talk on the boat about consciousness and memory (the titular Ghost in the Shell). In this respect, the film strongly evokes *Blade Runner* (see INSPIRATIONS). Motomo talks about feeling fear and hope and she then asks Bateau how much of him remains human. One of the film's motifs, and Motomo does seem imbued with this (especially in the final scene), is that of the doll. When Motomo is savaged by the tank it slings her around like a dog with a rag doll in its jaws. The reverie of the city as Motomo passes through it ends with an image of shop mannequins. Motomo expresses reservation about humanity's romance with technology.

STYLISH TOONS: *Ghost in the Shell* is stylish in the best sense of the word, its action centred around a clearly defined and expressive visual design. It has a real visual logic and coherence to it in its presentation of the city and its characters. In even the widest shot of a street, animated passers-by move completely and believably. It feels as if a world exists beyond the frame that captures the animation. The film's prologue, alone, is a vibrant and compelling 'short film' showing the film's main character in the moment of creation and birth.

The film is also notable for its dynamic sense of light. Shadows fall powerfully across people's faces and bodies throughout, plunging their eyes into darkness. The world of *Ghost in the Shell* is morally shadowy and the visual scheme helps reinforce this. The scene that shows Motomo being fabricated is terrifying and dreamlike, a particular strength that anime possesses.

Building on the immense cityscapes presented in *Akira*, *Ghost in the Shell* portrays the shifting perspectives of the tower blocks as vehicles drive along. In contrast to this urban sprawl and intensity the film is equally notable for its detail such as the droplets of water on Motomo's diving mask when she resurfaces from under the sea.

The film's believable environment is also enhanced by the quality of lights as on the buses and cars. The rainfall creates a kaleidoscope of colour at one point.

In its promotional material, the film receives an accolade from James Cameron. The film's visual design and kinetic energy is very akin to Cameron's live-action science-fiction films *The Terminator* (1984), *Aliens* (1986) and *Terminator 2: Judgment Day* (1991).

One of the most astonishing features of the film is its sound. There is a real sense of sounds moving nearer and further away as the characters run down back alleys or as helicopters swoop in overhead. The film immerses its audience through what they see and what they hear. Intriguingly, before any explosion of gunfire (and there is much in the film) a fractional moment of silence is 'heard'.

Thankfully, the film is not afraid of quiet, stiller passages and at critical points the sound and fury give way to a tone that is more lyrical in its meditation on the energy and deprivation of the city. For several minutes the film seemingly slows down as Motomo moves through the city on a boat. The terrain is mesmerising.

The film begins with a similar sense of rapture as Motomo, rather like Batman, crouches on a rooftop high above the city, the view vertiginous from so high up. Consider too the scene where she goes diving, lost in the peacefulness of the sea beyond the city. When she resurfaces what she sees first is a gloriously perfect golden sky. The cold blues and greys of the city seem distant and irrelevant.

The film's recurrent visual motif is of birth and liquid. Motomo is shown being born as a piece of technology and much is made of the moment when she resurfaces from her dive. When she leaves Bateau's apartment at the end of the film she goes out into the world quoting a line about not being a child and thinking childish thoughts any more.

CHARACTER SKETCH: Major Motomo, for all her cyborg resilience, is a melancholy and lonely figure grappling with her place in the world. She is in many ways an innocent and emotionally fragile.

Bateau is the good work partner, lending a degree of cynicism to Motomo's sincere investigations into the world and herself. Bateau is almost all human apart from his optical technology eyes.

TOON TUNES: As with *Akira*, the film is marked by an intense music score that is notable for its choral element. This approach readily picks up on audience association of the choral with the spiritual, connecting with the film's preoccupation with matters of the heart and their collision with technology.

The track listing for the soundtrack is: 'Making a Cyborg', 'Ghosthack', 'Puppetmaster', 'Virtual Crime', 'Ghost City', 'Access', 'Nightstalker', 'Floating Museum', 'Ghostdive', 'Reincarnation', 'See You Everyday'.

TOON TALK:
Bateau: 'Even a doll can seem to have a soul.'

Motomo: 'If man realises technology is within reach he achieves it, like it's damn near instinctive.'

Motomo: 'Memory cannot be defined but it defines mankind.'

OTHER SIMILAR FILMS: In its thematic concerns and its movement, the film must surely have inspired *The Matrix* trilogy, which itself utilises computer animation immensely in the realisation of its cyber world. Also check out the film *Appleseed* by the same director. So popular was *Ghost in the Shell* that a sequel, *Ghost in the Shell 2: Innocence*, has since been produced. The film, directed again by Mamaru Oshii and produced by the Production IG studio, focuses on the character of Bateau.

RECOGNITION: The *San Francisco Examiner* felt that the film was an 'Extraordinarily artful and highly adult creation . . . an effectively melancholy and intensely cerebral contemplation of what it means to be human.' However, *Time Out* was less complimentary: 'The *Blade Runner* theme of identity as function of memory is raised but not explored.'

AWARDS: *Ghost in the Shell* was given a simultaneous worldwide theatrical release on account of the intense following of comic book and anime fans for the work of the creator of the project Masamune Shirow. The film's director Mamoru Oshii is also a figurehead of anime. The film won the awards for Best Theatrical Feature Film and Best Director of a Theatrical Feature Film at the 1997 World Animation Celebration Awards.

COMMENT: 'The kind of film James Cameron would make if Disney ever let him.' *Empire.*

VERDICT: It is most obvious to compare *Ghost in the Shell* with an equally powerful and well-known Japanese animated feature *Akira*. To these eyes, though, *Ghost in the Shell* is a more controlled and focused story that crystallises several of the thoughts and preoccupations on display in the earlier film.

Ghost in the Shell is notable for its concision and its ebbing and flowing pace. It is not a relentless assault. It is more meditative than that and that is hugely in its favour.

While some of the dialogue (at least in translation) may sound clunky and clumsy as characters consider their situations, it elevates the animated form and again reminds audiences of just how arrestingly serious the format can be. The Japanese animation industry is to be saluted repeatedly for its blurring of the line between adult and child audiences when it comes to this way of telling stories.

Ghost in the Shell is melancholy, lyrical and savage. It is also very beautiful and belongs as readily in an overview of science-fiction cinema as *Things to Come* (William Cameron Menzies, 1936), *Forbidden Planet* (Fred McLeod Wilcox, 1956), *Solaris* (Andrei Tarkovsky, 1972), *Silent Running* (Doug Trumbull, 1971) *Close Encounters of the Third Kind* (Steven Spielberg, 1977), *The Terminator* (James Cameron, 1984) and *AI: Artificial Intelligence* (Steven Spielberg, 2001).

This is a very human film whose major achievement is to dramatise, through the prism of science fiction, issues that are common to everyone.

Princess Mononoke (1997)

(128 minutes)

Directed by Hayao Miyazaki
Written by Hayao Miyazaki
(English language adaptation by Neil Gaiman)
Produced by Toshio Susuki
Executive Produced by Yashyoshi Tokuma
Music: Jo Hisaishi
Cinematography: Atsuki Okui
Editing: Hayao Miyazaki and Takeshi Seyama
Animation Directors: Masashi Ando, Yoshifumi Kondo,
Katsuya Kondo, Kitaro Kosaka

BUDGET: 2.35 billion yen ($19.4 million)

ANIMATED FILMS Princess Mononoke

BOX OFFICE: 18.65 billion yen ($154 million)

RELEASE DATE: 12 July 1997 (Japan) 29 April 2000 (USA)

CERTIFICATE: PG13

VOICES: Yoji Matsuda (*Prince Ashitaka*), Yuriko Ishida (*San, The Princess Mononoke*), Yuko Tanaka (*Eboshi-gozen*), Kaoru Kobayashi (*Jokio-bo*), Masahiko Nishimura (*Kouroku*), Tsunehiko Kamijo (*Gonza*), Sumi Shimamoto (*Toki*), Tetsu Watanabe (*Yama-inu*), Mitsuru Sato (*Tatari-gami*), Akira Nagoya (*Usi-kai*), Akihiro Miwa (*Moro-no-kimi*), Mitsuko Mori (Hii-sama), Hisaya Morishige (*Okkoto-nusi*)
English language cast: Gillian Anderson (*Moro*), Billy Crudup (*Prince Ashitaka*), Claire Danes (*San, The Princess Mononoke*), Keith David (*Okkoto*), John DeMita (*Kohroku*), John DiMaggio (*Gonza*), Minnie Driver (*Lady Eboshi*), Jada Pinkett Smith (*Toki*), Billy Bob Thornton (*Jigo*)

TAGLINE: The fate of the world rests on the courage of one warrior.

STORYLINE: It's seventeenth-century, north-east Japan. A rural village is besieged by a wild boar in the form of a hideous demon, covered with bloody wormlike tendrils. Young Prince Ashitaka rides out to confront the beast and slays it, but not before being infected by its demon spirit. Ashitaka is branded with a mark on his arm and must be exiled from the village, never to return. Ashitaka sets out on his steed, Yakul, to discover what has caused the boar to manifest such a demonic spirit, so hell-bent on destroying humans.

Ashitaka's quest takes him westward across the expansive country. He comes across a village being attacked by samurai and when they chase him, Ashitaka fires arrows with ferocious outcomes, beheading and dismembering every victim. He clearly has a power within him that is highly destructive. At a provincial market, Ashitaka is befriended by a man called Jigo who explains the story of the spirit of the forest and how it is dangerous for man to go there.

Ashitaka rides on and comes across two men near death, who were part of the team of workers making their way back to Iron Town with food. As they did so they were attacked by forest wolves and a young woman who rides with them, Princess Mononoke. In the forest, Ashitaka looks and sees a young girl with a white wolf. The young woman, Princess Mononoke, says nothing before returning into the trees. Ashitaka takes the men back to Iron Town, run by the strong-headed Lady Eboshi. Ashitaka's arm begins to hurt as his demonic strength increases. Ashitaka chastises Eboshi for ravaging the forest in order to mine the iron.

Suddenly, the town is visited by Princess Mononoke who rides in to kill Eboshi. The Princess's name is revealed as San (see **THE DRAWING BOARD**) and she has been raised by wolves. Ashitaka intervenes and saves her from Eboshi. Ashitaka leaves the town and goes into the forest with San who takes him to the revered Great Forest Spirit who cures Ashitaka of his pain.

The tribe of boars come to San and the wolves and say that it is time to avenge the humans for their destructive ways. They say that San is human and therefore a threat but her wolf mother says she is not. Lord Okkoto, of the boar tribe, wonders if Nago's curse can be lifted (Nago is the boar who was killed by humans initially).

In Iron Town, Lady Eboshi realises there will be a battle between boars and humans. The boars are on the march. At the same time, Lady Eboshi's Iron Town is under attack from a local lord who wants a share of her business. The battle ensues and many boars die. Eboshi goes into the forest to hunt and slay The Forest Spirit, wanting its head.

Okkoto becomes a demon and takes San into his jaws. Ashitaka rides to rescue her, leaping into the mass of tendrils to free her. Ashitaka is near death and plunges into a forest pool. He revives and resurfaces. The Forest Spirit puts Okkoto to die and Eboshi then shoots the Forest Spirit and its head falls. The Forest Spirit, though, rejuvenates. Mononoke and Ashitaka return the head to the Spirit and it restores itself and in turn the ravaged land is healed and reborn. Ashitaka says goodbye to San, saying he cannot live in her forest world but he will always go and visit her there.

THE DRAWING BOARD: Studio Ghibli's trademark interest in the child's perception of the world is key to *Princess Mononoke*.

Miyazaki's intention was to create a piece of very human fantasy that drew on Japanese folkloric tradition. Significantly, *Princess Mononoke* was regarded as being specifically about Japanese mythology and cultural reference points. Previous Miyazaki films, unquestionably artful and dynamic, had been more genre-based and less culturally engaged. *Princess Mononoke* more explicitly expresses certain Japanese cultural tropes and concerns, which enhanced the film's immense popularity in its home country.

Originally the film was to have been titled *Ashitaka Tekki* (The Tale of Ashitaka). Mononoke means ghost, rather like a poltergeist, so the title is, loosely, *Ghost Princess*. The film contrasts with the science-fiction centred anime of *Ghost in the Shell* and *Akira*. Many of the scenes and ideas of the film were inspired by a 1980s manga by Miyazaki called *Shuna no Tabi (The Journey of Shuna)*.

INSPIRATIONS: Evidently Japanese folklore and mythology inform the fantasy and adventure: boars, for example, have a place in Japanese folklore. There is, in the ethical debate of the story, a fundamental humanism behind the wonder, miracles and violent intensity.

TOON TEAM: The project was produced at Studio Ghibli, now recognised as one of the great animation studios following the success of this film and *Spirited Away*. In essence Studio Ghibli began with *Nausicaa*, which was produced at another studio, but the film embodied the style and content that would largely define the studio's output over the coming years. Studio Ghibli was begun properly in 1985 when Miyazaki directed the successful *Laputa: Castle in the Sky* (Tenku no Shiro Laputa, 1986). Studio Ghibli has been compared to the UK's Aardman Animation by Andrew Osmond in *Sight and Sound*, in that 'Both studios are the subjects of local pride and affection . . . and have a reputation for integrity.'

Osmond goes on to note a general tendency for the Ghibli films directed by Miyazaki to be more immediately accessible while those directed by Isao are a little less narratively inclined – though far from obscure. Isao's films under the Ghibli banner are *Grave of Fireflies* that is set in post-nuclear Tokyo; *Only Yesterday* (Omoide Poro Poro, 1991), a low-key tale of a Japanese woman and memories of her childhood; *Defenders of the Forest* (Hesei Tanuki Gassen Pompoko, 1994) that serves as an allegory of Japanese leftist activism. (Miyazaki sympathised with leftist politics in the 1960s, being part of the 60s Anpo movement that opposed a Japan–America Security Agreement. This concern with superpower military bases being set up in small territories partly informs *Nausicaa*.)

The other Isao film to come out of Ghibli was *My Neighbours the Yamadas* (Hohokekyo Tonari no Yamada Kun, 1999) which is a loosely plotted portrait of a family.

VOCAL TALENT: For the English language version of the film, Gillian Anderson of *X Files* fame voices the wolf mother. Billy Crudup of *The Hi-Lo Country* (Stephen Frears, 1999), *Almost Famous* (Cameron Crowe, 2000) and *Big Fish* (Tim Burton, 2003) voices Prince Ashitaka. Billy Bob Thornton is Jigo. His directing credits include *Sling Blade* (1998), *All the Pretty Horses* (2000) and as actor *Monsters Ball* (Marc Forster, 2001) and *Intolerable Cruelty* (Joel Coen, 2003). Clare Danes (San) has appeared on TV in *My So Called Life* and on film in *Romeo and Juliet* (Baz Luhrmann, 1996) and *The Rainmaker* (Francis Ford Coppola, 1997). Jada Pinkett Smith features in *The Matrix Reloaded* (Andy & Larry Wachowski, 2003).

INK, PAINT AND HARD WORK: Production on the film began in August 1994 and ran through until June 1997. 144043 cels were used and 550 colours.

THEME: This film is abundant with metaphor and symbolism. It invests its faith in youth as the source of the world's future and its ecological theme dominates the action. The film also validates a respect for the spiritual and elemental. It may be one of the most pantheistic fantasy films yet made, alongside the tree sections of *The Lord of the Rings: The Two Towers* (Peter Jackson, 2002).

The film explores the conflict of commerce and nature and how best to strike a balance. The world is shown as both corrupt and nurturing, both qualities existing within the same person.

The narrative even finds space to express something about the Japanese culture around women; the women who work in Iron Town are all ex-prostitutes.

As an epic adventure the film adheres to the growth of a hero character which is essentially a way of charting anybody's journey from innocence to experience and back again. Ashitaka comes to understand the world's complexity and also how he can find his place in it. His valour and commitment are what save him more than his dexterity and bravery.

Intriguingly, the demonic curse that gives him such power is a major element of the story as he struggles with it. In this regard it recalls the narrative thrust of the film *Akira*, where a teenage boy is found to possess a powerful psychokinetic power that can be harnessed for good and bad.

In *Princess Mononoke* it is nature that emerges victorious over human folly and endeavour, forever strong and able to adapt and survive, just as the maimed Great Spirit does at the climax of the story.

Above The Nightmare Before Christmas: Jack Skellington and Sally find true love

Above left Jiminy Cricket and Pinocchio read a life-changing note from the Blue Fairy in *Pinocchio*

Left General Woundwort perishes in *Watership Down*

Above **Gertie the Dinosaur** and the beginnings of American animation

Above left Ray Harryhausen breathes life into one of his stop-motion miracles

Left **Jason and the Argonauts:** Jason meets his match in the skeleton crew – a stop-motion miracle

Above Walt Disney
ponders concept art for
Bambi

Right Jan Svankmajer at
work

Left Eddie Valiant and
Roger Rabbit surrounded
by the good, the bad and
the cartoony in *Who
Framed Roger Rabbit?*

Right Princess Mononoke:
the Princess and her
guardian wolf Moro
contemplate the challenges
ahead

Below The Iron Giant: the
eponymous giant and his
friend Hogarth get a
better view of the world

Above Shrek, Princess Fiona and the Donkey go adventuring in *Shrek*

Below The scientists discover a dinosaur and the movie audience discovers the wonder of computer animation in *Jurassic Park*. It's a long way from *Gertie the Dinosaur*

One of the most stirring qualities of the film, and other Japanese anime, is the moral seriousness and the sombre, mature tone. It is a long way from the vaudevillian energy and high spirits of other adventure-based animated films. The film's simple narrative allows for sequences to dwell on mood and emotional resonance rather than endlessly adding new plot twists.

STYLISH TOONS: The film combines highly kinetic sequences, such as the opening boar attack and Princess Mononoke's arrival in Iron Town, with stunningly quiet sequences such as the key phase of the story when Ashitaka is rejuvenated in the forest. It is hugely realistic in its deployment of tone.

The film's brief prologue economically encapsulates the overall concern and conflict of the film. A misty mountain range is accompanied by a voice-over explaining how man and beast lived in harmony before the forests were destroyed by man in a hunger for wealth. 'Those were the days of gods and of demons,' intones the voice. One image shows beautiful grass being torn up by an unidentified creature's foot, scarring the ground with every step.

The film brims with rich details. In the forest, for example, butterflies and dragonflies flit across much of the action and in doing so complete a sense of environment. Further fidelity to a believable natural atmosphere is evident in the smoke and rain effects and the glistening of rivers and pools of water.

The detail present in creating moss, water effects and sunlight streaming through trees is as compelling and fascinating as the more obvious elements of the storytelling. The forest is endowed with special majesty, mystery and magic, recalling Akira Kurosawa's images of trees and forest in his short film segment, 'Sunshine in the Rain' from his film *Dreams* (1990).

Stylistically, *Princess Mononoke* spans a wonderful tonal range that arcs from the bloody, visceral demon appearance at the start and close of the film to the cute forest sprites and the elegant movement of the characters.

Throughout the film, silence is used as powerfully as the most thunderous or exotic sound effect. When Ashitaka first sees a vision of The Forest Spirit it is a very quiet, epiphanic moment: almost silent, the silhouette of the Spirit looks at him in a golden haze before moving on. The sequence possesses lyrical power. Similarly, when Mononoke attacks Iron Town she moves with silence, expressing her superhumanity. In the Forest Spirit instance, silence suggests peace and in the latter example it is used to suggest an undetected threat.

139

Tilts and pans of the camera add a live-action dynamism to the sequences. The speed lines and blurring of backgrounds in high-action shots such as Ashitaka racing to rescue San emphasise character over all else.

There is great subtlety in facial expressions that sits neatly alongside the expansive fantasy images and apocalyptic moments. Appealingly, in an age of cinema that emphasises very fast cuts and rapid pacing, the film is not afraid to take its time and dwell on environments and moments. Even the very end of the film, where we know the land is about to be reborn, a wide shot lingers on the dead earth, silently. It makes the characters and audience wait for what they want to see, namely the rejuvenation of the world. Ultimately, *Princess Mononoke* stylistically treats the fantasy of its subject with an immense feeling of naturalism.

CHARACTER SKETCH: *Princess Mononoke* is replete with a wide range of human and fantasy characters and the world that Miyazaki creates feels very coherent.

Despite the film's title, the central character is Prince Ashitaka.

Ashitaka is a character very much attuned to nature and the environment. Ashitaka's connection to the natural world is first evidenced through his attachment to his steed, Yakul, a yaklike animal who can sense danger and power in nature. The young Prince is the classic hero figure journeying into an unknown world that opens up his understanding.

Like the audience, the Prince is learning about the world he finds himself in. He is a very charming and appealing character – intelligent, physically competent and accomplished. He is also charged with a strong moral viewpoint.

San (Princess Mononoke) is an orphan. Abandoned by her parents in the forest, San was cared for by the wolves, not unlike Mowgli in Rudyard Kipling's *The Jungle Book*. San is focused, brave and committed. Her flaw is being unable to side with the humans.

Lady Eboshi is both compassionate and mired in a lust for financial wealth. Her disrespect for nature is her undoing.

With great accomplishment, the film renders the beasts, the wolves, boars and apes at once terrifying, awesome and caring. The forest sprites that appear in two key sequences are many but very well defined as protective and nurturing, like a cross between *Casper the Friendly Ghost* (Joseph Oriolo, Seymour Reit), fairies and the Pilsbury Dough Boy.

There is a universality to the characters. The Great Spirit is like a super-stag with a more simian, tiger-striped face, but again its calm authority and ability to walk on water connects to a range of other cultural figures and deities. Evidently, the Japanese heritage that inspires the story does not preclude it from accessibility, again proving that mythic situations and characters are universal in their great appeal and resonance.

TOON TUNES: The music was composed by one of Japan's most well known and revered musicians, Jo Hisaishi who has a successful career that began in the early 1980s and is a fan of the Westerns of John Ford. He has become a core collaborator with Hayao Miyazaki. Alongside his concert works, Hisaishi has become the John Williams of Japanese film, composing for both live action and animation to great success.

Of Japanese animation Hisaishi has noted that he would not typically score for the form saying that 'Japanese animation in general has a unique characteristic that I find rather too detail orientated so I don't do them. The exception to this rule is . . . Miyazaki.' For Hisaishi the aim of a score is to represent the world view of a given film.

The film's orchestral score is lush and melodic but never overwhelming. Hisaishi is a fan of the Westerns of John Ford, and when Ashitaka arrives at Iron Town this Western influence can be heard in the musical score. The music's frequent large scale is countered by its small scenes such as those featuring the kodama (the forest sprites) where their gentility and the benevolence of the forest is represented by a gentle musical motif.

Hisaishi's other film credits include the live action *Hana Bi* (Takeshi Kitano) and also *Nausicaa of the Valley of the Winds, Sonatine, The Water Traveler, Kids Return, Kiki's Delivery Service, Laputa, Arion, Porco Rosso, Venus Wars* and most recently *Spirited Away*.

Princess Mononoke soundtrack: 'Legend of Ashitaka', 'Demon God', 'Journey to the West', 'Demon Power', 'Land of the Impure', 'Encounter', 'Forest of the Gods', 'Evening at the Ironworks', 'Demon God II: The Lost Mountains', 'Lady Eboshi', 'Tatara Women Work Song', 'Furies', 'Young Man from the East', 'Requiem', 'Will to Live', 'San and Ashitaka in the Forest of the Deer', 'Princess Mononoke Theme Song', 'Requiem II', 'Battle Drums', 'Battle in front of the Ironworks', 'Demon Part II', 'Requiem III', 'Retreat', 'Demon God III', 'Adagio of Life and Death', 'World of the Dead', 'World of the Dead II', 'Adagio of Life and Death', 'Adagio of Life and Death II', 'Ashitaka and San', 'Princess Mononoke Theme Song', 'Legend of Ashitaka Theme'.

TOON TALK:

Jigo: 'These days there are angry gods all around us.'

Ashitaka: 'To see with eyes unclouded by hate.'

Wolf Mother: 'I listen to the pain of the forest.'

OTHER SIMILAR FILMS: Miyazaki followed up *Princess Mononoke* with the equally well-received *Spirited Away* (*Sen To Chihiro No Kamikakushi*) which was released in Japan in 2001 and in Europe and North America in summer 2003 to great acclaim, critics and audiences alike swooning to its dreamy images. The film won an Oscar for Best Animated Feature in 2003 and shared the Golden Bear award at the 2002 Berlin festival. *Spirited Away* tells the story of a little girl, Chihiro, who is separated from her parents and finds herself in a Japanese bath house populated by gods and spirits. Characters include a six-armed man and a character called No-face.

The story is set in modern-day Japan, but the fantasy world exists right alongside it. Apparently, Miyazaki was motivated to make the film to remind children of the traditions of their nation as he sensed a real apathy in the young towards the country's heritage. The original ending for the film focused on a supernatural fight between Yubaba, Haku and Yubaba's sister to restore Chihiro's name and break the spell over her parents. The film grossed $15.8 million on its opening weekend in Japan and continued to build its success. After three months the film had sold one ticket for every six people living in Japan.

Miyazaki has said of the film's success: 'I think a small number of the people will understand the film and that is more than enough. Some think being popular in the United States is the best thing, but I think it is wrong to think that way.' John Lasseter, who directed Pixar's *Toy Story* (1995) has overseen the American release version of the film in 2003. Miyazaki once said that children should only watch his films on their birthday, as there is much else of interest for them to do.

Miyazaki's earlier films may be difficult to access but they are notable for their humour and richness of storytelling. *Princess Mononoke* continues the engagement with fantasy and the fragility of human existence laid down in his other notable features *Nausicaa of the Valley of the Wind* (*Kaze no Tani no Naushika*), which is set in a world where human civilisation has been destroyed after The Seven Days of Fire. Only some scraps of the human race endure and a poisonous jungle called The Fukai now covers much of the world. Giant insects dominate the land.

As with *Princess Mononoke*, the protagonist Nausicaa is a young woman with a penchant for exploration. As in *Princess Mononoke*, *Nausicaa* inventively explores the relationship between human endeavour and interference with the natural balance.

The follow-up to *Nausicaa* was *Laputa: Castle in the Sky* (1986) in which the miotiar are intrigued by a fortress in the air. The adventure begins when a young girl falls from the sky after being pursued by air pirates. This film may be released by Disney in North America with a new score by Jo Hisaishi.

Another of Miyazaki's fantasy movies is *My Neighbour Totoro* (*Tonari no Totoro*, 1988) which tells of a tree spirit called Totoro who is befriended by a little girl called Mei when she moves to the country with her family. The following year, Miyazaki directed *Kiki's Delivery Service* (*Majo no Takkyubin*) in which a thirteen-year-old witch named Kiki begins her first year away from home so that she can learn her job independently in a town that does not yet have a witch.

A smaller-scaled Miyazaki film, *Porco Rosso* (1992) began as a 30 to 45-minute in-flight piece for Japanese airlines. Miyazaki ran with the idea to feature length and the film tells the story of an Italian Air Force pilot who leaves military service in reaction to the rise of Fascism. He takes on the profession of bounty hunter, going by the name of Porco Rosso. This film was based on a Miyazaki manga called *Hikoutei Jidai*.

At the time of writing, anime fans are uncertain whether Miyazaki will direct another feature.

RECOGNITION: 'The story has simplicity and force, with captivating images and gutsy narrative ideas recalling Kipling, Ovid and Homer' said the *Guardian*, while *Salon* felt that it was 'More than a terrific animated film. It's a great work of fantasy . . . suffused with enough adult sadness and realism that its world brushes awfully close to ours.'

Interestingly, after *Princess Mononoke* failed to make much of a popular impact on its North American release it was felt that one of the other Studio Ghibli films could have been better used to introduce audiences to Miyazaki's films.

AWARDS: The huge popular success of the film was matched by its awards success. It received the Japanese Academy Award for Best Picture. It won Best Movie, Best Animation and Japanese Movie Fans' Choice award at the 52nd Mainichi Movie Competition. Miyazaki won Best Director at the Takasaki Film Festival. It won Best Composer and

Best Album production at the 39th Japan Record Awards. The film won the Saturn Award for Best Home Video Release in 2001 and at the Annie (animation) Awards in 2000 it was nominated in the category of Outstanding Individual Achievement for Directing in an Animated Feature Production.

In 2000 the film was nominated for a Sierra Award by the Las Vegas Film Critics' Society Awards for Best Animated Film and at the Motion Picture Sound Editors awards in 2000 was nominated for a Golden Reel Award in the category of Best Sound Editing for an animated feature.

COMMENT: 'We are not trying to solve the global problems . . . even in the middle of hatred and killings there are still things worth living for. A wonderful meeting or a beautiful thing can exist.' Hayao Miyazaki.

VERDICT: In the summer of 1999, *Star Wars: Episode 1 – The Phantom Menace* (George Lucas) was released, its space adventure images very Japanese in their design and influence, from the highly adorned Queen Amidala to the samurai spins and duels of the Jedi Knights. Lucas's film was unfavourably compared with *Princess Mononoke*, which combines kinetic, highly cinematic energy with wonderful pastoral silences. *The Phantom Menace*, with its plot strand around the Gungans and Naboo, is also as ecologically minded.

Perhaps the greatest sequence in *Princess Mononoke* is that where Ashitaka is taken to the pool in the forest to be revived. The film is a masterpiece that really is as emotionally affecting as any live-action fantasy and is certainly preferable to the lumbering *Lord of the Rings* films. *Princess Mononoke*'s humanity, ecological commitment and emphasis on the potential for harmony over discord is potent. This film should be ranked alongside *Star Wars* (George Lucas, 1977), *The Wizard of Oz* (Victor Fleming, 1939), *ET: The Extra-Terrestrial* (Steven Spielberg, 1982), *Back to the Future* (Robert Zemeckis, 1985) and *Edward Scissorhands* (Tim Burton, 1990) as a genuinely cinematic fantasy with very real emotions.

This film is utterly accessible and thrilling, displaying the best that the adventure format is capable of.

Pix and Mix: When Live Action Met Animation

Since the earliest days of animation there has been much success (commercially and creatively) found in combining live action with animation. Certainly stop motion has been used in this way countless times to put men and monsters in the same frame. This chapter is concerned with cel animation. Two films come to mind as exemplary of the technique. The first is *Mary Poppins* and the second *Who Framed Roger Rabbit?* though other movies, such as *Bedknobs and Broomsticks* (Robert Stevenson, 1971) and *Pete's Dragon* (Don Chaffey, 1977) have used the form. Obviously, virtually every visual-effects film is a variation on this concept but these two films foreground the illusion as fantasy comes crashing and dancing into reality.

Mary Poppins (1964) was directed by Robert Stevenson, the film was produced by Walt Disney and Bill Walsh with original music by Richard M Sherman and Robert B Sherman. The film's vivid special visual effects were supervised by Peter Ellenshaw, Eustace Lycett and Robert A Mattey. For the now-famous animated sequences (representing, at that time, the most intricate interaction of live action and animation) Disney called on several of his long-standing animators, namely Hal Ambro, Ward Kimball, Milt Kahl, Eric Larson, John Lounsberry, Hamilton Luske (Animation Director), Cliff Nordberg, Ollie Johnston, Frank Thomas, Jack Boyd. Considered for the role of Mary Poppins were Bette Davis and Mary Martin but when Disney saw Julie Andrews on stage in *Camelot* he knew he had found his actress. The actress Jane Darwell was asked by Walt to appear in the film even though she had retired. Her character of The Bird Woman encapsulates the concept of caring and charity.

For the role of Bert, Disney hired hugely popular TV star Dick van Dyke. Ed Wynn played the 'laughoholic' Uncle Albert and David Tomlinson played the father, Mr Banks. Karen Dotrice and Matthew Garber played the children, Jane and Michael.

With a budget of $5 million, the film was a massive success, made a star of Julie Andrews and has embedded itself as the touchstone of family film fantasy. Its initial box office take was $45 million.

The film experienced a laboured development period. Walt Disney had been intrigued by the stories of *Mary Poppins* by PL Travers that had been published in the early 1940s and early on he had attempted to convince the author he could do justice to the character. Disney was a little unprepared for the strength of Travers's resistance, yet he remained focused on making an adaptation somehow and one that seemed suited to the musical format. In time, the film became a vast project for the studio and for many was Walt's last great fantasy project. He had said of the proposed film that it 'would combine cartoon and live action in an enormous fantasy'.

The eventual film production served to employ all that the studio had developed and learned since its inception in the early 1920s. Certain aspects of the project were regarded as 'firsts' notably the *Jolly Holiday* sequence which at that time became the most long-running and most involved combination of live action and animation. The film also contained its fair share of dance numbers, choreographed by Marc Breaux and Dee Dee Wood.

Prior to *Mary Poppins*, of course, the Disney studio had made other live-action–animated shorts. In the earliest years of the Disney studio they had very successfully produced the *Alice in Cartoonland* series and prior to World War Two had produced the *Saludos Amigos* and *Three Caballeros*.

Initially, Disney had not realised PL Travers's books were collections of short stories but one of Disney's daughters enjoyed reading them.

Roy Disney, Walt's brother, visited Travers during a stay in New York and he attempted to interest her in a film adaptation of her character. Travers, who had just had her latest Poppins title published, *Mary Poppins Opens the Door*, remained reluctant. Walt invited Travers to Los Angeles to the studio and they talked through the possible project more comprehensively but Travers stayed firmly reticent and the project was put back on the shelf.

On a business trip to London in the 1950s, Disney met with Travers once more, in another attempt to nurture her enthusiasm. This time Disney returned to LA with Travers's blessing and got the film project moving. Disney's first move was to involve Richard and Robert Sherman, a songwriting team, in the development. Disney gave them the mission of going through the *Mary Poppins* books and choosing what they felt were the six best short stories. From this they created a storyline and several early song sketches. Amazingly, when Disney met with them he had marked up the same six short stories as most movie-friendly. Bill Walsh and Don DaGradi were hired to craft the screenplay.

Meanwhile, The Sherman Brothers began work on what became 37 possible songs. In 1961, with work under way at the studio, PL Travers went to see Disney and voice her concerns. Walt was unprepared for such strong and well-articulated opinion regarding the adaptation process. Nonetheless, Disney and Travers worked well together, perhaps *because* of this creative tension.

Inevitably, certain planned sequences had to be cut such as Mary Poppins on a trip around the world and an underwater sequence. This sub-aquatic scene would be revised in another Disney animation and live-action movie, *Bedknobs and Broomsticks* (Robert Stevenson, 1971). It was Travers who suggested the 1930s setting be moved to that of Edwardian England.

At the time in Disney's merchandising history, *Mary Poppins* generated the most licensing of product promoting the film. Indeed, the marketing push had its effect as an estimated 200 million people saw the film in its initial release.

Special effects included showing Mary Poppins on a cloud over London, a tea party on the ceiling and most significantly chalk pavement pictures coming to life.

For many years, the film stood as a benchmark as the most sophisticated combination of classical animation and live action characters interacting. It was warmly received, acknowledged for both its dramatic, comic and fantasy charm and also for its technical accomplishments. Reviews included this: 'one of the most magnificent pieces of entertainment ever to come from Hollywood'. (Hollis Alpert, the *Saturday Review*) and, more recently, indicative of the film's enduring appeal, this: 'a magnificent job of adapting PL Travers's character to the screen, using cinematic effects to the full in creating an enchanting story'. (George Perry, BBCi Film reviews.)

The film won five Academy Awards in the categories of Best Song (*Chim Chim Cher-ee*), Best Score, Film Editing, Special Effects and Best Actress. *My Fair Lady* (George Cukor) beat the film in the Best Picture category. For many the film represents the pinnacle of Walt Disney's personal storytelling and producing skills.

A little over twenty years later the Disney Studio would again be largely responsible for taking the format of drawn animation and live action further yet in the landmark feature, *Who Framed Roger Rabbit?*

Who Framed Roger Rabbit? (1988)

(103 minutes)

A Buena Vista Release of a Touchstone and Amblin Entertainment presentation, in association with Silver Screen Partner III
Directed by Robert Zemeckis
Produced by Robert Watts, Frank Marshall
Executive Producers: Steven Spielberg, Kathleen Kennedy
Written by Jeffrey Price and Peter S Seaman from the novel
***Who Censored Roger Rabbit?* by Gary K Wolf**
Cinematography: Dean Cundey
Editor: Arthur Schmidt
Music: Alan Silvestri
Sound: Tony Dawe, Michael Evje
Animation Director: Richard Williams
Production Design: Elliot Scott and Roger Cain
Special Visual Effects: Industrial Light and Magic
Visual Effects Supervisor: Ken Ralston
Mechanical Effects Supervisor: George Gibbs
Costume Design: Joanna Johnston
Production Managers: Patricia Carr and Jack Frost Sanders
Supervising Animators: Andreas Deja, Russell Hall, Phil Nibbelink, Simon Wells
Animation Effects Supervisor: Christopher Knott
Animation Consultants: Chuck Jones, Walt Stanchfield, Stan Green
Associate Producers: Steve Starkey, Don Hahn

BUDGET: $50 million

BOX OFFICE: $130 million

RELEASE DATE: 24 June 1988

CERTIFICATE: PG

CAST/VOICES: Bob Hoskins (*Eddie Valiant*), Christopher Lloyd (*Judge Doom*), Joanna Cassidy (*Dolores*), Marvin Acme (*Stubby Kaye*), Alan

Tilvern (*RK Maroon*), Richard LeParmentier (*Lt Santino*), Joel Silver (*Raoul Raoul*), Betsy Brantley (*Jessica, performance model*), Kathleen Turner (*Jessica, voice*), Charlie Fleischer (*Roger* Rabbit, voice), Amy Irving (*Jessica, singing*), Lou Hirsch (*Baby Herman*), Joe Alakey (*Yosemite Sam*), Mel Blanc (*Daffy Duck, Bugs Bunny, Tweety Pie, Sylvester, Porky Pig*), June Foray (*Wheezy, Leena Hyena*), Richard Williams (*Droopy*), Wayne Allwine (*Mickey Mouse*), Minnie Mouse (*Russi Taylor*), Tony Pope (*Goofy*), Cherry Davis (*Woody Woodpecker*), Peter Westy (*Pinocchio*), Frank Sinatra (*Singing Sword*)

TAGLINE: A man, a woman and a rabbit in a triangle of trouble.

STORYLINE: RK Maroon presents a Roger Rabbit cartoon which is being filmed and then comes to a crushing halt when Roger flubs a gag and a line. Roger Rabbit is a cartoon who lives and breathes in the human world, one of a roster of animation stars working alongside Mickey Mouse, Bugs Bunny and Betty Boop to name just a few. Roger Rabbit is anxious, something is unnerving him and Maroon needs to know why as it is making the film run over budget. Eddie Valiant is hired to investigate. Going to the Ink and Paint Club, where toons entertain humans, Eddie watches Roger's wife Jessica sing a sultry song. After the show, Eddie takes snaps of Jessica with Marvin Acme, the owner of Toontown, in her dressing room. Acme is then found dead and Roger is the criminal everybody points to. Roger goes on the run and hides out at Eddie's office and apartment.

Eddie is reluctant to associate with toons and therefore reluctant to help. Complicating the investigation is the intrusion of Judge Doom, a maniacal and twisted character who has invented a way to kill toons, namely a fluorescent green dip. The Judge tracks Roger down, in hiding at Eddie's favourite bar, and almost dips him when Eddie intervenes and runs with the rabbit. They hitch a ride in Benny the cartoon cab.

Eddie then goes to see RK Maroon only to witness him killed by an unseen assassin. Eddie sees Jessica and follows her to the last place he wants to go, namely Toontown, located not far from the Maroon studio. Eddie drives into Toontown to find Roger and is met by Jessica who tells Eddie that Doom killed Maroon. Eddie untangles the intrigue and realises that Doom is intending to destroy Toontown and the moviemaking studio in order to make way for a vast moneymaking enterprise named the freeway. Doom has bought up and will make obsolete the tram network.

Eddie, against his better judgement, must journey into Toontown as part of his mission. In Toontown, Eddie is aided and abetted by some legendary characters and is then caught by Doom who takes Eddie and Jessica to the Acme factory as his prisoners. Roger rides out of Toontown and with Benny the Cab races to the rescue. Roger bursts in on Doom in an attempt to save his wife and gumshoe pal. Roger and Jessica are tied up and the dip gun is aimed at them. Doom and Eddie fight one another and Doom's real identity is shown – he too is a cartoon in human disguise. Doom perishes and Eddie rescues Roger and Jessica from the dip just in time. Doom's dip machine is knocked out of commission and smashes through the factory wall, revealing Toontown beyond.

Eddie, Roger and Jessica are met by dozens of cartoon characters who all sing along to the song 'Smile Darn Ya Smile' as Eddie, Jessica and Roger walk off into the Toontown sunset.

THE DRAWING BOARD: 'There was a lot of suffering on Roger' is how Robert Zemeckis recalled the creative process of bringing Roger Rabbit to the screen.

One of the quintessential fantasy movies of all time, and one of the best studio spectacles of the 1980s, *Who Framed Roger Rabbit?* began life as a novel by Gary Wolf entitled *Who Censored Roger Rabbit?* The premise of the novel was that cartoons were actually photographed for comic strips. In Wolf's imagination there was mileage in fusing this with a film noir-style story. The cover of the novel showed Roger in bright yellow trousers with a green flower pattern and red braces. He is approaching a very wary-looking Eddie Valiant. A speech bubble hangs over Roger's head saying 'Help! I'm stuck in a mystery of double crosses, steamy broads, and killer cream pies.' The novel was published in 1981 and was originally considered by Disney as a feature. Rather like Tim Burton's concept for *The Nightmare Before Christmas*, also pitched in the early 1980s, Wolf's novel was turned down. Wolf has since gone on to write *Who P-Plugged Roger Rabbit?*

Director Robert Zemeckis, one of the great Hollywood fabulist screenwriters and directors (with *Romancing the Stone* (1984) and *Back to the Future* (1985)) had read the book in the early 1980s and thought it had potential but was not really in a position to do much about it. Prior to commercial and critical success with *Romancing the Stone*, his two directorial-screenwriting efforts had failed commercially, *I Wanna Hold Your Hand* (1978) and the excellent and brattish *Used Cars* (1980), which is a fantastically snappy kinetic comedy, and he and his writing partner Bob Gale had written *1941* (Steven Spielberg, 1979) which had been a critical and commercial disappointment.

For a period Joe Dante, a director specialising in fantasy movies (*Piranha*, 1979, *The Howling*, 1980, *Gremlins*, 1984, *Explorers*, 1985) was involved in the development of the film but in time committed to other work. Indeed, Dante's most recent film, *Looney Tunes: Back in Action* has been a live-action–animation combo for Warner Brothers.

After the worldwide success of *Back to the Future*, Zemeckis was very hot property. The story goes that one day Zemeckis was in Steven Spielberg's office soon after the release of *Back to the Future*. Zemeckis saw Wolf's novel on Spielberg's desk and enthused about it. According to Zemeckis, Spielberg said something to the effect of 'Why don't we think about doing it?' The project became the first and only collaboration between Spielberg (through Amblin' Entertainment) and the Walt Disney Company.

Preparation for the film was extensive and hugely detailed, representing as much a furthering of animation and visual effects as *Star Wars* had ten years before. *Roger Rabbit* was one of the last pre-digital effects movies, still dependent on a mass of practical effects for its illusion. The film shot from December 1986 until April 1987 at Elstree Studios in London with pick-up photography in December 1987.

At the time of the film's release, Williams enthused to the now-defunct *Films and Filming* magazine (August 1988): 'These things would come over and we wouldn't recognise our own animation. It's so good you can't believe it.' The film employed 35 animators, about 150 paint and trace artists, 100 people working on mattes and rotoscopes, 30 assistant animators and 40 in-betweeners, plus 90 people in Los Angeles.

Key to the success of the film was animator Richard Williams who directed the animation on the film from his London base (see **TOON TEAM**). Significant in the film's visual design was Zemeckis's trademark kinetic camera movement. Typically, any live-action film with animation in frame worked with a locked-off frame making the job that bit easier in terms of scale and perspective but this was not the case on *Who Framed Roger Rabbit?* Zemeckis (who had seen a reel of Richard Williams's life work *The Thief and the Cobbler*) knew that Williams was the man. 'The guy who has the right feel for the movie in terms of style and humour was Richard Williams . . . And I do think, as Chuck Jones has said, he's the only true animation genius working today.'

The screenplay for *Who Framed Roger Rabbit?* was written by Jeffrey Price and Peter Seaman whose credits also include *Wild Wild West*

(Barry Sonnenfeld, 2000). Certainly, Zemeckis, as a writer himself, was heavily involved in refining the screenplay. In Wolf's novel the characters speak with speech bubbles but this would have been infuriating and redundant in a movie. In another change to the novel the film introduced the character of Judge Doom whose ambition for a new transport system in LA echoed *Chinatown* (Roman Polanski, 1974).

INSPIRATIONS: Much of the film is inspired by the legacy of Hollywood animation, manifested by the films of the Disney, MGM and Warner Brothers studios. The Fleischer Studio is also acknowledged with an appearance by Betty Boop (in black and white). She appears as an usherette at The Ink and Paint Club telling Eddie Valiant, 'I still got it, Eddie. Boop boop de boop.' She also seems to be quite keen on Roger Rabbit, citing Jessica as a 'lucky goil' for being married to him.

The film made animation very cool again, with its crazy 'dynamite down your pants' brand of humour to borrow Robert Zemeckis's description. Zemeckis wanted to combine the following touchstones of popular animation: the characterisation of the Warner Brothers cartoons, the articulation of the Disney characters and the Tex Avery humour.

One of the early challenges of the film was securing copyright clearance for a wealth of animated characters. 'I really feel we're making this film for Walt,' Steven Spielberg remarked during the film's production. Warner Brothers lent Sylvester the Cat, Tweety Pie, Porky Pig, Yosemite Sam, Daffy Duck and Bugs Bunny to the production.

Given Zemeckis's credentials as a writer, the screenplay went through numerous drafts, creating frustration for the preparation of visual effects. Thus, Baby Herman was at one point the villain and then Jessica Rabbit. The last script received by Ken Ralston had the new villain, Judge Doom.

TOON TEAM: Robert Zemeckis had two key collaborators on the film. The first was visual-effects supervisor Ken Ralston, with whom Zemeckis had worked since *Back to the Future*.

Ralston supervised not just ILM's shadowing effects on each animated character, as well as their integration into the live action; he also oversaw the extensive blue screen work that believably threw Eddie Valiant into the bendy, twisty, bright and breezy world of Toon town where buildings really do taper to infinity rather like the cliffs in a *Road Runner* cartoon. Blue screen permitted Eddie to plummet apparently to his doom before being handed a parachute by those well-known aeronauts, Mickey Mouse and Bugs Bunny.

Ralston and Zemeckis are currently at work on the equally groundbreaking adaptation of Chris Van Allburg's lush children's picture book, *The Polar Express*, which involves the actors being motion captured and animated within a computer-rendered environment that closely approximates the style of the book's glowing and magical pastel images. Tom Hanks, as the Conductor, will also be rendered as a boy for the film.

The other key collaborator on *Who Framed Roger Rabbit?* was animation director Richard Williams, whose name is near legend in animation circles. Williams had worked in England since the 1960s and, alongside his award-winning work for commercials and short pieces of animation, what Williams was most renowned for was his personal project, *The Thief and the Cobbler*. An expansive Arabian adventure, Williams had worked on it since the mid-1960s as a feature film. It was finally released in the mid-1990s and is rightly regarded as the victim of too much studio interference.

The Thief and the Cobbler is one of the great cause célèbres of animation history. Ironically, it was an excerpt from this film that prompted Zemeckis to contact Williams about involvement in *Who Framed Roger Rabbit?* Zemeckis had seen the excerpt in the mid-1980s when Williams was trying to raise further funding for it in Hollywood. Earlier in his career, Williams had contacted several of Disney's nine old men, veterans of the earliest Disney features. Frank Thomas, Ollie Johnston and Milt Kahl guided Williams in the fundamental and the spirit of classical animation.

Working alongside Richard Williams as director of animation were noted lead animators Andreas Deja and Simon Wells. Deja had been a Disney animator since the mid-1980s, with movies such as *The Black Cauldron* (Richard Rich, Ted Berman, 1985) and *Basil the Great Mouse Detective* (Ron Clements, David Michener, 1986). Simon Wells, great grandson of the author HG Wells, is a British animator who has gone on to co-direct *An American Tail: Fievel Goes West* (with Phil Nibbelink, 1991) for Steven Spielberg's Amblimation company. Wells also directed *We're Back* (1993) and *Balto* (1995). He went on to co-direct *The Prince of Egypt* (1998).

Helping Robert Zemeckis bring the live action world into which the cartoons would easily and believably live, breathe, bend, squash and bound was Dean Cundey, a cinematographer with a special affinity for lighting fantasy movies. Cundey's dazzling credits include *The Thing* (John Carpenter, 1982), *Romancing the Stone* (Robert Zemeckis, 1984), *Back to the Future* trilogy (Robert Zemeckis, 1985, 1989, 1990), *Hook* (Steven Spielberg, 1991) and *Jurassic Park* (Steven Spielberg, 1993).

In an age before digital effects, *Who Framed Roger Rabbit?* depended greatly on interactive practical effects to sustain the illusion of the cartoon characters interacting with the real world. Responsible for overseeing this aspect of the film's creation was George Gibbs whose other credits include *The Meaning of Life* (Terry Jones, Terry Gilliam, 1983), *Indiana Jones and the Temple of Doom* (Steven Spielberg, 1984) and *Labyrinth* (Jim Henson, 1986).

VOCAL TALENT: For the voice of Betty Boop the original voice artist Mae Questel returned to her character. Mel Blanc and his son Noel provided voices for Bugs Bunny, Tweety Pie and Porky Pig. Charlie Fleischer was the voice of Roger Rabbit and Lou Hirsch voiced Baby Herman. Kathleen Turner was the husky voice of Jessica Rabbit and her singing voice was that of Amy Irving.

INK, PAINT AND HARD WORK: The animation was produced at a studio in Camden Town, London. For many of the live-action scenes, shot at Elstree Studios (home to so many favourite fantasy films) the sets were built about ten feet off the ground, allowing puppeteers to orchestrate devices to allow for the animated characters to believably engage in the human world of offices, diners and clubs. The animation cost around £118,000 per minute. The Industrial Light and Magic produced the 'comps', the composite shots of the animation placed into the live-action footage.

On location, the character of Roger Rabbit was voiced by stand-up comedian Charlie Fleischer, who would provide the voice for the finished film. Sometimes Fleischer wore a rabbit in red dungarees outfit and big bunny rabbit ears. On location George Gibbs, legendary live-effects supervisor, whose other credits include *Labyrinth* (Jim Henson, 1986), *Indiana Jones and the Temple of Doom* (Steven Spielberg, 1984), *Alien* (James Cameron, 1986) and *Indiana Jones and the Last Crusade* (Steven Spielberg, 1989) provided interactive set-ups that mimicked the effects of the cartoons on the real environment. A rubber Roger Rabbit figure true to his eventual on-screen height was used as an eye line reference. The task of integrating the animation with the live action was dubbed 'multidimensional interactive character generation'.

Cinematographer Dean Cundey had to ensure interactive lighting would marry with the animation.

On set, Richard Williams would sketch the action of the characters in a given scene so that Zemeckis would have a more comprehensive idea of how to block a scene out and allow for the cartoons. Zemeckis improvised new pieces of action on set that would challenge or change the storyboarded material.

One of the most elaborate sequences was the appearance of Jessica Rabbit on stage at the Ink and Paint Club. A live-action motion-control camera tracked the stand-in actress to Stubby Kaye's table. The actress reached down and polished an apple on Kaye's head. The camera panned over and followed the actress to where Hoskins was sitting. She reached into frame from outside what would eventually be a split screen. Hoskins pantomimed everything so that it would correspond with the animation. The camera re-ran for shots of the crowd and again for the spotlights on Jessica and these images would be combined. Eventually the stand-in's images were replaced by a blank plate of the set and Jessica was drawn in.

THEME: Robert Zemeckis's best films are marked by a real zest and *Who Framed Roger Rabbit?* is no exception – an all-out carnivalesque fantasy, it is a celebration of humour.

It also offers an anti-racist storyline where the best humans in the story have no problem with the Toons. 'We were very aware of what we were doing, although we drew the line at calling The Dip the Final Solution,' said Zemeckis.

Judge Doom's dreams of a highway in place of a movie studio and movie culture are presented as hugely evil. For Zemeckis the film celebrates the improving value of fantasy in our daily lives. Eddie learns from Roger and in the film's climax it is his sense of playfulness that saves the day and protects the legacy of cartoons. Smile, darn ya, smile, indeed.

In his book *7 Minutes*, Norman Klein writes that, 'It is a folk tale about the last two decades before cartoons essentially vanished from movie theatres; as well as a folktale about how we misremember the past, nearly get it right, then settle for the movie.' He also notes that the film characters represent essential American spirit and that at the end of the story these 'Antic characters get to keep their unique ecosystem.'

Who Framed Roger Rabbit? centres on the important role that the playful cartoon has in everyday life. Roger endlessly attempts to make glum Eddie laugh and by the end of the film Eddie has learnt his lesson.

Judge Doom embodies the unhealthiness of disrespect for the past and also the importance of play and imagination. Ultimately these failings prove his undoing in real horror-movie fashion, his final moments recalling the death of the Wicked Witch of the West in *The Wizard of Oz* (Victor Fleming, 1939).

STYLISH TOONS: Critical to the film's believability (you would never call it realistic unless you had been born and raised in Toon town) is not just the richness and fluidity of the animation but the subtlety with which it is integrated into the live action. Heading up this part of the process was one of the great visual effects supervisors, Ken Ralston. A contemporary of Dennis Muren and Phil Tippett, Ralston had worked at Industrial Light and Magic on *Star Wars, The Empire Strikes Back* (Irvin Kershner, 1980), *Raiders of the Lost Ark* (Steven Spielberg, 1981) *Dragonslayer* (Matthew Robbins), *Return of the* Jedi (Richard Marquand, 1983) *Indiana Jones and the Temple of Doom (*Steven Spielberg, 1984), *Star Trek III: The Search for Spock* (Leonard Nimoy, 1984) *Cocoon* (Ron Howard, 1985), *Sabrina* (Sydney Pollack, 1995), and *Men in Black* (Barry Sonnenfeld, 1997).

ILM had 900 effects shots to create, mostly compositing live action and animation but also overseeing some model work and blue screen.

The shadow passes were shot separately and then integrated with the animation which, initially, was all flat. A single ten-second piece of action might typically take two weeks and 1440 pieces of artwork. The volume of work was daunting. However, there were two particularly challenging pieces of animation: the opening camera move that transits from the cartoon world to the sound stage world of Maroon Studios (which was critical to establishing the illusion); and the film's finale in which the Toon town characters come crashing through a brick wall to see Eddie, Roger and Jessica (and for which it was necessary to ensure that each character retained their individual characteristics within the swell of a crowd scene).

One of the key scenes in the film is the moment when the opening cartoon sequence segues into live-action footage, revealing that the cartoon characters are in fact actors on a Hollywood set, and that all the shelves, chairs and settings the audience has just seen in the dazzlingly kinetic animated scene are real props. The fridge that Roger drops on himself at the end of the take is indeed a real fridge. The scene is gasp-worthy and immediately sucks the audience into the new reality of the world of Roger Rabbit. While the animation is fluid, what truly sells the image is the camera move as it tracks back from the cartoon Roger Rabbit to reveal a live-action scene unfolding.

The film inevitably brims with scenes of astonishment and the best moments tend to be the less large scaled. Yes, Benny the Cab (a bright yellow cartoon cab) being driven by human Eddie Valiant is quite something, and when Roger and Eddie are handcuffed is amusing and wondrous all at once, but even more dazzling is when Eddie pushes Roger under the water in the sink to hide him from the weasels on his tail. When the weasels depart Roger leaps up out of the water, gasping for air.

For the chaotic and kinetic climax of the story, the film uses animation to bring back to life Judge Doom who has apparently been flattened by a mechanised roller vehicle. The Judge re-animates, walking along with the jerky motion of a stop-motion figure, any roundness to him lost.

The film finds time for subtler animation in its occasional quieter moments. We really feel for Roger when his big soft eyes glaze with a tear.

The film's nostalgia for the animation genre is accentuated by the glowing presentation of old LA permanently bathed in golden sunlight.

One can only wish Jessica Rabbit's flying lips were a special effect allowed in real life.

CHARACTER SKETCH: Roger Rabbit is a fusion of all our favourite animated characters, a real post-modern rabbit. Richard Williams identified Roger's cashew-shaped head, being inspired by Tex Avery characters such as Droopy. The overalls were inspired by Oswald the Lucky Rabbit (an early Disney character), and Roger sports Mickey Mouse gloves in their Fred Moore iteration and Porky Pig's bow tie. In a point of supreme detail it was Spielberg who suggested Roger's mouth resemble the mouth of Thumper the rabbit from the Disney production of *Bambi*.

Richard Williams thought of Roger as a 'Frankenstein's monster' in the sense that he synthesised so many familiar cartoon forms into one über toon. Roger Rabbit is the toon's toon. Roger is by turns manic, compassionate, softhearted and humanly anxious. By the film's end, though, even he has undergone a believable character arc that sees him become the hero he was never really able to be at work in the cartoons.

Paradoxically, the live human world is where he is most effective, so that when he leaps to Jessica's rescue he says 'I'd love to embrace you but first I have to satisfy my sense of moral outrage.' Roger's all-out, undiluted commitment to the power of laughter is astonishing and is what saves the day.

For Eddie Valiant, life does not seem worth living in the shadow of his beloved brother's death. Roger partly fills the void and as the storyline develops their buddy potential is assured as they bicker and ally themselves with one another to solve Roger's dilemma.

Eddie's experience helping Roger reawakens a spirit of play and fun. Eddie and his brother used to travel in the circus with their father, as one newspaper cutting on Eddie's desk shows. What gets Eddie out of a fix in the film's climax is his renewed sense of having a lark. Fantasy and reality fuse to enriching emotional effect and salvation, no less, for the human hero. Adding to his redemption is the revival of the relationship with Dolores, the woman he thought he had lost in a fog of self-pity and drink.

Dolores is the calm centre of this ink and paint, film noir storm. She tolerates the toons and understands Eddie, even though their best romantic days are behind them. Joanna Cassidy, who portrays Dolores, has something of a Lauren Bacall quality to her. Cassidy had memorably appeared in another essential 1980s fantasy film, *Blade Runner* (Ridley Scott, 1982) as the snake-dancing replicant, Zora.

As a big, joyful thank-you to American animation history, the film cameos not just the more obvious characters like Mickey Mouse and Bugs Bunny but even Koko the Clown from the 1920s Fleischer Studio series, *Out of the Inkwell*, which itself combined live action and animation. It is Koko that Eddie waves hello to as he leaves the Maroon Studios lot to hop on the back of a tram.

Dumbo's cameo very particularly evokes memories of his appearance in *Dumbo* and that moment when he hoovers up a slew of peanuts as he soars through the air.

The film is bursting with detail and visual fun and invention. The opening cartoon relishes the opportunity to be its own complete short, mimicking the energy of the Tex Avery style and maybe even exceeding it with its low-height camera as Roger rolls rollercoaster-like around the kitchen on a rolling pin.

The Ink and Paint Club scene is notable for its endlessly moving camera and the appropriately shifting perspectives of the animation. When Jessica Rabbit passes in front of a spotlight, the play of light and shadow seems real.

TOON TUNES: Alan Silvestri composed and conducted the score (played by The London Symphony Orchestra), continuing his marvellous collaboration with director Robert Zemeckis. Their collaboration includes *Romancing the Stone* (1984), the *Back to the Future* trilogy (1985, 1989, 1990), *Death Becomes Her* (1992), *Forrest Gump* (1994), *Contact* (1997), *What Lies Beneath* (2000), *Castaway* (2000) and the upcoming *The Polar Express* (2004).

Alan Silvestri's orchestral score ably and humorously pastiches the vibrant orchestral scores of the animated shorts of MGM and Warner Brothers, and this device is especially evident in the opening animated segment of the film. The music anxiously leaps and dives to intensify the already intense scrapes that Roger Rabbit and Baby Herman find themselves in when Roger is left on babysitting duty. The music also suggests the noirish, 40s aspect of the story with its melancholy sax theme for Eddie Valiant. For Toon town, Silvestri's music is suitably chaotic and carnivalesque. The song, 'Smile, Darn Ya, Smile!', which rounds out the film, sung by all the animated characters, is in fact a song from a 1931 *Merrie Melodie* animated short.

Who Framed Roger Rabbit? soundtrack listing: 'Maroon Logo', 'Maroon Cartoon', 'Valiant and Valiant', 'Weasels', 'Hungarian Rhapsody', 'Judge Doom', 'Why Don't You Do Right?', 'No Justice for Toons', 'Merry-Go Round Broke Down', 'Jessica's Theme', 'Toon town', 'Eddie's Theme', 'Gag Factory', 'Will', 'Smile Darn Ya, Smile!/That's All Folks!', 'End Title'.

TOON TALK:
Eddie Valiant to RK Maroon: 'Forget it, I don't work Toon town.'

Dolores (when Eddie hides Roger in his overcoat): 'So, tell me Eddie is that a rabbit in your pocket or are you just happy to see me?'

Dolores to Eddie about Roger: 'Is he always this funny or only on days when he's wanted for murder?'

Jessica Rabbit innocently to Eddie: 'I'm not bad, I'm just drawn that way.'

OTHER SIMILAR FILMS: *Mary Poppins* would obviously deserve a mention here for its integration of classical animation with live action. So too would *Monkeybone* (Henry Selick, 2001). This film fuses live action and stop-motion animation. Ultimately, though, perhaps the range of films that best inspired *Who Framed Roger Rabbit?* are the animated shorts of Tex Avery and Chuck Jones.

After the success of the film, three *Roger Rabbit* shorts were produced between Amblin' and Disney. The first was *Tummy Trouble* (1989), released as a short that played before *Honey, I Shrunk the Kids* (Joe Johnston, 1989). *Tummy Trouble* follows in the frantic tradition of the original short and tells of Roger's typically failed babysitting of Baby Herman. The Baby swallows a rattle. Roger hurtles Baby Herman to hospital (St Nowhere) and when Baby coughs up the rattle, Roger swallows it and is taken into the operating theatre where the nightmare begins. Jessica cameos as an, unsurprisingly, curvaceous nurse.

The next Roger Rabbit short was *Rollercoaster Rabbit* (1991) in which Roger is left to look after Baby Herman at a fairground. When Baby loses his red balloon Roger goes to get another, leaving Baby alone. Baby Herman goes and explores the fairground, imperilling himself in shooting galleries and dart boards. The story culminates with Roger and Baby racing on a miles-high rollercoaster – more twisting and convoluted than a plate of spaghetti.

The final Roger Rabbit short to date is *Trail Mix Up* (1993) in which Roger is left to look after Baby Herman on a camping trip. Baby Herman is intrigued by a beaver, thinking it is a dog, and follows it. Roger races to save Baby from a range of dangers, including a sawmill. Jessica Rabbit cameos as a Forest Ranger in a ridiculously impractical short skirt. Each Roger Rabbit short concludes with a live-action segment showing Roger and Baby crashing into the set after the cartoon action is over. In *Trail Mix Up*, Roger and Baby are shown hanging from the title card. The film is also notable for Roger even managing to destroy Mount Rushmore. You can only feel sorry for the good-hearted, overanxious rabbit.

For many years a Roger Rabbit feature-length sequel that followed Roger's early days in Hollywood and perhaps even pitted him against the Nazis was talked about – Indiana Jones with floppy ears. Such was Roger's popularity that Lucas clearly took some inspiration for the character of Jar Jar Binks in the film *Star Wars: Episode 1 – The Phantom Menace*.

RECOGNITION: '*Who Framed Roger Rabbit?* which triumphantly mixes human and animated characters, captures everything we have ever loved and hated about cartoons . . .' said David Denby of *Rolling Stone* and Jonathan Rosenbaum of the *Chicago Reader* was also very positive about the film: 'After about a decade of the spurious mysticism of Spielberg and Lucas . . . here at last is a giddy and glittering labour of love and a grand entertainment that validates their approach to filmmaking if any movie does, or can.' The *Washington Post* agreed that the film worked: 'Robert Zemeckis' multidimensional free-for-all is not only a technical tour de force, it crackles with entertainment.'

Famously, Steven Spielberg said of the film in 1988 that the first time he saw film history unfold was with *Star Wars* and the second time was with *Who Framed Roger Rabbit?* The film was released to great success on 24 June 1988.

AWARDS: *Who Framed Roger Rabbit?* was rightly acknowledged for its filmmaking craft and innovations at awards time in late 1988 and early 1989. The film won the 1989 Oscar for Best Effects, Sound Effects Editing; Best Visual Effects and Best Film Editing. Richard Williams also received a Special Achievement Award for his work on the film. The film won the 1989 Saturn Award for Best Director (Fantasy Film) and Best Visual Effects. It was nominated for an Eddie Award from the American Cinema Editors awards and at the BAFTA awards won for Best Special Effects.

The film was nominated for BAFTA awards in the categories of Best Adapted Screenplay, Best Cinematography, Best Editing and Best Production Design. At the French Cesar Awards the film won Best Foreign Film and Robert Zemeckis was nominated by the Directors Guild of America for Outstanding Directorial Achievement. The film won Best Actor for Bob Hoskins at the Evening Standard British Film Awards. At the Golden Globes, the film was nominated for Best Motion Picture, Comedy/Musical and Best Performance by an Actor in a Musical or Comedy. The film was nominated for a Writers Guild of America award for Best Screenplay Based on Material from Another Medium.

HOME VIEWING: The film has long been available on VHS. In 2003 it was finally made available on DVD. The significant difference between Region 1 and Region 2 versions is that the Region 1 version features a commentary (taken from the earlier Laserdisc version of the early 1990s). The DVD features the three Roger Rabbit shorts, a trivia feature that runs text on-screen during the film, a short *Making Of* featurette that does no justice at all to the work involved in creating the film. For this information it would be much better to track down the original hour-long documentary *Roger Rabbit and the Secrets of Toon town* that ran on TV when the film was released theatrically in 1988.

COMMENT: 'The one I'm proudest of to this day (as producer) is *Roger Rabbit* . . . that movie, for me, was as emblematic of a Bob Zemeckis picture as anything he has ever done.' Steven Spielberg.

'The idea of mixing film noir and animation was so outrageous, I felt it had to be done.' Robert Zemeckis

VERDICT: *Who Framed Roger Rabbit?* remains a dazzling film, fifteen years on from its original release. Its energy and wit outsmart many of the more recent special-effects spectacles. The film manages to be both a dazzling piece of 'eye candy' and an emotionally strong drama about a private eye who gets his life back. Key to the success of the film's storytelling must be that it is shot as though it is a live-action film and so there is no sense of lifeless compositions for the animation to be placed in.

It is an exhilarating film that, like *Back to the Future*, suggests the importance of some sense of history and community. In this respect it is a truly entertaining movie, bursting with colour and good humour.

The Digital Toon: How the Computer Exploded on to the Animation Scene

In the early part of the twenty-first century audiences and filmmakers can let their jaws drop at what has just passed – namely the establishment of a new form of filmmaking called computer animation. Rather like the introduction of sound and then colour into film what appeared like a novelty has become a completely legitimate new tool and one that allows for stories to be told in certain new ways. While the general movie-going public may only have become aware of the concept of digital animation since the mid-1990s, the effort to apply computers to animation has been ongoing since the early 1960s with the work of computer scientists such as Steve Coons, Rich B Reinfeld, Robin A Forrest, Brian Barsky and Pierre Bezier laying the groundwork for the investigations of the late 1970s and early 1980s into how the technology could be applied aesthetically. Bezier developed the technology with which to build curves in the computer.

Entirely computer-generated animation seems to have become many people's preferred form of animation, though that says more about the power of novelty value than the inefficacy of other animation media.

Animation had always been used to enhance visual effects and live-action sequences, for instance at the end of *Raiders of the Lost Ark* (Steven Spielberg, 1981) for all the lightning and animated energy unleashed by the Ark of the Covenant. But the prospect of computer animation was different, as it married a virtual, untouchable, almost intangible world with the physical, photographic domain of film. The marriage of computing and animation reached as far back as the 1960s and 1970s with the bold, abstract work of Stan Vanderbeek, who made several animated shorts called Poemsongs in collaboration with Bell Lab's technical computer expert, Ken Knowlton. They used the BEFLIX computer language on an IBM 7094.

In the late 1970s, George Lucas, with Industrial Light and Magic increasingly productive in visual effects, decided it would be worth investing in the development of digitally produced images that could augment optically produced effects work on *Star Wars*. He considered that digitally produced images might one day be standard and not the exception. How right he was. Turning to the New York Institute of Technology, Lucas recruited a team of thinkers and doers who could think the future. Leading the effort under the newly named LucasFilm Computer Division was Ed Catmull.

It was 1982 that yielded a major leap for the introduction of computer-generated animation into live action. The science-fiction film *Star Trek II: The Wrath of Khan* (Nicholas Meyer, 1982) featured a sequence called the Genesis Sequence in which a once-dead planet was shown to revive, the camera apparently racing fast and low across the reviving globe at superspeed as the rocks became green with life. The sequence ran a matter of seconds but it showed how things might develop. Twenty years later, the place of computer-animated elements in fantasy and science fiction is a given. However, that summer another feature had been released which failed to prove popular though twenty years on it has a keen following. The film was *Tron* (Steven Lisberger) and had been produced by the Walt Disney Company. The film pitted two humans into the virtual world of a computer where they assumed a gladiatorial aspect which included racing around a matrix on Light Bikes. *Tron* was a live-action film that was packed out with intriguing computer-generated backgrounds and other animated elements, such as vehicles.

With the success of the *Star Trek* sequence proven, Lucas utilised computer animation for a brief part of *Star Wars: Return of the Jedi* (Richard Marquand, 1983) for the scene where the Rebels plan their attack on the Death Star. An image is activated by one of the characters that shows a wire model of the Death Star suspended in mid-air. The model is shown to zoom in track around the shape which eventually explodes as per the attack plan of the plucky Rebel pilots.

In 1984, a film was released called *The Last Starfighter* (Nick Castle, 1984). Regarded as yet another *Star Wars* rip-off at the time, the film was hugely enjoyable, telling of a teenager who is an ace at arcade games and who is subsequently recruited to pilot a real spaceship in a real space battle. The film's computer effects supervisors, John Whitney Jr and Gary Demos, had established their company Digital Productions in 1981 and their aim was to revolutionise computer imaging. The film is notable for its extensive use of computer-animated spaceships and its 25 minutes of computer-generated animation was unheard of at the time. The creation of the Gunstar vehicles, and others, was made possible by storing the computer data on the most powerful computer of the time, the Cray XMP-2. The look of these spaceships built in a computer and combined with a backdrop was unique.

By the late 1980s, after some caution about the success of integrating computer-animated elements into live action, a second attempt was made at fusing the real and virtual worlds and this time the results were far more productive.

There had been one exception to the slight lull in the mid-1980s in the application of computer animation and that was the highly entertaining film *Young Sherlock Holmes* (Barry Levinson, 1985) written by Chris Columbus who would go on to direct *Harry Potter and the Philosopher's Stone* (2001). Alongside the humorous scene in which various cakes seem to come to life before the eyes of a hungry young Watson (stop motion being used to create the illusion) the film also featured a breakthrough as significant as the *Star Trek II* Genesis sequence.

Again produced by Industrial Light and Magic and overseen by the great Dennis Muren, the scene centred on a stained-glass window coming to life as a knight and marching through a church at night with sword raised. The scene is quite beautiful and can be regarded as the first piece of computer-generated character animation in a live-action film. The process is now often used far more subtly so that live-action actors are replaced by digital actors for stunts too dangerous to contemplate. The *Young Sherlock Holmes* example, though, is completely convincing and wonderful to watch.

First, live-action reference footage of the knight was shot to determine its movement and positioning. A wire frame model was built in the computer and animated according to the live-action reference material. The colours of the knight's stained-glass form were then painted on to the animated figure using a cathode ray tube and an electronic paint box. All of the data appeared on a monitor and was stored on a computer, and rearranged to allow for different angles. This piece of computer animation was the first to be scanned directly on to film using a laser.

The work – the first computer-animated character to be painted directly on to film with a laser – was overseen by Eben Otsby and Bill Reeves. The ambitious thirty seconds of on-screen animated action required six months of work.

In the light of the stained-glass knight's success, computer-animated characters seemed increasingly viable. In the sword and sorcery fantasy *Willow* (Ron Howard, 1988) Dennis Muren (again) saw the chance to advance computer animation through what became known as morphing (short for metamorphosing). A key scene where a sorceress named Fin Raziel changed from a bird to an old woman, via an ostrich, a goat and a tiger was a critical moment in proving how fluid computer-generated animation could be.

It was the director James Cameron who elevated the character potential of computer animation in his science-fiction films, *The Abyss* (1989) and *Terminator 2: Judgment Day* (1991). For *The Abyss* computer animation allowed for the believable illusion of an otherworldly subterranean water tentacle to seemingly live, breathe and emote as it encounters humans beneath the waves. The 75 seconds of screen-time allotted the gorgeous animated character required eight months of concept and animation effort. The effect was achieved by initially creating a transparent resin model that allowed the computer animators to see how light was reflected and refracted by water. In the film, the human actors interact with the playful water creature. At one point the creature mimics the facial expressions of the humans. The effect is one of the most graceful visual effects ever and in keeping with the overall concept of *The Abyss* there is something angelic in its animated spirit.

In contrast to the benevolent water creature, Cameron and his computer animators unleashed an evil cyborg called the T-1000. Human in surface appearance, beneath the synthetic flesh there is a chrome robot that can assume a range of forms, liquefying and then solidifying in a moment. An appropriately thunderous image is used to announce the spectacle of this effect. After a huge truck and motorcycle chase, the T-1000 disguised as a bike cop emerges from the flames of the burning truck in all his silver, chromatic glory.

Audiences worldwide sat agape at the image and the film continued to delight in the apparently impossible animated images of a chrome villain who could slip and slide like water through shattered glass and across floors. For Dennis Muren the project was a risk because the creation of the T-1000 was so dependent on new technology. ILM created fifty or so shots. 'When I saw the storyboards, my first reaction was "There is nothing in the world like this," ' he says. For the T-1000's action, Robert Patrick was shot doing the moves, then an empty plate was shot to use as a background into which to composite the eventual metal character. Morphing was used to smooth transformations (Michael Jackson's *Black or White* pop promo of the same year was filled with morphing and this new animation too quickly became overly familiar everywhere).

* * *

The next leap occurred in the film *Jurassic Park* (Steven Spielberg, 1993) when computer-animated dinosaurs replaced the initially planned stop-motion versions. The moment when the human protagonists first see a brachiosaurus amidst the trees and then a vista of dinosaurs emerging from a lake is arguably one of the greatest instances in cinema history.

The animals move with great fluidity, the animation at a point where computer-generated skin appears to move supply and in tandem with the function of muscle and bone beneath. These computer-animated creatures match almost seamlessly with their physical live-action alternatives. The animation creates dinosaurs at rest and in motion, and dinosaurs in nurturing mode and super-hungry mode. The T-Rex attack on the jeeps is a highlight action sequence made all the more real by the detail of a computer-animated foot slamming down in a puddle and water splashing everywhere at the bottom of the film frame.

As progress on *Jurassic Park* was made it became apparent to the director that he could rework the finale. There was a legitimate space for the T-Rex to make a triumphant return appearance. Originally, Alan Grant (Sam Neill) was to have completed his showdown with the velociraptors by manning a forklift truck. Ultimately, his salvation was to be the T-Rex crashing into frame in broad daylight, its computer-animated head swinging and thrashing right up to the camera without any fracture in the illusion. The success of the film, artistically and commercially, finally put the stamp of approval on the computer-generated animated character in live action.

Jim Carrey starred as *The Mask* (Chuck Russell, 1994). An ancient mask allows Stanley Ipkiss to unleash his inner, more animated, self in a raucous homage to the spirit of Tex Avery and Chuck Jones characters. For example, at one point Stanley wolf-whistles at a beautiful woman and reincarnates the wolf from *Red Hot Riding Hood*, the Tex Avery classic that put eyes on stalks.

Two other fantasy projects that played more naturalistically with digital animation were *Casper* (Brad Silberling, 1995) and *Jumanji* (Joe Johnston, 1995). In *Casper*, an adaptation of the Harvey Comics character *Casper the Friendly Ghost*, computer animation brought all the ghouls to life. Originally, the characters were to have been realised in part as puppets but this approach was considered an undeniable failure as the motion was not fluid enough to create a convincing illusion of a ghost. Computer animation allowed Casper to hew very closely to his comic-book form and also do all the things that friendly ghosts do so well, such as passing through walls, making breakfast and sitting on rooftops in the moonlight with the girl they feel deeply for. *Casper* was the first motion picture with a digital, computer-animated character as its protagonist.

The film *Jumanji*, based on Chris Van Allsburg's picture book, met the challenge of creating realistic animals such as rhinos, lions and elephants as they go on the rampage through a small town, unleashed by the greatest board game never made. The animals moved with the same ease and fluidity as the dinosaurs of *Jurassic Park* but the real technical breakthrough was in the creation of synthetic hair with the monkey characters. Critical to the illusion of the animals charging through the real world was getting the animation to match certain live-action, animatronic puppet versions, notably the lion and the pelican. When Alan Parrish confronts the lion, the combined use of an animatronic lion and a computer-generated one is satisfyingly real and Alan's courage is put to the test. When the elephants stampede over parked cars, the weight of these bodies impacting on metal can almost be felt. Nature triumphed again courtesy of technology.

The following year, the most complex computer-animated character thus far was created (by stop-motion ace Phil Tippett) for the film *Dragonheart* (Rob Cohen, 1996). The dragon's face resembled that of Sean Connery in its mannerisms as Connery was providing the voice for the character. Draco befriends a down-on-his-luck knight called Bowen (Dennis Quaid) and they team up in a buddy system to bring down the rule of an evil tyrant. Draco possesses a leonine grace and a density of detail not previously seen as he strides proudly across European hillsides and fields and races through forests.

A major challenge in the creation of this gracious beast was that so many of his scenes were set in broad daylight. Phil Tippett's grand design of the character was immensely detailed in it scales, bones and plates of armour. Another critical issue was maintaining the computer-animated character's gracefulness both in air and in repose. What the animators did realise was that no matter how fluid and expressive the facial movements were, without accurate animation of the eyes the sincerity of emotion was not quite there. Even for a computer-animated dragon the eyes are the window of the soul.

James Cameron, who had done so much to prove the dramatic intrigue of computer animation with *The Abyss* and *Terminator 2: Judgment Day*, utilised computer animation again in his sprawling film, *Titanic*. To furnish the computer-created ship with crew and imperilled passengers, computer-animated characters were used to great effect. To create realistic movement, the technique of motion capture was employed.

Even Stanley Kubrick engaged, from beyond the grave as it were, with computer animation through *AI: Artificial Intelligence*, one of the boldest most emotionally affecting science-fiction films of recent years and one of Steven Spielberg's greatest directorial achievements. Famously, Kubrick had been developing the film since the early 1970s after reading the Brian W Aldiss short story, *Supertoys Last All Summer Long*. Kubrick bought the rights to the story and used it as the basis for a feature film project with a tortuous history of development. In 1984, Kubrick confided the idea to Steven Spielberg and over the years they discussed the project. Kubrick suggested Spielberg would be the better director for the material with its *Pinocchio* motif (added to the film to Aldiss's chagrin).

When Kubrick died in March 1999, Spielberg found himself taking up the challenge of realising the science-fiction fairy tale. Kubrick had grappled with building an animatronic lead character for the robot boy David, but ultimately a real human essayed the role. In effect, by adapting the screenplay from a ninety-page treatment by Ian Watson based on Kubrick's notes, Spielberg created a new kind of *Wizard of Oz* story. A quest for love and belonging, *AI* features a third act dominated by very beautiful computer-animated characters. Earlier phases of the film feature a Jiminy Cricket-like teddy bear who looks out for David. The final phase of the film, taking place 2,000 years in the future, is dependent largely on animated characters for its mystery and resolution. At this point it is as though Spielberg has unleashed images he has had dancing around for years. Computer animation brings the Blue Fairy character gracefully to life in a way that recalls the Blue Fairy in *Pinocchio*. When animators were having difficulty animating her mouth, Spielberg instructed them not to bother animating any lip synch. After all, the Blue Fairy was a statue only imbued with life and meaning by David's imagination and compulsion for love. An element of computer animation helps round out the final image of the film as Teddy walks across David's mother's bed to be with David who lies next to her. Spielberg said, 'The heart of the story is a boy's love for his mother, and everything that goes with it.'

The other key computer-animated characters are those that Spielberg calls 'the Specialists' in his screenplay. Mistaken for aliens by many movie-goers, they are in fact highly advanced robots, supertoys of the highest order. Chris Baker, who had worked with Kubrick in designing the film prior to Spielberg's involvement, offered simple yet highly effective 3-D animations of the Specialists' ship. For the Specialists, Kubrick's original concept had been for them to be leather clad with their faces exposed. Spielberg went for a look more redolent of a Giacometti sculpture.

Intriguingly, it emerged that one of the Kubrick designs for the aliens of 2001 had been along this Giacometti line. The Specialists move with grace and gentility befitting their insight and intelligence. The film embeds them in the live-action photography so that we see their elegant, glasslike hands brushing ice away from the windscreen of the vehicle in which David lies frozen.

The Specialists' translucent appearance comprised three layers: illuminated circuitry, opacity and the refraction of light. The faces even register subtle expressions despite the fact that there are no eyes or mouths to speak of. These characters might be mechanical but deeper down their illuminated minds are far more angelic and help round out the affecting spiritual dimension of the film.

Computer animation is frequently put to less obvious use than the creation of space creatures, emotionally savvy robots and stained-glass knights. Robert Zemeckis is a prime exponent of computer animation and his film *Cast Away* uses it to render the curious eye of a whale passing by Chuck Noland at night as he floats on his raft at sea.

Even Spielberg's animatronic wonder, ET, was enhanced by computer animation for the Twentieth Anniversary release. This reinstated a scene of ET and Elliot in the bathroom, and ET was rendered as a computer-animated figure, allowing him to interact easily with the filled bath. Computer animation also smoothed out some of his facial expressions.

These computer-animated enhancements were made with Spielberg's editorial approval. In each instance the changes are slight and, to the casual viewer, will most likely go unnoticed. The changes are: ET is shown running to try and catch his ride home at the beginning of the film; in the middle section of the film ET is shown submerging himself in the bathtub and blowing bubbles; when he drinks from the beer can his Adam's apple (or whatever it might be called on his home planet) is visible; dressed up in Gertie's clothes, ET's eyes are more expressive in their computer animated form; when Elliot zips up the body bag containing the revived ET, ILM re-animated his face; for the farewell scene, ET's hand was reanimated for its touch to Elliot's forehead; finally, purple flames were added to the base of ET's ship for its lift-off at the film's operatic conclusion.

Surprisingly the re-release failed to be quite the popular hit everyone expected. Perhaps ET had become too soft for our hard world.

The children's book *Stuart Little* was also realised using computer animation for the mouse in New York. Animation director Rob Minkoff directed this live-action–computer-animation hybrid.

The leading visual-effects animation studios contributing to this creative boom in computer animation were Industrial Light and Magic, PI, Rhythm and Hues, Blue Sky and Digital Domain.

In the spring of 1999 a new science-fiction movie was released called *The Matrix* (The Wachowski Brothers). Refreshingly not an adaptation of a pre-existing novel, TV series or comic book, the film's dynamism proved compelling and swiftly generated an appreciative following. The film tapped into today's information technology lifestyle in its story of a computer programmer who enters a virtual reality world that he is charged with the mission of saving. Machines are threatening the existence of human civilisation. The film was a rich and engrossing adventure movie, combining a new-looking surface with a very traditional, classically inspired story (with references to *Alice in Wonderland*, the Bible, Greek mythology). The highly detailed fantasy inevitably was dependent on special effects to bring it to life and computer-generated animation was a key element of making the unreal believable.

The film's trademark was its bullet time effect, whereby time seemed to freeze and extend as the camera appeared to track around frozen action. Examples of this include Trinity about to air-kick a cop or Neo and his nemesis Agent Smith engaged in aerial fisticuffs. Computer animation brought to life the chilling biomechanical monsters, the Sentinels, who moved like squids but were armed with high-tech tentacles, guarding the underworld.

The Matrix was massively successful, instantly creating a loyal following romanced by its exploration of technology and human experience. A sequel followed, *The Matrix Reloaded* (The Washowski Brothers, 2003). The film is notable, though, for its computer-animated action sequences notably the Burly Brawl in which Neo is confronted by dozens of Agent Smiths.

While dramatically very tedious and certainly outstaying its welcome, the sequence represented another push for computer animation. Motion capture was used to generate fluid body movement that was then expanded by applying muscle and 'flesh' to the characters. The actors portraying the characters in the fight then had their facial expressions videoed by five cameras arranged in a semicircle around the actor's face. This footage of real faces was mapped on to the computer bodies and heads. In turn, photographed clothing was mapped on to the bodies. For John Gaeta, visual effects supervisor, this particularly piece of computer animation represented true virtual reality.

Computer-animated action is present at other points in the film too and a nicely animated robot can be glimpsed in a stunning vista of the heroes' hideaway as their ship docks for landing.

As a precursor to the release of the sequel, a series of animated shorts was produced under the title *The Animatrix*. Intriguingly, the anthology of stories, set in *The Matrix* world and expanding on it, was created in the style of Japanese animation. Seven anime directors were brought on to the project, each to direct an animated short, making clear the filmmakers' aesthetic debt to the anime tradition in the kinetic energy of their action, and also the inclusion of a Samurai warrior ethic in their character of Morpheus. The pervasive anime aesthetic extends even to a sequence in *Kill Bill: Volume 1* (Quentin Tarantino, 2003) and has, just a little, also shaped the look of the animated *Star Wars* characters in the new *Clone Wars* animated series.

In stark and playful contrast to these realist examples of computer animation, director Richard Linklater's film *Waking Life*, based around lucid dreaming, applies animation in a different and very intriguing and appropriate way. The live-action material was shot on digital video and then each frame painted over using a computer-animation system, the animation being supervised by Austin, Texas animator Bob Sabiston. Subsequently the images have a very vivid, often comic-book appeal and certainly a distinct, hypereal identity perhaps befitting the visions that lucid dreaming allows.

The year 1995 also marked the coming of age of the computer-animated feature film with the release of Pixar Studios' debut feature, *Toy Story*. Pixar had begun life in the early 1980s as part of LucasFilm when George Lucas was keen to investigate the potential of computers married with film.

In 1986 Lucas sold off his Computer Division that became known as Pixar after one of the core pieces of animation software it had developed during the LucasFilm years. (Interestingly, in spring 2003, an emerging computer animation company, LucasFilm Animation, was announced.) Pixar began producing short pieces of character-based computer animation that got noticed and highly praised.

In 1984, Pixar (still at LucasFilm then) had produced a short that ran under two minutes called *The Adventures of Andre and Wally B* about a bee who gives a man a hard time as he tries to take it easy in a blissfully sunny forest. Significant in this film was the creation of motion blur, which is to say the lack of definition that moving objects have as they pass through a space. Short though the film was, it took months of computer power to process, using, as had been on *The Last Starfighter*, the Cray computer systems. Following on from this first effort were *Luxo Jr*, *Knick Knack Tin Toy* and *Red's Dream*. Indeed, Tinny the hero of *Tin Toy* was initially going to be a central character in *Toy Story* until Buzz Lightyear was dreamt up. Amusingly in retrospect, the Pixar software in 1986 was referred to as 'a rich kid's toy' by the former General Manager of ILM, Thomas G Smith in his immense book *Industrial Light and Magic: The Art of Special Effects*.

Digital Animation and Live Action

Star Wars: Episode 1 – The Phantom Menace (1999)

(130 minutes)

Directed by George Lucas
Produced by Rick McCallum
Screenplay: George Lucas
Music: John Williams
Special Visual Effects: John Knoll, Dennis Muren, Rob
Coleman, Scott Squires/ILM
Costume Design: Trisha Biggar
Production Design: Gavin Bouquet
Concept Design: Doug Chiang, Ian McCaig

BUDGET: $120 million

BOX OFFICE: $330 million

RELEASE DATE: 19 May 1999

CERTIFICATE: U

CAST: Liam Neeson (*Qui Gon Jinn*), Ewan McGregor (*Obi-Wan Kenobi*), Natalie Portman (*Queen Padme Amidala*), Ian McDiarmid (*Palpatine*), Hugh Quarshie (*Captain Panaka*), Ahmed Best (*Jar Jar Binks*), Anthony Daniels (*C-3PO*), Kenny Baker (*R2D2*), Brian Blessed (*Boss Nass*), Ralph Brown (*Ric Olie*), Terence Stamp (*Chancellor Valorum*), Ray Park (*Darth Maul*), Pernilla August (*Shmi Skywalker*), Frank Oz (*Yoda*)

TAGLINE: Every saga has a beginning.

STORYLINE: A Trade Federation dispute rages and the Jedi Knights Qui Gon Jinn and his apprentice, Obi-Wan Kenobi, are sent in to resolve the dispute between the Neimodians and the Naboo people whose planet has been blockaded. Things go awry and the Jedi flee to Naboo where they befriend a creature called Jar Jar Binks who leads them to safety. The Jedi protect Queen Amidala and on board her ship break through the blockade.

Needing to fix the damaged ship, the Jedi direct it to the forgotten planet of Tatooine. On Tatooine, the Jedi befriend a young boy named Anakin Skywalker. Anakin is very adept at making things and Qui Gon detects a strong sensitivity to the Force in the boy. Obi-Wan is less sure. The Jedi are confronted by a Sith enemy called Darth Maul who is on their trail.

The Jedi fly to Coruscant where Queen Amidala becomes embroiled in politics. Senator Palpatine is elected to higher office from where he becomes Chancellor (and eventually the evil Emperor). Qui Gon asks for Anakin to be inducted into the Jedi Younglings training plan but the Jedi Council are reluctant. Yoda relents and Anakin falls into the care of Qui Gon and Obi-Wan. Darth Maul continues on the trail of the Jedi. Naboo has been overtaken by the Trade Federation and a military presence.

The Jedi, Queen Amidala, Anakin and Jar Jar return to Naboo. Jar Jar leads them to the ancient Gungan temples where the Gungans are in hiding from the Trade Federation. Jar Jar is instrumental in reuniting the Gungans and the humans of Naboo. The Jedi set about liberating Naboo in an all-out battle. Anakin becomes accidentally embroiled in the space battle above Naboo and Jar Jar helps lead the Gungan army against the Battle Droids of the Trade Federation.

The Jedi Knights are confronted by Darth Maul in a severe and thrilling duel. Qui Gon is killed. The Trade Federation is destroyed and the Gungans overcome the high-tech robot army. Obi-Wan kills Darth Maul and then assumes guardianship of Anakin. Qui Gon is given an honourable funeral and peace is restored. Obi-Wan looks on with some concern at the lavish ceremony to celebrate the return of order.

THE DRAWING BOARD: Much has already been written about this film and the space fantasy saga of which it is the first instalment. The history of the *Star Wars* saga's realisation for the cinema is itself part of popular culture. Some deserves recounting, though, notably George Lucas's struggle to get the first film (Episode IV) financed in the early and mid-1970s though he had proved his facility with both science fiction with the brilliant *THX-1138* (1971) and with actors and emotional warmth with the dazzling *American Graffiti* (1973).

Star Wars, its early development funded by profits from American Graffiti, fused the fantasy of the first film and the humanity and youthful energy of the second. Both films also had their downbeat qualities and this certainly underpins The Phantom Menace, a title that was famously baulked at when announced online on 25 September 1998. It set the tone for the film's eventual reception.

Perhaps it is best to regard The Phantom Menace as part live action and part animation, utilising computer-generated animation to render alien characters that by their design would not easily accommodate human performers inside suits.

Even the way Lucas organised the project's preparation mirrored an animated feature, the screenplay being written simultaneously with the development of concept art, characters and environments. Where the original trilogy had featured an alien creature – the lumbering, doglike Wookie Chewbacca – by putting a performer in a mohair suit and mask, The Phantom Menace's central creature would be the Gungan Jar Jar Binks, an amphibious cross between a dinosaur, Roger Rabbit and an over-eager puppy, realised through animation inserted into the live action.

Jar Jar, though, was mocked for his slapstick tendencies in the Star Wars universe, but he offered appropriate relief and symmetry with the über seriousness of the Jedi and their dilemma with the Sith. Jar Jar was a more concentrated version of the slapstick present in a scattered form through the original trilogy. Lucas did not give his design team much to work with initially in the creation of the character, describing him as a clumsy, amphibious creature. So Jar Jar was given the head of a hadrosaur on a swan's neck early on.

Concept designer, Terryl Whitlatch, struggled to define Lucas's thoughts. Inevitably, the gold dust was to be found in the margins of her work. Lucas saw a sketch she had doodled during work on Jumanji and this began to sum up what Lucas was after. The sketch showed a nervous-looking froglike character. Lucas's work shares much in common with the late great Jim Henson who was originally to have performed Yoda in The Empire Strikes Back, though Frank Oz eventually essayed the role. Henson and Lucas collaborated on Labyrinth (Jim Henson, 1986) and his influence can be seen in the humour and characterisations of the Pixar films.

With Lucas beginning to see the basis for Jar Jar Binks, Whitlatch continued developing the character with input from Doug Chiang and Ian McCaig. The process took eighteen months to reach the approved design that made the film. The floppy ears were Lucas's suggestion and, when the character reached the computer-animation phase, he was originally to have something of a Tex Avery-styled grin. Lucas retracted this element in order to keep Jar Jar a little more realistic.

INSPIRATIONS: Lucas and his animators looked to silent film for guidance on the visual comedy of Jar Jar Binks and, of course, the original *Star Wars* movies indicate the tone and pace of action. Japanese images and African art influence the design of creatures and droids respectively. It is a real fantasia of a movie, perhaps more so than the earlier *Star Wars* films. It feels fanciful like *The Wonderful Wizard of Oz* is and the American tradition of Howard Pyle, L Frank Baum and Winsor McCay is continued by Lucas.

TOON TEAM: To create the computer animation, Lucas worked with supervisors John Knoll (a veteran of *The Abyss* which had showcased very graceful, angelic effects), Scott Squires and the legendary Dennis Muren who had worked on the original *Star Wars* movies. Muren had also overseen the animation of computer-generated dinosaurs on *Jurassic Park* (Steven Spielberg, 1993) and *Jurassic Park: The Lost World* (Steven Spielberg, 1997), computer-animated ghosts in *Casper* (Brad Silberling, 1995) and also did a computer-animated human, albeit of monstrous proportions, on *The Hulk* (Ang Lee, 2003). John Knoll had supervised work on *Mission: Impossible* (Brian De Palma, 1996). Scott Squires had been heavily involved on *Dragonheart* (Rob Cohen, 1996) which featured a computer-animated dragon as a central character.

Rob Coleman served as animation supervisor on the film and would continue in this capacity on *Episode II – Attack of the Clones*, focusing especially on the creation of the computer-animated Yoda.

VOCAL TALENT: Ahmed Best lends his voice to the ultra inverted and flip-floppy speech patterns of Jar Jar Binks. Brian Blessed voices Boss Nass and Andy Secombe voices Watto. Again, Frank Oz reprised the role of Yoda, which has almost become the defining voice of the *Star Wars* story.

INK, PAINT AND HARD WORK: *Star Wars: the Phantom Menace* synthesises the lessons of the preceding twenty years of adventures in computer animation folding all of the developments and refinements into one enormous feature film.

For Lucas, the breakthrough moment was when he was supervising *Jurassic Park*'s post production when Steven Spielberg was in Poland shooting *Schindler's List*. Lucas realised that computer animation could help achieve the subtlety of movement that computer-animated fantasy characters would need in order to be believable illusions.

In November 1994, Lucas began work on the screenplay for what would be titled *The Phantom Menace*. During this process, Lucas also oversaw the *Star Wars* original trilogy, Special Editions, which not only introduced the films to a new audience of young people, priming them for the prequel trilogy, but also allowed Lucas the chance to test-run his plans for computer animation (and indeed the digital backlot). In terms of computer animation, *Star Wars: A New Hope* was hot-rodded to reincorporate Jabba the Hutt as an animated character interacting with live-action footage of Harrison Ford. Jabba may look a little slim but the trick of matching eye lines and lighting and shading is accomplished. Lucas uses computer animation to refine a practical effect from *Return of the Jedi*, giving the Sarlaac Pit a threatening beak to go with its tendrils.

As Brad Bird, the director of *The Iron Giant* has noted, Lucas organised production of *The Phantom Menace* in such a way that it resembled more an animated movie wherein screenplay development ran parallel with visual concepts and planning.

For animation supervisor Rob Coleman: 'I specifically wanted to make fantasy digital characters have the same kind of life and breadth that humans do, which was daunting.'

Initially Jar Jar was going to be a combination of live action and computer animation, with the head being computer animated and the rest of the character being the photographed actor in costume on set. During production of the film, Lucas described Jar Jar as Yoda times ten in the difficulty of nailing the spirit of the character.

Critical to the believability of Jar Jar, one of the first digital characters in a live-action feature, was that he appeared embedded into the live-action footage. Thus, the actors had to be acutely aware of eye lines that would match with the animation. To enhance the illusion further Jar Jar was shaded and lit to match the light of the live-action footage. Digital clothes were also designed that moved with the flow of muscles. Such was the detail of the performance that Jar Jar walked in subtly different ways depending on the ground beneath his feet. Animators also had to establish whether Jar Jar's top lip was made of cartilage or flesh, as this would impact on the realism of the way his lips closed and interacted. Jar Jar's initial broad, cartoony smile was dropped as Lucas felt that might be a bit too far from the realism of his project.

Ultimately Ahmed Best portrayed Jar Jar on set, running through several rehearsal takes and then leaving the action for a take that left the frame empty of Best so that it could be filled by the animated Jar Jar. The rehearsals allowed the other actors to familiarise themselves with Jar Jar's eventual action and eye lines. Best wore a Jar Jar hat that approximated his head height and eye lines for the actors. In several cases, Lucas preferred the rehearsed and filmed footage in which Best was included. The ILM crew had to erase Best from the frame and then put in the computer-animated Jar Jar, a real fairy-tale sidekick, something of an Ugly Duckling.

The Phantom Menace is a carnival and celebration of digitally animated characters of which Jar Jar is the slapstick star. There is also Boss Nass, leader of the Gungan race. His jowls were modelled after an improvised element in Brian Blessed's live-action performance.

Computer animation also brought to life highly detailed forest animals, from knee-high beasts to huge dinosaurlike creatures, all of whom feature fleetingly as the Jedi Qui Gon Jinn flees the Trade Federation tanks.

Compounding the challenge of the end battle out on the fields was that the action occurred in bright sunlight. Dennis Muren rose to the challenge and ensured that the perfection of computer animation was given a little more grit by factoring in camera shake and other inconsistencies to mimic live-action photography. The 5,000 animated droids were given walk cycles of 200 frames but typically only seventy frames were used per shot so variety was relatively easily accomplished. For the crowds of Gungans and droids, a hero character was made the focus of the shot around which the more generically animated characters would move. There were motion cycles for droids walking, shooting and running.

THEME: As a *Star Wars* film *The Phantom Menace* focuses on the resonances of family ties and the repetitions of family history. The film also dramatises the childhood of the boy who becomes Darth Vader, centring on the critical moment when he enters the world of the Jedi which he will ultimately deviate from and imperil.

The film also has an ecological undertone and a welcome embrace of diverse cultures. Obi-Wan initially resents Jar Jar Binks's involvement in their odyssey but it is Qui Gon who reminds him of a sense of openness.

STYLISH TOONS: Lucas's stylistic approach was to create a film consistent with the look of the earlier *Star Wars* films. Obviously, this is apparent in ways of framing action. The creation of digital characters rather than latex ones, however, creates a distinct but not necessarily harmful disparity between the earlier cycle of movies.

The Phantom Menace is packed out with computer-animated detail from flocks of birds to the hustle and bustle of the pod-race starting grid. Other animated highlights include the little worker droids and the lethal destroyer droids who challenge the Jedi early on. For the animation of the movement of these droids, wolf spiders were studied.

The Gungan world is largely visualised through animation and one of the highlight sequences of the film is the underwater journey where a range of computer-animated monsters pursue the Jedi heroes in a submarine. Lucas makes deep sea as potentially adventurous as deep space. The sea creatures move with stealth and a real sense of heavy weight, just like Monstro the whale does in *Pinocchio* (Ben Sharpsteen, 1940).

The expansive battle between Gungans and battle droids at the climax of the film is entirely synthetic, a fully animated sequence with super-realistic lighting and textures.

The scene where Jar Jar Binks is introduced is fanciful and fairy tale-like, and so vividly real even down to Obi-Wan ducking to avoid the swing of one of Jar Jar's ears as he nervously spins around. Look at the reflection caused by his moist skin and the play of the light and shadow thrown by the trees. A camera shot tracks with Jar Jar as he walks and talks with the Jedi, further enhancing the animated character's believability. His expressions register his confusion and juvenile nature. When Jar Jar rejects a notion, watch how his hand gestures amplify the response, as though he is pushing the idea away. His nervous smile is constant and there is a real sense of weight to his legs as he clomps through the terrain. In the scene that soon follows with Jar Jar, Qui Gon and Obi-Wan in the Gungan submarine, watch how Jar Jar's eyes go out on stalks incredibly briefly as he registers shock at an encroaching, very big fish. Jar Jar's eyes then wearily hold close together to suggest his distress and exhaustion. He is a sidekick innocent, about to be plunged into a shadowy world of violence and duplicity.

CHARACTER SKETCH: Jar Jar's clumsiness is what saves him and he not only recalls Roger Rabbit in his hapless, good-hearted energy and accidental heroism but also Dumbo. Like Dumbo, it is Jar Jar's apparent clumsiness and oddity that saves the day, for example in the battle between the Gungans and the Battle Droids. Charlie Chaplin, Jimmy Stewart and Danny Kaye were other informing sources for the soft-hearted helping hand, whose smiley high jinks are countered by his evident sadness at the funeral pyre at the end of the film where he looks more real than ever in the firelight.

The animated character of Watto the junkyard owner is a creature driven by profit, but who has a soft spot for the boy who works for him, Anakin Skywalker. In the film's sequel *Attack of the Clones,* Watto punches at the air with approval when Anakin visits him as a trainee Jedi, Watto clearly proud of what the boy has become.

For the pod-race scene, computer-animated characters prevail from the naturalistic to the far more cartoony-looking. Animated beasts of burden fill out the background of the film and help maintain a sense of a world existing beyond the action being captured by the camera.

TOON TUNES: George Lucas has famously compared his *Star Wars* cycle to silent film where music is vital to tone, meaning and energy. John Williams has likened them to cartoons in turn and his music for *The Phantom Menace* is almost non-stop. When the film was released, those interested speculated on what familiar themes would be reused. The Force theme and main *Star Wars* theme return and 'The Imperial March' becomes the gentle theme for Anakin Skywalker. For Jar Jar Binks, a playful theme is introduced.

John Williams is a major name in the history of orchestral film music and his extensive list of credits include a phenomenal collaboration with Steven Spielberg, as well as fruitful team-ups with Oliver Stone and Mark Rydell. Williams's scores include *The Rare Breed*, (Andrew V MacLaglen, 1966), *The Cowboys* (Mark Rydell, 1971), *Cinderella Liberty* (Mark Rydell, 1973), *Jaws* (Steven Spielberg, 1975), *The Eiger Sanction* (Clint Eastwood, 1975), *The Missouri Breaks* (Arthur Penn, 1976), *Close Encounters of the Third Kind* (Steven Spielberg, 1977), *Dracula* (John Badham, 1979), *The Empire Strikes Back* (Irvin Kershner, 1980), *Raiders of the Lost Ark* (Steven Spielberg, 1981), *ET: The Extra-Terrestrial* (Steven Spielberg, 1982), *Return of the Jedi* (Richard Marquand, 1983), *The River* (Mark Rydell, 1984), *Space Camp* (Harry Winer, 1986), *The Witches of Eastwick* (George Miller, 1987), *Born on the Fourth of July* (Oliver Stone, 1991), *JFK* (Oliver Stone, 1995) *Nixon* (Oliver Stone, 1995) *Sleepers* (Barry Levinson, 1996), *Stepmom* (Chris Columbus, 1998), *Harry Potter and the Philosopher's Stone* (Chris

Columbus, 2001) and *AI: Artificial Intelligence* (Steven Spielberg, 2001). He has also composed themes for numerous Olympic games and for a Millennium montage by Steven Spielberg.

Star Wars: Episode 1 – The Phantom Menace soundtrack listing: 'Star Wars Main Title and The Arrival at Naboo', 'Duel of the Fates', 'Anakin's Theme', 'Jar Jar's Introduction and The Swim to Otoh Gunga', 'The Sith Spacecraft and The Droid Battle', 'The Trip to the Naboo Temple and The Audience with Boss Nass', 'The Arrival at Tatooine and The Flag Parade', 'He is the Chosen One', 'Anakin Defeats Sebulba,' 'Passage through the Planet Core', 'Watto's Deal and Kids at Play', 'Panaka and the Queen's Protectors', 'Queen Amidala and the Naboo Palace', 'The Droid Invasion and The Appearance of Darth Maul', 'Qui Gon's Noble End', 'The High Council Meeting and Qui Gon's Funeral', 'Augie's Great Municipal Band' and 'End Credits'.

TOON TALK:
Jar Jar Binks to the Jedi: 'Maxi big da Force.'

OTHER SIMILAR FILMS: *Star Wars: Episode Two – Attack of the Clones* (2002) is the film to watch as it builds on and expands the palette of an animated live-action movie hybrid that *The Phantom Menace* so clearly was. The climax in the gladiatorial arena is very much in the sprit of a Ray Harryhausen monster movie, especially when Obi-Wan uses a spear to confront a huge praying mantis-like creature having a very bad day, a homage to *Mysterious Island* (Cy Endfield, 1961) in which a man faces off against a giant crab.

Attack of the Clones features Jar Jar Binks in an extended cameo in which he is dressed in ceremonial robes. In that film, the main focus of computer animation of a character is Yoda. To date he had only been a latex puppet with the exception of a wide shot at the end of *The Phantom Menace*.

While Jar Jar Binks's screentime is minimal, a new character, diner owner Dexter Jettster, refines the fluid movement and idiosyncrasies that can be realised in the medium. This big old-time space critter hugs Obi-Wan Kenobi and sits with him in a diner booth helping solve a mystery. Dexter's dirty, ripped T-shirt rolls out over his big belly and his four thick arms flex and hang most believably, his eyes sparkling and his mouth smiling with a piratical love of adventure.

By contrast, the Kaminoan aliens are intensely graceful, very much in keeping with the generally accepted idea of what an extra terrestrial might look like. Their long necks and bulbous heads with large dark eyes recall the animatronic alien at the end of *Close Encounters of the Third Kind* (Steven Spielberg, 1977).

The Kaminoans move with great elegance, their robes sliding easily across their Giacometti-like bodies. To some degree they are angelic successors of the water creature in *The Abyss* (James Cameron, 1989) and the Specialists in *AI: Artificial Intelligence* (Steven Spielberg, 2001). Computer animation is also used briefly to showcase one of Lucas's long-held favourite designs, a winged whale that blasts out of the waters in an establishing shot of the Kaminoan world. Lucas has had this design as part of the *Star Wars* world since work on *The Empire Strikes Back* (Irvin Kershner, 1980).

The computer-animated beasts move wildly and frantically in this action sequence, lunging at the foreground, slamming into the ground, leaping and lashing out. The film also computer animates a clone army of white armoured soldiers. These soldiers move with heroic determination in the onslaught of bad-guy force and it is tiny computer-animated Yoda who, amid the immense vista of battle and landscape, leads the effort proving his maxim that 'Size matters not. Judge me by my size do you?'

Also check out the similarly rich fantasy of *Princess Mononoke* (Hayao Miyazaki, 1997) and *Spirited Away* (Hayao Miyazaki, 2001), two Japanese animated features. Lucas has long been a fan of Japanese cinema and these two very recent fantasy pieces fall within the same kind of fantasy that Lucas engages with.

RECOGNITION: The expectation and hype for *The Phantom Menace* was unprecedented. In time the film will benefit from being just another film worth watching. On its initial release it was derided by many for its apparently ineffectual human performances and tedious premise that lacked the set-up of the original trilogy where the sense of evil was more apparent. *Sight and Sound* felt 'the biggest problem with *The Phantom Menace* is that it lacks narrative coherence.'

AWARDS: *The Phantom Menace* was nominated for Academy Awards in 2000 for Best Visual Effects and Sound. At the Academy of Science Fiction, Fantasy and Horror awards the film won Saturn awards in the categories of Best DVD, Best Costumes and Special Effects. The film was also nominated for Best Actor (Liam Neeson), Director (George Lucas), Makeup and Best Performance by a Young Actor (Jake Lloyd and

Natalie Portman). The film was nominated for a BAFTA for Best Achievement in Special Visual Effects amnd Best Sound. At the Brit and Grammy awards the film was nominated for Best Soundtrack. At the Las Vegas Film Critics Society Awards the film won a Sierra for Best Costumes and nominated for Best Production Design and Best Visual Effects.

HOME VIEWING: *Star Wars: Episode 1 – The Phantom Menace* is available on VHS and DVD. The DVD contains a multitude of additional features including a production documentary called 'The Beginning', numerous interviews and deleted scenes and a commentary track over the movie.

COMMENT: 'Writing the script was much more enjoyable this time around because I wasn't constrained by anything.' George Lucas.

VERDICT: *The Phantom Menace* is markedly different from the original trilogy in its scale and visual scope. In terms of its design it also feels refreshingly unfamiliar with a strong Oriental aspect to much of its visual sense. The animated characters are real highlights, capable of emotion and reaction.

Computer-Animated Films

Toy Story (1995)

(81 minutes)

Directed by John Lasseter
Written by John Lasseter, Andrew Stanton, Pete Docter, Joe
Ranft (story and screenplay), Joss Whedon, Joel Cohen and
Alec Sokolow (screenplay)
Produced by Bonnie Arnold, Ralph Guggenheim
Executive Producer: Ed Catmull and Steve Jobs
Music: Randy Newman
Editor: Robert Gordon, Lee Unkrich
Art Direction: Ralph Eggleston

BUDGET: $30 million

BOX OFFICE: $191.8 million

RELEASE DATE: 22 November 1995

CERTIFICATE: U/G

VOICES: Tom Hanks (*Woody*), Tim Allen (*Buzz Lightyear*), Don
Rickles (*Mr Potato Head*), Jim Varney (*Slinky Dog*), Wallace Shawn
(*Rex*), John Ratzenberger (*Hamm*), Annie Potts (*Bo Peep*), Wayne
Knight (*Al*), John Morris (*Andy Davis*), Laurie Metcalf (*Andy's Mom*),
Estelle Harris (*Mrs Potato Head*)

TAGLINE: The toys are back in town.

STORYLINE: In a boy's bedroom in a suburban house on a bright
sunny day, Andy is playing cowboys with his favourite toy, Woody. It is
Andy's birthday and when his mother has called him downstairs Woody
and the other toys come to life. The toys are gathered together by Woody
and they send the toy soldiers downstairs to see what new toys Andy has
got, fearing they may be replaced. Sure enough, Andy receives a new toy
called Buzz Lightyear. Andy later leaves Buzz on his bed and Woody

confronts him, suspicious of Buzz's appeal. Buzz believes he really is an intergalactic superhero. Woody expends energy trying to convince both Buzz and the other toys that Buzz is not quite what he thinks. But soon Buzz has befriended all the toys in the room.

Envious of Buzz's popularity, Woody tries to hide him but accidentally sends Buzz out of the bedroom window. The toys chastise Woody for his behaviour. Andy and his mother go and get pizza and Andy takes Woody with him. Buzz leaps up into the car and is reunited with Woody. They find themselves at Pizza Planet and are embroiled in a range of escapades. At the Pizza Planet is Andy's nefarious neighbour, Sid who enjoys putting toys on to firework rockets and watching them go. Much to their horror, Woody and Buzz are taken home by Sid.

Woody and Buzz are imprisoned in Sid's bedroom and try to make an escape, but must negotiate Scud, Sid's dog. Woody and Buzz escape just as Andy and his mother pull away from home to follow the removal van, as they are moving house that day. They make a daring last-minute race to get on board the moving van where all the other toys are. Using a remote-control car and one of Sid's fireworks, with Buzz attached to it, Woody and Buzz get close to their family and finally Buzz launches into the air. He and Woody drop down through the sunroof of the family car. At Christmas in the new house, the toys wait to see what gifts Andy has got. He gets a puppy and the toys are dismayed.

THE DRAWING BOARD: *Toy Story* stands as a landmark movie and a touchstone in animated features, representing the immensely well-resourced American film industry at its best. *Toy Story* took four years to make and was the first-ever computer-animated feature.

John Lasseter had begun his animation career at Disney, the studio that released *Toy Story* and subsequently *A Bug's Life, Toy Story 2, Monsters, Inc.* and *Finding Nemo*. Prior to *Toy Story*, one of Lasseter's endeavours had been giving talks about the potential of computer animation. In 1987 he had an article published in *Computer Animation* in which he stated that it would be possible to apply many of the rules of traditional animation to the aesthetics of computer animation.

After the success of the *Luxo Jr* and *Tin Toy* shorts (the latter winning an Academy Award), Pixar anticipated producing some kind of thirty-minute TV special. Surprisingly, though, Disney suggested they move straight into creating a feature project.

By the time of *Toy Story*'s inception, many animated features produced in Europe and North America had proved successful when incorporating a musical element. Later in the project an executive at Disney questioned them about where they would be putting their eight songs. Ultimately, the film has three songs in it, all written by Randy Newman.

John Lasseter did not want to go down that route with their first project and instead focused energies on creating some kind of buddy movie. Buddy movies, after all, had long been a staple of Hollywood filmmaking and had been made especially popular with films like *Butch Cassidy and the Sundance Kid* (George Roy Hill, 1969) *Lethal Weapon* (Richard Donner, 1987) and *Midnight Run* (Martin Brest, 1988). What are the Laurel and Hardy films but hilarious buddy movies?

One of the key impulses for John Lasseter was that 'We wanted to create a sense of nostalgia for the adults in the audience.'

Originally, *Toy Story* was to have opened with a Buzz Lightyear cartoon. This 'prologue' was abandoned but essentially reinstated at the beginning of *Toy Story 2*.

INSPIRATIONS: Pixar's own short, *Tin Toy* contained the germ of the *Toy Story* concept, namely the emotional secret life of a toy. For the *Tin Toy* short, Tinny had to have forty facial muscles virtually created in the computer. Prior to this there was *Luxo Jr* which happened a little by chance. Lasseter had a Luxor desklamp on his desk and began measuring its dimensions and inputting them and then animating them. When Lasseter also considered the movement of a colleague's baby, *Luxo Jr* was born.

Rather obviously, one of the inspirations for the film were all the toys that were available in a typical toy shop and one of the early tasks was to secure the permission of various toy manufacturers so that toys' likenesses (such as Mr Potato Head) could be used as central characters.

At a more aesthetic level a key visual influence on the Pixar look is the artwork of American painter Maxfield Parrish 'because of the richness of light in his paintings'. Parrish was noted for hyper-real painting such as *Riverbank Autumn* (1938) which emphasises, not his typical 'Parrish blue', but instead the warm orange of the autumn sunlight. Parrish was also noted for his paintings of fairies. His paintings and illustrations seem to shine with some inner glow.

TOON TEAM: A large writing team was put in place to develop the storyline and then the emerging screenplay, developed in tandem with conceptual artwork. On *Toy Story* the team comprised Joss Whedon of

Buffy the Vampire Slayer fame, Andrew Stanton (who went on to direct other Pixar features), Joel Cohen and Alex Sokolow. The team worked from an original story by John Lasseter, Pete Docter, Andrew Stanton and Joe Ranft.

John Lasseter had begun his career studying animation at the California Institute for the Arts (usually abbreviated to CalArts) where several veteran Disney animators taught character animation. Lasseter's fellow students included Tim Burton, John Musker (who went on to be an animation director at Disney) and Brad Bird, who worked on *The Simpsons* and who directed the great *The Iron Giant*.

Early in his career, Lasseter worked as an animator on *Mickey's Christmas Carol* (Burny Mattinson, 1983) while in another part of the Disney studio other animators were working on *Tron* (Steven Lisberger, 1982). Lasseter became intrigued by the computer animation element of that film so he and animator Glen Keane produced a thirty-second in-house project that fused hand-drawn images with computer-generated backgrounds. Initially the computer had been considered as a way of rendering environments until computer imaging guru Ed Catmull suggested that the computer could animate characters. Lasseter soon became involved at the LucasFilm Computer Division being headed up by Ed Catmull who was a computer scientist and frustrated animator.

VOCAL TALENT: Tom Hanks stars as Woody Pride. By the time of this role, Hanks had established himself as a major Hollywood star with films such as *Splash* (Ron Howard, 1984), *Big* (Penny Marshall, 1988), *Sleepless in Seattle* (Nora Ephron, 1993), *Philadelphia* (Jonathan Demme, 1993), *Forrest Gump* (Robert Zemeckis, 1994) and *Apollo 13* (Ron Howard, 1995).

Hanks went on to reprise the Woody role in *Toy Story 2* (2000) as well as star in *Saving Private Ryan* (Steven Spielberg, 1998), *You've Got Mail* (Nora Ephron, 1998), *The Green Mile* (Frank Darabont, 1999), *Cast Away* (Robert Zemeckis, 2000) and *Catch Me If You Can* (Steven Spielberg, 2002). In November 2004, Hanks will star in a new computer-animated project entitled *The Polar Express* (Robert Zemeckis, 2004) for which live action has been shot and over which computer-animated versions of the actors will be placed. The film is a fantasy based on Chris Van Allsburg's beautiful picture book of the same name in which a boy takes a trip to the North Pole.

Tim Allen (Buzz Lightyear) starred in the sitcom *Home Improvement*, the comedy movie *The Santa Clause* (John Pasquin, 1994) and *Galaxy*

Quest (Dean Parisot, 1999). Don Rickles as Mr Potato Head can be seen in *Casino* (Martin Scorsese, 1995).

Andy's mother is portrayed by Laurie Metcalf, co-star of 1980s sitcom *Roseanne*. She was also in *Internal Affairs* (Mike Figgis, 1990).

John Ratzenberger voices Hamm and is most famous as Cliff the postman in the sitcom *Cheers*. He also appears, very briefly, in *Star Wars: The Empire Strikes Back* (Irvin Kershner, 1980). He has gone on to voice characters in *A Bug's Life* and *Monsters, Inc.*

INK, PAINT AND HARD WORK: The scale of the *Toy Story* endeavour can be seen in the number of gigabytes of computer power used in its creation – 1,000 as opposed to a mere 100 used to create the dinosaurs of *Jurassic Park*. In all, around 800,000 machine hours were needed to render all the film's images.

Though *Toy Story* is set in the suburban bedroom of a child and occasionally on the road outside, a slightly exaggerated aesthetic was employed so that doors were that bit taller and so on. It is a very rich and fun-looking environment.

Once a screenplay had been approved, storyboards mapped out the entire movie. Maquettes of the characters were made and some of these were scanned in to the computer. For Pixar a key challenge was animating human characters.

Each completed character had their movement blocked out. Once a shot had been composed it was then passed on to the animation department.

The animators began by listening to the voice track of the vocal talent and also referring to video footage of them performing their dialogue. As a reference for the character of Woody, a doll was made up out of parts of other toys to allow the animators a better sense of fabric move and scale.

THEME: The film's fantastic premise and situations play out on themes of identity and purpose. The film demonstrates the importance of toys and play in the imaginative life of children. As a buddy movie, the film celebrates the coming together of apparently disparate characters who work well as a team.

More subtly, the film's second half revolves around a sense of value that the protagonists do or do not feel: Buzz's self-confidence flies out the window when he realises that he is just a toy. At this point the rest of the adventure for him is a way of finding and determining his value again and that's why his firework flight to freedom with Woody really has an emotional power to it.

STYLISH TOONS: One advantage of computer camera moves (virtual positioning) is that they can be completely free-ranging, unencumbered by real spatial limitations. For *Toy Story*, a key decision was made to make the virtual camera positions close to live set ups, so that nothing was too 'off the wall'. A virtual crane camera was built inside the camera which allowed the crew to select the kind of virtual lenses they wanted to use for each shot. In keeping with this attention to naturalistic detail a major effort was put into meeting the challenge of dressing the virtual sets.

Another key challenge of the film, and one that truly extended the creative palette of Pixar, was the creation of believable human skin. The studio also had to address and then express the ways in which light played off surfaces. *Toy Story* is packed with characters with very shiny surfaces that reflect light.

Although much of the film centres on the terrain of Andy's bedroom, for the film's climax – the chase sequence through suburbia – the story steps outside into the very big, very wide world. For this sequence, 243 shots were made and two miles of virtual road was constructed in the computer. Two weeks were spent storyboarding the chase and one of the key reference materials was the train sequence at the end of the glorious *Back to the Future Part III* (Robert Zemeckis, 1990). Other films referenced were *Ben Hur* (William Wyler, 1959), *Bullitt* (Peter Yates, 1968) and *Raiders of the Lost Ark* (Steven Spielberg, 1981).

As with so much character animation, whether classically styled, stop motion or computer animated, capturing believable human facial expression is critical to a level of emotional realism and *Toy Story* is rich with these instances. Just watch Woody as he thinks through his little scheme to get back at Buzz.

The film's production design does much for the tone of the image. Compare the bright world of Andy's room and its sky-blue and cloud-patterned wallpaper with the sense of decay and doom in Sid's room with its low-key lighting and grim green walls. Details fill out the effects such as raindrops on windows and the nicks and dents in Andy's bedroom door.

CHARACTER SKETCH: Woody Pride suffers from a serious case of jealousy when Buzz Lightyear comes into the world of Andy's bedroom.

For all of Woody's easygoing, cowboy charm he has to confront his own selfishness and ego. Woody's most appealing feature is his genuine good faith in the need for toys in a child's life, claiming early on that 'What matters is that we're here for Andy when he needs us.' On the surface, Woody is a very easygoing old cowboy toy but deeper down he is racked with anxiety.

Buzz Lightyear's delusion about his identity is very amusing and his despair later in the film, when he realises that he is only a toy after all is genuinely affecting. The montage sequence of Buzz befriending the other toys is a highlight. In the DVD documentary about the film John Lasseter notes how, initially, Buzz was more of a Dudley Do-Right kind of figure, but through Tim Allen's performance became more of a cop. Buzz's original name was Lunar Larry.

The character of Sid is memorable and the 'mechanimal' toys he has created are genuinely creepy, contrasting neatly with the sunny spirit of most of the film.

In conceiving the main characters, a general principle was applied that the way a toy had been put together was reflected in its personality. Thus, Mr Potato Head tends to be a grouchy rabble rouser because he is so annoyed at his ever-changing appearance.

Another principle was that all the toys regarded their relationship with their child owners as a job.

TOON TUNES: Randy Newman's playful and tender score enriches the drama no end and is by turns sweet and frightening. It represented the first of several fantastic collaborations with the Pixar studio. Newman went on to score *A Bug's Life*, *Toy Story 2* (John Lasseter, 2000) and *Monsters, Inc.*

Toy Story soundtrack listing: 'You've Got a Friend in Me', 'Strange Things', 'I Will Go Sailing No More', 'Andy's Birthday', 'Soldiers' Mission', 'Presents', 'Buzz', 'Sid', 'Woody and Buzz', 'Mutants', 'Woody's Gone', 'Big One', 'Hang Together', 'On the Move', 'Infinity and Beyond', 'You Got a Friend in Me' (Lyle Lovett).

TOON TALK:
Woody to Buzz: 'That wasn't flying. That was falling with style.'

OTHER SIMILAR FILMS: As the first Pixar feature, *Toy Story*'s success led to *A Bug's Life*, *Toy Story 2*, *Monsters, Inc.* and *Finding Nemo*.

Perhaps the most significant film to view though is *Tin Toy*, the 1988 short that Pixar produced, with John Lasseter directing. It tells of Tinny, a one-man band toy who, seeing a baby crying, sets out to make him smile again. In doing so, Tinny is terrified by the immense-looking baby who chases him all over the room. Tinny even finds other toys cowering in terror beneath a sofa.

The short contains the same sunny lighting and dynamic tracking shots as the action builds. Most significantly it imbues a toy with real emotion. Though he never speaks, he clearly registers happiness, terror and sadness. Amazingly, it is the expression communicated by the toy's eyes that contributes most. *Tin Toy* was the first computer-animated short to win an Oscar, building on the success of *Luxo Jr* (1986).

The original concept for *Toy Story* starred Tinny who gets lost and befriends a ventriloquist's dummy. Together they hit the road and end up in a safe haven – a preschool where they can never get lost.

Like *Toy Story*, the subsequent Pixar features form something of a coherent whole all focusing on families and the fundamentals of childhood, and also of what an adult might hold most special in their memory of growing up. *Toy Story 2* is even more acute and emotionally potent in this regard than the original film. Surprisingly, given the mega success of *Toy Story*, the sequel was originally going to be a direct-to-video release. However, when Disney saw the film's story reel they committed to releasing it theatrically, investing more money and resources into the project. Subsequently, certain changes had to be made to the narrative.

Enhancing the integrity of the sequel is the returning original cast, rounded out by new additions Kelsey Grammer as Stinky Pete, Joan Cusack as Jessie and Wayne Knight as Al McWhiggin.

Toy Story 2 developed and refined many of the lessons learned on *Toy Story* and *A Bug's Life*. For the Zurg space opening 240,000 individually articulated robot models were created and fifteen different cycles of action were used to create some sense of variety. Of the Emperor Zurg opening, John Lasseter says it is '*Star Wars* simmered for a long time and boiled down to a nice, rich sauce.'

For the shots of Woody's old time TV show, the image was given twenty layers of fake degradation. One of the benefits of computer-based work is easy access to archives of material. Thus, the film could use trees and leaves previously created for *A Bug's Life*. The project also refined a 3-D paint system from *A Bug's Life*. The Pixar team developed a more sophisticated camera style (virtual) for this film. A year of research and development was given over to refining lighting and shading.

Again, there were humans in the film, more extensively featured than before. Alongside Andy and his mother was the nemesis of the story, the toy collector and trader Al. Al had 150 facial controls. Buster the dog had 4 million hairs.

The film was set in eighteen different virtual locations and this time they were even able to backlight suburban trees. Camera shots were also going to need to contain both human and toy perspectives on the action. Of *Toy Story 2*, Lasseter observes, 'One of the things that's different about this film is that it's one of the rare times that a sequel actually changes genre from the original.'

RECOGNITION: Of *Toy Story, Box Office* magazine said 'The characters are as emotionally complex and poignantly sympathetic as those any flesh and blood actors could portray' while the *LA Times* were surprised at 'how much cleverness has been invested in story and dialogue . . .' *Time Out* mentioned *Toy Story* within its history and surroundings: 'Randy Newman songs, mutant toys, reminiscent of Bosch and Svankmajer and a surprisingly effective foray into existential crisis . . .'

Toy Story's sequel, *Toy Story 2* garnered equally positive reviews such as: 'A sequel that takes chances and hits pay dirt with emotional nuances and riotous satire' (SFGate.com) and 'an extremely sophisticated, surprisingly melancholy understanding of the importance, resonance and tragically brief shelf life of the average plaything.' (*Sight and Sound*).

AWARDS: *Toy Story* was a landmark of animation history just as *Snow White* and *Who Framed Roger Rabbit?* had been, and the film was duly acknowledged and hailed for so successfully fusing technique with storytelling heart. The film won Randy Newman the ASCAP award for Top Box Office Film while at the 1996 Oscars the film was nominated for Best Music, Original Musical or Comedy Score (Randy Newman), Best Music for the song 'You Got a Friend in Me'. The film also received Oscar nominations for Best Screenplay written directly for the screen (Joel Cohen, Peter Docter, John Lasseter, Joe Ranft, Alec Sokolow, Andrew Stanton, Joss Whedon).

Toy Story won the Annie award for Best Animated Feature, Best Individual Achievement in Directing (John Lasseter), Best Individual Achievement in Music (Randy Newman), Best Individual Achievement in Producing (Bonnie Arnold and Ralph Guggenheim), Best Individual Achievement in Production Design (Ralph Eggleston), Best Individual Achievement in Writing (Andrew Stanton, Joss Whedon, Joel Cohen and Alex Sokolow).

At the BAFTA awards in 1997, the film was nominated for Best Achievement in Special Visual Effects (Eben Otsby and William Reeves) and at the Chicago Film Critics Association Awards the film won for Best Original Score. At the Golden Globes in 1996 the film was nominated for Best Motion Picture (Comedy or Musical) and Best Original Song ('You Got a Friend in Me'). The film was nominated for a Hugo award in the category of Best Dramatic Presentation and at the 1995 Los Angeles Film Critics Association Award won Best Animation.

COMMENT: 'I've been inspired all my life by Walt Disney films.' John Lasseter.

VERDICT: *Toy Story* is a mesmerising film that balances the spectacle of a new form of computer animation with the accepted conventions of classical storytelling to create a film that is utterly traditional in narrative but very forward looking in technology. For all its enjoyment, the film's sequel, *Toy Story 2*, is the better film rather in the way that *The Godfather Part II* (Francis Ford Coppola, 1974) is to *The Godfather* (Francis Ford Coppola, 1971).

A Bug's Life (1998)

(96 minutes)

Directed by John Lasseter and Andrew Stanton
Written by John Lasseter, Andrew Stanton, Joe Ranft, Dan McEnery, Bob Shaw
Produced by Darla K Anderson and Kevin Reher
Music: Randy Newman
Cinematography: Sharon Calahan
Edited by Lee Unkrich
Production Design: William Cone

BUDGET: $45 million

BOX OFFICE: $162,792,677

RELEASE DATE: 25 November 1998

ANIMATED FILMS A Bug's Life

CERTIFICATE: U/G

VOICES: Dave Foley (*Flik*), Kevin Spacey (*Hopper*), Julia Louis-Dreyfus (*Atta*), Hayden Panettiere (*Dot*), Phyllis Diller (*Queen*), Richard Kind (*Molt*), David Hyde Pierce (*Slim*), Joe Ranft (*Heimlich*), Denis Leary (*Francis*), Jonathan Harris (*Manny*), Madeline Kahn (*Gypsy*), Bonnie Hunt (*Rosie*), Michael McShane (*Tuck/Roll*), John Ratzenberger (*PT Flea*), Brad Garrett (*Dim*)

TAGLINE: An epic of miniature proportions.

STORYLINE: Glorious summertime. Ant Island is a bucolic haven for an efficient ant colony. Complicating their routine is the need to preserve their safety by gathering a food offering for the grasshoppers who protect the ants from other, larger bugs.

One of the ants, a young male named Flik, clumsily causes the food offering to topple just when the grasshoppers turn up. The grasshoppers attack and threaten the colony and Flik is put before the Queen and her council. Flik offers to go and find help in fighting off the grasshoppers, leaving the ants to gather food before the start of autumn.

Flik undertakes his mission and ventures to the city, a rubbish pile near a trailer and car. Performing in a makeshift circus are the performing bugs of PT Flea and, despite their best efforts, their scant audience is not entertained. Flik is thinking he will never find other, bigger bugs who are happy to help when he enters a bar and sees the circus troupe, at that moment striking a suitably heroic pose. The bugs think Flik is a talent scout and readily follow him when he expresses interest in them. Flik is flown back to Ant Island and en route tells them more about his mission.

Back at Ant Island, the bugs finally understand what it is they have really been recruited for and they make a quick departure. Flik is unable to convince them to stay and ventures out beyond the cover of the island. Dot, the youngest daughter of the Ant Queen and friend of Flik, follows him and she is attacked by a bird. Flik and the bugs ride to the rescue and return to Ant Island as heroes.

The Ant Princess makes Flik the liaison between ants and bugs and in thinking about how to defeat Hopper a plan is hatched to create a fake bird to scare him away for good. The ants and bugs work together.

Hopper and his cronies are getting eager to return to Ant Island especially when Hopper reminds them that the ants could easily overthrow them because of their sheer numbers.

At Ant Island, the circus bugs have become part of life and, at the critical moment, PT Flea turns up looking for his actors. Only now do the ants realise the true identity of the supposed warrior bugs. Flik is banished for lying to the colony and he leaves with the bugs.

The last leaf of summer falls and the grasshoppers arrive at Ant Island. Dot and her friends hide and Dot learns that Hopper wants to wipe out the Queen ant. She flies to tell Flik and convinces him to return. The ants fight back with the help of the bugs and the model bird. Flik confronts Hopper who savagely attacks him. Finally, the ants mob the grasshoppers and Hopper is caught by the real bird.

Order returns to the colony and the circus bugs depart once again. Flik, Dot and the Princess look proudly over the colony as another summer begins.

THE DRAWING BOARD: *A Bug's Life* was in development at Pixar before *Toy Story* had been released to massive critical and commercial success. With *A Bug's Life* the challenge was to advance the technology to new subtlety, refinement and richness. *Toy Story* had proved the level to which you could direct and design every element of the frame, controlling it absolutely for emotional and thematic impact. Four years went into the development of the film and the staff went from 175 members in 1995 to 400 in 1997.

The screenplay was developed extensively. Every shot was storyboarded. This development period took half of the four-year production period. Twenty-six sequences comprised the film's narrative and some sequences were reconfigured up to thirty times before being approved.

The original concept for the film featured a central character called Red who was part of a group of down-on-their-luck circus ants. Inadvertently they become the solution to the ant colony's problems with the grasshoppers. Six months of storyboards were worked up and were ready to become the story reel when the decision was made to overhaul the notion which was deemed to create too many plot-holes. Joe Ranft of Pixar calls it 'stor – re – boarding', emphasising the process of reworking a concept until it is just right.

A new concept was devised about a lonely hero who goes and seeks help for his family. Red became Flik. The circus ant element of the story remained a part of *A Bug's Life* after the revision. However, a key question that had to be answered was why the circus troop would stay with the colony when things became rough. This was worked through as the story team plotted out the sequence called Dot's Rescue, in which a bird attacks the insects and the circus ants inadvertently save Dot and are greeted as heroes of the hour.

INSPIRATIONS: The concept for *A Bug's Life* was inspired by an Aesop's fable about the busy ants working through the summer to prepare for the harsh winter while a neighbouring grasshopper lazed around, reaping the rewards of his laziness.

TOON TEAM: *A Bug's Life* assured audiences that *Toy Story* was not a fluke. This follow-up film was more expansive, intricate (in plot and design) and busier in action. John Lasseter led the effort again with co-director Andrew Stanton. The story for the film was by John Lasseter, Andrew Stanton and Joe Ranft who had served in the same capacity in *Toy Story*. Ranft had also contributed to storyboard supervision on *James and the Giant Peach*, a film with a similarly expansive outdoorsy feel of adventure across terrain and the landscape of the heart. Andrew Stanton also co-wrote *Toy Story 2* with John Lasseter, Peter Docter and Ash Brannon.

VOCAL TALENT: The actors were recorded separately and their dialogue then mixed together. As with *Toy Story* and *Monsters, Inc.*, the vocal talent for *A Bug's Life* featured several well-known names. Kevin Spacey voiced the nefarious Hopper. Spacey's other credits include *The Usual Suspects* (Brian Singer, 1997), *American Beauty* (Sam Mendes, 1999) and *The Shipping News* (Lass Hallström, 2001). Denis Leary, *Wag the Dog* (Barry Levinson, 1997) and *Small Soldiers* (Joe Dante, 1998), voiced Francis the ladybird and Madeline Kahn, *Nixon* (Oliver Stone, 1995), voiced the spider. Pixar regular John Ratzenberger features as PT Flea. Ratzenberger was the voice of Hamm in the *Toy Story* movies and the voice of the Abominable Snowman in *Monsters, Inc.*

INK, PAINT AND HARD WORK: For *A Bug's Life* the RenderFarm, the hub of computer power at Pixar, was dialled up by a factor of twelve over *Toy Story*, indicative of the intense detail of surfaces, character animation and environments.

To get a better sense of the world at our feet, a Bugcam was made by fixing a tiny video camera to a pole that was then run through the grass. The translucency of the world at that level was a critical aesthetic discovery and a programme for translucency was written. John Lasseter commented, 'Imagine being in a world where all the buildings are stained glass – that's what the insect world is like.'

Typically, an animator or animating team will zero in on a specific character. At Pixar this is not the rule of thumb and animators work on a variety of characters. A small core team will animate the earliest shots of a character to establish persona and a standard to work to, but beyond that animators come and go.

Each frame of the film has what is called an 'eye fix', namely a visual element that the audience is immediately drawn to, no matter how busy the rest of the frame.

Lasseter and his team decided that they wanted to present the film in CinemaScope because of the wide vistas they wanted to show. Disney agreed to the unusual decision.

As on all of their films, Pixar employed many live-action film techniques such as the use of shallow focus whereby foreground characters are placed in focus and the background is thrown out of focus, allowing the audience to concentrate on the characters.

At one point on *A Bug's Life* the unforeseen occurred when the computer-processing rate seriously slowed because of the density of detail and animation it was handling.

Where, on *Toy Story*, shots were transferred on to video tape for editorial comment, on *A Bug's Life* everything was digitally formatted from the start.

THEME: The ant colony is very much set in its ways and must learn to think afresh in order to defeat its enemy. The value of community and good faith in one another helps save the heroes and, rather like Dumbo, Flik comes to realise his own potential through his own shortcomings. It is his eagerness to please that sets him on his journey out into the world, returning like a real hero to save his world.

STYLISH TOONS: One of the key breakthroughs was the creation of subdivision surface modelling software, which was a combined effort of shading and lighting departments to create an illuminating model for translucent effects and virtual lighting variations.

The film brilliantly conjures the heat and bright light of summer and similarly the pinks and cooler colours of autumnal mornings. Just watch the scene where the grasshoppers race in at summer's end to get the food from Ant Island.

The film's opening moments replicate the natural world with real subtlety, so that the first image is of the blazing sun and flares. The camera then reveals water and then pushes in softly on a tree swaying in a summer breeze. The camera pushes through the grass and in the sharply focused midground appear ants. The foreground and background blades are out of focus.

As with *Toy Story* and *Monsters, Inc.*, *A Bug's Life* brims with kinetic energy and delicate facial animation. Just look at Flik's forlorn face throughout the film, especially as he sits in the back of PT Flea's wagon towards the end of the story.

A stand-out sequence is the bird attack on Dot, where the bird screeches and roars rather like the velociraptors in *Jurassic Park* (Steven Spielberg, 1993. Both films share the same sound designer, Gary Rydstrom.

Visual comedy is abundant, notably in the set-piece scene that introduces the hapless circus troupe at work. *A Bug's Life* has a real Tex Avery-inspired sense of action and comedy. Contrast this energy with the more violent action of Hopper towards the ants at the end of the film, such as when he slams his foot down on Flik.

The film also has fun concocting bug versions of human accoutrements, notably Flik's leafy baseball cap and the raindrop telescope. In the bar scene there is even a mosquito who drinks a Bloody Mary and then explodes in a possible reference to Winsor McCay's exploding mosquito in his animated short, *How a Mosquito Operates*.

Lighting subtleties enrich the action no end so that even Dim the beetle has wonderfully iridescent wings, shown in close-up as Flik rides back to Ant Island with his supposed warriors.

CHARACTER SKETCH: The hapless Flik is a classic young hero who, like so many before him, must find his place in the world and in true hero fashion get out beyond the safe confines of home in order to undertake an adventure that draws out his best nature. Flik returns to his community with a gift that saves the others. Flik stands up to the bullying Hopper and even finds a little romance with Princess Atta. It is Flik's capacity to dream and imagine the colony can save itself that wins the day. He regards himself as a clumsy failure through most of the film but ultimately redeems himself through his courage and bravery.

Hopper is the unrepentant villain of the film, marked by the savage scar just below his right eye. His exoskeleton is very armourlike in contrast to the soft-looking, frail ants. Hopper is more than just bullying for food. He fears that the grasshopper way of life could be eradicated if the ants ever realised just how much they outnumbered the grasshoppers.

The circus bugs are vividly drawn, all of them desperate for approval and belonging. Like Flik, they recognise their potential and find a place in the world.

Princess Atta is a strong-willed young woman who is afraid of getting things wrong.

Dot is a cute supporting character who just wants to fly.

TOON TUNES: Watching *A Bug's Life*, one is reminded how Randy Newman's music has become the sound of Pixar. For *A Bug's Life*, Newman's music is truly epic and suggests *The Magnificent Seven* influence with its bold, brass hero statement. For the action sequences the music is seriously melodramatic and intense and when Flik arrives in the city Newman easily parodies the Gershwin musical portraiture he provided for New York in pieces such as *Porgy and Bess*.

The soundtrack for *A Bug's Life:* 'Time of Your Life', 'The Flik Machine', 'Seed to Tree', 'Red Alert', 'Hopper and His Gang', 'Flik Leaves', 'Circus Bugs', 'City', 'Robin Hood', 'Return to Colony', 'Flik's Return', 'Loser', 'Dot's Rescue', 'Atta', 'Don't Come Back', 'Grasshoppers Return', 'Bird Flies', 'Ants Fight Back', 'Victory', 'Bug's Life Suite'.

TOON TALK:
Manty to Flik: 'You have rekindled the long dormant embers of purpose in our lives.'

Hopper to the ants: 'It's a bug eat bug world out there.'

OTHER SIMILAR FILMS: *A Bug's Life* owes a debt to the live-action drama, *The Seven Samurai* (Akira Kurosawa, 1954) about the titular seven samurai coming together to protect a village from marauders. The premise also plays out in *The Magnificent Seven* (John Sturges, 1960).

RECOGNITION: While *Sight and Sound* felt 'The film has fun mixing bug-world givens with anthropomorphism' and *Time Out* wrote that 'The computer generated imagery . . . is exceptional throughout', the *Chicago Sun-Times* got to the heart of the matter, saying they enjoyed 'the use of animation to visualise a world that could not be seen in live action and not be created with special effects.'

AWARDS: *A Bug's Life* was nominated for the 1999 Oscar for Best Music, Original Musical or Comedy Score. At the 1999 Academy of

Science Fiction, Fantasy and Horror Films it was nominated for a Saturn Award as Best Fantasy Film. At the 1999 Annie Award it was nominated for Outstanding Achievement, recognition for Animated Theatrical Feature, Direction, Production Design and Screenwriting. In 1999 it won the Broadcast Film Critics Association Award for Best Animated Film (tying with the classically animated *The Prince of Egypt*). At the Golden Globes the film was nominated for Best Original Score. At the 2000 BAFTA awards it was nominated for Best Achievement in Special Visual Effects.

COMMENT: 'With Flik, he grows quite a bit, but more importantly, everyone around him, because of his influence also grows a tremendous amount.' John Lasseter.

VERDICT: Alongside *Toy Story 2*, *A Bug's Life* is Pixar's strongest effort to date. With its wide vistas and epic adventure scale it differs significantly from the more enclosed world of *Toy Story* and *Monsters, Inc.* and anticipates the aquatic quest of *Finding Nemo*.

A Bug's Life also knows how much terror to lay on alongside the sunny wit and all-American energy. The spookiest element of the film is the crazed ant who is kept on a chain and who pursues Dot late in the story.

The film ably spoofs and honours the conventions of the adventure genre and features a level of violence that is a little more intense than any to be found in other Pixar films.

Monsters, Inc. (2001)

(92 minutes)

Directed by Peter Docter, David Silverman, Lee Unkrich
Written by Robert L Baird, Jill Culton, Pete Docter, Dan Gerson, Jeff Pidgeon, Rhett Reese, Jonathan Roberts, Andrew Stanton
Produced by Darla K Anderson
Executive Producer: John Lasseter
Associate Producer: Kori Rae
Music: Randy Newman
Editor: James Austin Stewart
Production Design: Harley Jessup, Bob Pauley

Art Direction: Tia W Kratter, Dominique Louis
Sound Design: Tom Myers
Animators: Angus MacLane, Dave Mullins

BUDGET: $15 million

BOX OFFICE: $255,870,172

RELEASE DATE: 2 November 2001

CERTIFICATE: U

VOICES: John Goodman (*Sulley*), Billy Crystal (*Mike Wazowski*), Mary Gibbs (*Boo*), Steve Buscemi (*Randall Boggs*), James Coburn (*Henry J Waternoose III*), Jennifer Tilly (*Celia*), Bob Peterson (*Roz*), John Ratzenberger (*Yeti*), Frank Oz (*Fungus*), Dan Gerson (*Needleman/Smitty*), Steve Susskind (*Floor Manager*), Bonnie Hunt (*Flint*), Jeff Pidgeon (*Bile*), Sam Penguin Black (*George Sanderson*)

TAGLINE: You won't believe your eye.

STORYLINE: At Monsters, Inc., newly inducted monsters watch a scare training session operation. The artificial kid scares the monster more than the monster scares the artificial kid. Monstropolis, the city the monsters live in, is fuelled by the screams of children around the world. It is running low and needs to up its resources. James P Sullivan (Sulley) is Monsters, Inc.'s top scarer, followed closely by sneaky, creepy Randall Boggs. Sulley's pal, Mike, works with him in generating screams.

All is well with Sulley's world until he goes back to work after the shift is over and sees Randall Boggs sneaking about and cheating to increase his scare score. In the process, he unwittingly lets into Monstropolis a little girl, Boo, from the human world. There is no greater source of toxicity for the monsters. Randall Boggs sees this as his chance to see Sulley demoted.

Realising what has happened, Sulley goes to tell Mike, who is on a hot date, and when Boo appears the restaurant evacuates and the word is out. Sulley and Mike take Boo back to Sulley's apartment and try not to scare her even though they are themselves terrified. Sully realises that she is not to be feared.

For her protection Sulley and Mike disguise Boo as a monster and take her to work the next day where she escapes and runs amok. Mike wants to send Boo back through any door but Sulley insists she go back to her own bedroom. Boo goes missing at the factory. Randall realises that Sulley and Mike are responsible for letting a human child in. Boo discovers a secret tunnel that leads to The Scream Extractor, the device that Randall possesses to collect all the screams without the need for scaring the child by sending a monster in. Sulley tries to tell the boss Waternoose what is going on and it emerges that he is in league with Randall.

Sulley and Mike are exiled to the Himalayas and Boo is cast out too. Sulley and Mike meet the Abominable Snowman and Sulley goes to try and find Boo. Soon enough Mike and Sulley get back into Monsters, Inc. where Boo has been put in front of the Scream Extractor. Sulley rescues her and Randall attacks him. Sulley and Mike race to return Boo safely home and they take her up into the door archive to find her door.

Randall captures Boo and Sulley almost perishes in his rescue effort. Sulley finally evicts Randall and casts him into the human world. Sulley returns Boo safely home and then confronts Waternoose.

Sulley takes one last look at Boo in her bedroom. Waternoose is then confronted by the authorities and Sulley assumes control of Monsters, Inc. and decides to collect energy fuelled by the laughter of children and not their screams.

THE DRAWING BOARD: After three films set among the relatively familiar worlds of toys and insects, Pixar's next feature made a bolder leap into fantasy, with monsters central to the concept. For debut feature director Peter Docter, the notion of monsters began to occur during the production of *A Bug's Life*. Rather like being toys was a job for the toys in *Toy Story*, a similar thought occurred that maybe it was monsters' job to be monsters. For Docter, 'We began thinking there must be some reason why monsters scare kids and started playing with that notion . . . Our own fears are afraid of us!'

Released in autumn 2001 to typically positive reviews *Monsters, Inc.* reaffirmed the deft narrative punch of the Pixar approach, finding a potent way for the fantasy setting to brim with very real emotion. *Monsters, Inc.* perhaps also touched a chord with America at the time of its release, given that, post 11 September, the country was in an especially anxious state of mind.

As with many initial concepts that are abandoned in the development process, one of the early notions for the premise of *Monsters, Inc.* sounds fascinating. A thirty-year-old man is given a childhood book by his mother. Inside the book are a cluster of drawings of monsters he had made as a kid. These images come to life and play havoc with the grown man's working and romantic life. Ultimately, the man confronts his fears with the help of the monsters. This idea was seen as lacking in one critical area – the absence of any child at the heart of the story. The concept which eventually made the film was based on exploring the theme of fear. *Toy Story 2* had articulated a very poetic concern in terms of the passing of time.

The first eighteen months of the project were spent developing the concept and narrative. It was John Lasseter who suggested that the monsters should be scared of the children they are meant to be scaring. A critical balance had to be found between scary monsters and non-scary monsters. All the monster body shapes were fairly rounded which immediately minimised their sense of threat. Deleted scenes include one of Sulley making a scare and being more afraid of the child than the child is of him. At this stage in story development he was only an assistant scary monster.

Designing Sulley was a challenge. In his first iteration he was a clumsy, scary monster. He always had fur, though, and llama fur was used as the key reference for its movement and appearance.

For the home-video version of the film, an all-singing all-dancing ending was added to the film.

INSPIRATIONS: A local gas refinery inspired the look for the Monsters, Inc. base which is a huge sprawling factory.

TOON TEAM: Directing duties fell to Peter Docter who had been an animator on *Toy Story*. One of the key crew members was Harley Jessup, once of ILM and also an alumnus of *The Nightmare Before Christmas* and *James and the Giant Peach*.

VOCAL TALENT: Big actor John Goodman's warm, deep voice features as Sulley. Goodman had done similarly strong work in the little animated feature, *We're Back*, where he voiced a far-from-threatening Tyrannosaurus Rex in modern-day New York. Goodman's other credits include the TV show *Roseanne* and the films *Raising Arizona* (Joel Coen, 1987), *Sea of Love* (Harold Becker, 1989), *Always* (Steven Spielberg, 1989), *Barton Fink* (Joel Coen, 1990), *The Flintstones* (Brian Levine, 1994), *O Brother, Where Art Thou?* (Joel Coen, 1999).

Comedian and comedy movie star Billy Crystal is neurotic, wisecracking Mike. Crystal has been a movie staple since the late 1980s when he appeared in *Throw Momma from the Train* (Danny DeVito, 1988), *When Harry Met Sally* (Rob Reiner, 1989), *Mr Saturday Night* (Billy Crystal, 1991), *Analyze This* (Harold Ramis, 1998).

James Coburn, veteran of over a hundred movies including *The Magnificent Seven* (John Sturges, 1960) and *Our Man Flint* (Daniel Mann, 1966) portrays the bad guy Waternoose and Steve Buscemi is Randall Boggs, slimy of voice and creepy as can be. Buscemi has appeared in *Reservoir Dogs* (Quentin Tarantino, 1992), *Trees Lounge* (Steve Buscemi, 1996) and *Armageddon* (Michael Bay, 1999).

Pixar regular vocal performer (*Toy Story*, *A Bug's Life*) John Ratzenberger returns for a memorable cameo in *Monsters, Inc.* as the voice of the beleaguered Abominable Snowman.

INK, PAINT AND HARD WORK: One of the first parts of creating the film was to develop a colour strip which comprised postage stamp-sized pastel thumbnails showing the dominant colour of each scene. Viewed in whole it was an easy-to-read map of the entire film's colour scheme and hence some guide to the moods being presented. Specific sequences were then storyboarded out and from these basic-concept art images a screenplay was fashioned by Andrew Stanton and Dan Gerson.

Sessions to record the dialogue typically ran about four hours. There were around fifteen sessions with Billy Crystal and John Goodman, both of them recording together which is quite unusual. This allowed for them to develop a real rapport that adds so much warmth to the film.

The accepted character drawings were sculpted by Jerome Ranft into clay maquettes. Full-sized heads were also sculpted that were marked with grids so they could be scanned into the computer as references.

In *Toy Story* and *Toy Story 2*, human figures were present, especially in the sequel. In *Monsters, Inc.* the young child Boo is central to the story but, wisely, is also not rendered in a naturalistic way.

The film's bad guy Randall Boggs was the trickiest to animate because of the number of legs.

One of the storytelling devices the film really employed was shifting focus and focus pulling to an extent not used in previous Pixar features.

The individual workstations in the factory area where the doors appear were modelled in part around the classic bowling alley and the idea was that the factory had been built in the early 1960s to maximise the Baby Boom era.

There are 5.7 million closet doors filling the door vault in which the film's action climax occurs.

THEME: Like the *Toy Story* saga, *Monsters, Inc.* deals with matters central to being a kid, in this case being scared. Sulley also learns the value of being responsible for someone and doing more than scaring, as he realises in the film's most affecting moment when he watches video playback of himself really being scary. As with *Toy Story* the power of the imagination is central to the warm meaning of *Monsters, Inc.*

STYLISH TOONS: Big, lumbering Sulley moves with gentle giant poise, his hair lilting as he goes. Monsters they might be, but Sulley, Mike and all the other workers at Monsters, Inc. have very human expressions. Just witness the critical scene when Sulley realises that Boo has got inside Monsters, Inc. Watch too the scene where he sleds to Boo's rescue through the wind and snow of the Himalayas. The animation to represent his windswept movement is astonishing, as is the glow of his lamp.

The film is rendered in a soft, pastel colour scheme. The film's opening titles playfully recall 1950s title sequences, invoking the spirit of Chuck Jones's classic short *The Dot and the Line*.

The film's climactic chase sequence through the archive of closet doors is a real suspenseful thrill, as kinetic and visually dynamic as an Indiana Jones caper. Certainly, it recalls the whoosh and thunder of a rollercoaster ride at a theme park, but the jeopardy is rooted in more than just a quick thrill. Sulley must rescue Boo and make good on his latent paternalism that is finally expressed in the film's coda.

The film bursts with stylish humour, never more evident than in its affectionate, fleeting nod to the animation great, Ray Harryhausen. The restaurant where Mike goes on a date is called 'Harryhausen's'. Ray Harryhausen is famous for animating monster characters in live-action special-effects movies.

The film's subtle animation is all pervasive. When Sulley, in a hurry, rushes into the restaurant to tell Mike about Boo, look at how Sulley's foot taps impatiently beneath the table. In the Abominable Snowman's ice cave, Sulley's expressions run from rueful, guilty and sad with real human subtlety.

For all the visual splash and panache and scale, the most all-out gorgeous image is of Boo's moonlit bedroom, dominated by blue moonlight and offset by a point of pink light from a moon-shaped plug-socket light. If there is one picture-book image in the film it is this, a visual paean to the sanctity and magic of a child's room, a retreat from the world.

ANIMATED FILMS Monsters, Inc.

CHARACTER SKETCH: Sulley is a bearlike, warm character which amplifies the mean spiritedness towards him later in the film. During his creation, Sulley was at one point orange-coloured and started out as a janitor at Monsters, Inc., then a clumsy loser who assisted a top scarer. Glasses and tentacles were also an early design style for him.

Mike is the older, slightly more wised-up 'brother' to Sulley.

Waternoose is a corrupt crustacean-like monster who has lost the spirit of the company, a slave to the bottom line. Sulley revitalises Monsters, Inc. with the power of laughter, in effect doing what animated movies do.

In a film packed with amusing characters, one of the most amusing is the Abominable Snowman who complains about his reputation, asking why he cannot be the Adorable Snowman. He certainly looks and sounds far from scary.

TOON TUNES: Randy Newman's playful jazzy score is as successful as his work on *Toy Story* and *A Bug's Life*. For the all action set-pieces, the score is far from jokey. As with *Toy Story*, Newman composes a nifty theme song. Randy Newman has composed numerous American-flavoured scores for films such as *The Natural* (Barry Levinson, 1984) and *Avalon* (Barry Levinson, 1990).

The *Monsters, Inc.* soundtrack: 'If I Didn't Have You', 'Monsters, Inc.', 'School', 'Walk to Work', 'Sulley and Mike', 'Randall Appears', 'Enter the Heroes', 'Scare Floor', 'Oh, Celia', 'Boo's Adventure in Monstropolis', 'Boo's Tired', 'Putting Boo Back, Boo Escapes, Celia's Mad, Boo Is a Cube, Mike's in Trouble, Scream Extractor', 'Sulley Scares Boo', 'Exile', 'Randall's Attack', 'Ride of the Doors', 'Waternoose Is Waiting', 'Boo's Going Home', 'Kitty', 'If I Didn't Have You'.

TOON TALK:

Waternoose: 'There's nothing more toxic or deadly than a child.'

Monsters, Inc. motto: 'We scare, because we care.'

Waternoose: 'Kids these days, they just don't get scared like they used to.'

Mike: 'You know, I am so romantic sometimes I think I should just marry myself.'

OTHER SIMILAR FILMS: *Monsters, Inc.* built on the popular successes of its predecessors *Toy Story*, *A Bug's Life* and *Toy Story 2* and also anticipated the success of its follow-up, *Finding Nemo* (Andrew Stanton, 2003). *Finding Nemo* concerns a father's search for his son and his son's desire to get back to his father. Nemo is a clownfish who is being taken to his first day at school by his father Marlin. Against his father's caution, Nemo heads out beyond the reef to explore a sunken ship. Nemo is picked up by a scuba diver and finds himself transplanted to a fish tank in a dentist's office in Sydney. Marlin teams up with a blue tang called Dory and begins the journey to find Nemo. In the tank, Nemo makes friends and devises a plan to escape and get back home.

The film refines computer animation ever further and makes a significant push in terms of lighting, making believable the play of light on water and the murkiness of the hidden depths.

As with Pixar's other films, *Finding Nemo* augments vivid, classically styled animation with a story of fundamental emotion.

The film was conceived by Andrew Stanton prior to the release of *Toy Story*. In its focus on a child aiming to get back home it recalls Don Bluth's *An American Tail* (1986) and *The Land Before Time* (1988), and also *Pinocchio* (which itself features its share of underwater action) and the brilliant *James and the Giant Peach*.

The big question is whether Nemo is named after Jules Verne's underwater hero Captain Nemo or is an allusion to animation pioneer, Winsor McCay's cartoon character, Little Nemo, who went adventuring through his dreams.

RECOGNITION: 'This movie is staggeringly generous with its witty lines, its allusions, above all with its sheer visual spectacle' said Peter Bradshaw in the *Guardian*, while *Sight and Sound* described it as 'An animated feature that refuses self consciousness and cultural irony.'

AWARDS: *Monsters, Inc.* won the 2002 ASCAP award for Top Box Office Film and also the Oscar for Best Music, Song 'If I Didn't Have You'. The film was nominated for Oscars for Best Animated Feature, Best Sound Effects Editing and Best Music, Original Score. It was nominated for a 2002 Saturn Award as Best Fantasy Film and Best Writing. At the Annie awards it won Outstanding Character Animation and was nominated for Best Animated Feature, Direction, Music, Production Design and Writing. At the 2002 BAFTA awards the film won the BAFTA Children's Award for Best Feature Film and also the Grammy for Best Song. At the Hugo Awards the film was nominated for Best Dramatic Presentation.

HOME VIEWING: *Monsters, Inc.* is available in both VHS and DVD formats. The DVD contains both pan and scan and widescreen versions of the film. It also includes a commentary track, a short called *Mike's New Car*, a series of games, abandoned concept material, and other behind-the-scenes material.

COMMENT: 'The overall design philosophy for Monstropolis was to think of it as our world – only monsters live there.' Peter Docter.

'I think somewhere midway through *Monsters*, we all started to sense, if we didn't watch ourselves, you'll be able to peg a Pixar movie.' Andrew Stanton.

VERDICT: The film is faithful to the possibilities inherent in animation aimed at young minds to be resonant and emotionally true. *Monsters, Inc.* plays on the power of fear and charts the journey of a character in understanding something of the complexity and inconsistencies of the world, all within a fast-paced, elegantly structured narrative that revels in the animation-friendly format of the rescue and chase.

Shrek (2001)

(90 minutes)

Studio: DreamWorks SKG
Directed by Andrew Adamson and Vicky Jenson
Screenplay by Ted Elliott, Terry Rossio, Joe Stillman, Roger
SH Schulman
Produced by Ted Elliott, Jeffrey Katzenberg, Aron Warner,
John H Williams
Executive Producers: Penny Finkelman Cox, Sandra Rabins,
Steven Spielberg
Music: Harry Gregson-Williams, John Powell
Editing: Sim Evans-Jones
Production Design: James Hegedus
Art Direction: Guillaume Aretos, Douglas Rogers
Supervising Animators: Rex Grignon, Raman Hui

BUDGET: $60 million

BOX OFFICE: $267,652,016

RELEASE DATE: 18 May 2001

CERTIFICATE: U

VOICES: Mike Myers (*Shrek*), Eddie Murphy (*Donkey*), Cameron Diaz (*Princess Fiona*), John Lithgow (*Lord Farquuad*), Pete Dennis (*Ogre Hunter*), Vincent Cassell (*Monsieur Hood*), Clive Pearse (*Ogre Hunter*), Chris Miller (*Gepetto and Magic Mirror*), Cody Cameron (*Pinocchio and Three Little Pigs*)

TAGLINE: The greatest fairy tale never told.

STORYLINE: An old, fairy-tale storybook opens up to reveal an illuminated manuscript and a story is told of a princess under a spell, locked away in a keep guarded by a dragon.

A beautiful, sunlit forest. Shrek the ogre prepares for another day, taking a mud shower and enjoying his quiet life. Somewhere nearby fairy-tale characters are being rounded up and caged by the soldiers of Lord Farquuad. One of the fairy-tale characters, a donkey, escapes and runs into Shrek who scares off Farquuad's soldiers. The donkey pleads to stay with Shrek who seems to have no enemies. Shrek reluctantly agrees.

That night, all of the evicted fairy-tale characters not taken by the soldiers gather in safety on Shrek's property where the soldiers are too scared to go. Shrek is angry and says he will go and sort the problem out with Farquuad. Shrek and the donkey head off immediately to the town of DuLoc where Lord Farquuad rules. He wants to be king but can only become so by marrying a Princess. He is told of the princess under the spell and instantly decides that she is the one. Being a coward, he must find someone worthy of getting to her in the dragon-guarded keep.

Shrek arrives at the castle where Farquuad is holding a tournament that he will use to determine who is worthy of going to rescue Princess Fiona and bringing her to him. The soldiers are ordered to attack the ogre but he dispatches all of them with ease. Farquuad strikes a bargain with Shrek. If he retrieves Fiona he can have his swamp back free of all the evicted fairy-tale characters. Shrek accepts the mission and heads off with Donkey.

Shrek and Donkey trek from the rolling green fields and sunlit forests to a barren volcanic land where a ruined fortress stands. Shrek and Donkey cross a perilous bridge suspended over a lava pit. They enter the keep and are confronted by a dragon who attempts to destroy them.

Shrek is inadvertently, but helpfully, thrown through the Princess's window by the dragon.

Fiona awakes sure that her true love has come to the rescue. Shrek rescues her as the dragon closes in again and Shrek, Donkey and Fiona run free of the keep. Fiona is delighted and is eager to see the face of her heroic rescuer beneath the helmet. Shrek reluctantly removes it and Fiona does not seem impressed. She says she will wait for Farquuad to come and rescue her as he must be her true love. Shrek has none of this and carries Fiona over his shoulder, taking her back to DuLoc.

En route across the countryside, Shrek and Fiona's friendship blossoms. They meet Robin Hood and his Merry Men and a fight breaks out in which Fiona knocks them all out to the astonishment of Shrek.

Camping out at an old mill close to DuLoc, Fiona goes inside the mill to sleep. Donkey goes in to speak to her and discovers that she too is an ogre just like Shrek. Shrek approaches the mill wanting to tell Fiona how he feels about her. He overhears Donkey and Fiona talking but misunderstands what he hears. He walks off to DuLoc and brings Farquuad back with him to meet his bride. Farquuad takes Fiona off to be married.

Shrek heads home and Donkey goes it alone in the woods. Shrek mopes around at home thinking of Fiona and Fiona mopes around at the castle thinking about Shrek.

Donkey and Shrek make up. Donkey tells Shrek that Fiona loves him. Time is running out before the wedding. Donkey calls the dragon in to help and flies Shrek to the castle.

Shrek interrupts the wedding ceremony and declares his love for Fiona. The sun goes down and she transforms to her ogre self. The soldiers rush in to grab both Fiona and Shrek and the dragon intervenes, blasting them away. Shrek kisses Fiona and she remains an ogre. Love wins out.

Back in the woods, Shrek and Fiona ride off into a picture-book sunset and Donkey leads the dancing-and-singing fairy-tale characters, celebrating true love.

THE DRAWING BOARD: DreamWorks SKG was a new movie studio established in 1994 by Steven Spielberg, Jeffrey Katzenberg and David Geffen to produce feature films, animation, TV, music and toys. Jeffrey Katzenberg had recently ended his tenure at Disney and in co-forming SKG was able to steer his destiny in terms of animation production. In 1998 the studio's first CG animated feature, *Antz*, was released. Based around an ant colony and the fight to overthrow a tyrannical military leader within the colony, the film's adult sensibility was well received but the film was not quite as popular as *A Bug's Life*, released in the same autumn period. DreamWorks' follow-up project, in collaboration with PDI, was *Shrek*.

With a screenplay by Ted Elliott and Terry Rossio, who had co-written the brilliant adventure movie *The Mask of Zorro* (Martin Campbell, 1998) and had worked on *Aladdin* (John Musker, Ron Clements, 1992) for Disney and uncredited on *Men in Black* (Barry Sonnenfeld, 1997), *Shrek* was an adaptation of William Steig's children's picture book, *Shrek!* which had been published in 1990.

For Ted Elliott and Terry Rossio, adapting the source material was about latching on to one key concept: 'The book is actually this Jungian journey of self discovery and self fulfilment.'

Not unusually for an animated feature, the development process was rigorous. The effort to approach the subject with the right treatment began in 1996 when producer John H Williams pitched the idea of the book to Jeffrey Katzenberg, who was enthusiastic.

Initially the film was going to be a combination of live action, stop motion and computer-generated elements with the comedian, the late Chris Farley, voicing Shrek. Farley was a well-known American TV celebrity from *Saturday Night Live*. Director Kelly Asbury began developing the project. Her previous credits included storyboard and layout work on *The Little Mermaid* at Disney and as production designer on *James and the Giant Peach*. Asbury was joined by a second director, Andrew Adamson and production designer James Hedegus. Their first thought was to fabricate and shoot a thirty-second proof-of-concept reel for Katzenberg, showing an idyllic fairy-tale world with a motion-captured Chris Farley inserted into the environment. To create just the two shots required, Illusion Arts were commissioned to generate a forest and field environment and a wider shot of a castle.

The decision was soon made for the project to be entirely computer generated, a decision in part prompted by *Antz* (1998).

The project hit a bump in December 1997 when Chris Farley died, at the age of 33. Director Kelly Asbury moved over to DreamWorks classical animation feature *Spirit: Stallion of the Cimarron* (2002) and Vicky Jenson took her place.

In designing the narrative for the film, Andrew Adamson noted that 'the thing about Steig's book was that it wasn't really a linear narrative. It was more a study of this character Shrek and his inverted way of looking at the world.' Steig's book contained a subplot about Shrek's parents kicking him out of the family swamp but this was not regarded as dynamic enough for the film and so the subplot revolved around the storybook invasion. An element of the book that was retained was the bovine dragon.

INSPIRATIONS: Two key old-time inspirations on the film were the American painters Grant Wood and NC Wyeth. Grant Wood (1891–1941) was a painter noted for the application of the Old Master technique to American settings and subject. His most famous image is *American Gothic* in which an old man and woman look sternly out of the painting with a pitchfork between them. NC Wyeth is known for his luminous images of the American landscape.

To develop a sense of how the castle in the film should look, some of the team visited San Simeon, where the Hearst Castle is located. Victorian fairy paintings, storybook illustrations and the art of Edmund Dulac were key to the visual design of the film. Dulac was a contemporary of illustrator Arthur Rackham. Dulac's work is defined by the way he often placed less emphasis on the human figures in an illustration than on the backgrounds, composed of watercolour washes. He illustrated *The Arabian Nights* (1907) and *Stories from Hans Andersen* (1912).

TOON TEAM: *Shrek* corralled four screenwriters and a 28-member story department at PDI, DreamWorks' computer-animation partners. Leading this story effort were Randy Cartwright and David Lowery.

VOCAL TALENT: Unusually, vocal talent was hired before the screenplay was completed. Mike Myers developed a Shrek voice which he adjusted through the process. Minor roles were vocalised by the animators. Myers came to movie prominence in *Wayne's World* (Penelope Spheeris, 1992) and went on to appear in *Austin Powers* (Jay Roach, 1997) and its sequels. He has also starred as The Cat in *The Cat in the Hat* (Bo Welch, 2003).

Eddie Murphy excels as Donkey. His delivery of some already snappy lines is hilarious and gives the film an energy and spark it might otherwise have lacked. Shrek represents another in a run of family-orientated films the comic actor has featured in lately. Murphy was a massive box-office star in the 1980s in a run of hits starting with *48 Hours* (Walter Hill, 1982), *Trading Places* (John Landis, 1983), *Beverly Hills Cop* (Martin Brest, 1984), *The Golden Child* (Michael Ritchie, 1986), *Beverly Hills Cop 2* (Tony Scott, 1987), *Coming to America* (John Landis, 1988). He was also hilarious in *Bowfinger* (Frank

Oz, 1999). The fast-talking, smart-ass roles of the characters in these movies is exactly what Murphy offers a family-friendly version of. Murphy also voiced a dragon sidekick in the animated feature *Mulan* (1998) to excellent effect.

Cameron Diaz, who voices Princess Fiona, instantly became a star the moment she walked into Stanley Ipkiss's life in *The Mask* (Chuck Russel, 1994). She has gone on to *There's Something About Mary* (The Farrelly Brothers, 1999), *Charlie's Angels* (Joseph McGinty, 2000) and *Gangs of New York* (Martin Scorsese, 2002). Originally the role of Fiona was to have been voiced by comedienne Janeane Garofalo, noted for her role in *The Truth About Cats and Dogs* (Michael Lehmann, 1995).

John Lithgow as Lord Farquuad is one of America's best character actors and has been on the movie scene since the early 1980s with films such as *The World According to Garp* (George Roy Hill, 1982), *Buckaroo Banzai* (WD Richter, 1984), *Harry and the Hendersons* (William Dear, 1987) and *Raising Cain* (Brian De Palma, 1991). He also starred in the mid-90s sitcom *3rd Rock from the Sun*.

INK, PAINT AND HARD WORK: Character sketches were worked up and the approved paper designs became sculpted reference models. Suffice to say, the film version of *Shrek* is far cuter than the Steig character in the book. In detailing character and movement, the animators had to minimise Shrek's double chin to allow the animated character to look down. In the book, Shrek wore bright red trousers. In the film he wears a golden plaid design and so is less garish.

In the Steig book Princess Fiona has bright red hair and a long, pointed nose though in the film she has softer features. Live donkey footage was studied and for the Donkey character to amplify his cuteness they gave him short legs that made him move like a (lovable) puppy.

To get the movement of mud splashing over Shrek when he takes his mud shower, one animator dressed in a coat and hat and had mud poured over him.

THEME: As with the best animated features, the animation conveys a simply drawn thematic line. In *Shrek* the notion of beauty being skin-deep is played out most evidently. Shrek's bravery and commitment to his mission are far more valuable than any physical appeal.

STYLISH TOONS: It took nine months to develop the quality of light and magic that envelop Fiona during her transformation at the end of the film.

This issue plugs the movie back into animation history as a similar question was addressed for the transformation scene of the Queen into the hag in *Snow White and the Seven Dwarfs*. The film's opening images of Shrek showering himself and getting ready for his day are gorgeous, the trees and grasses blowing gently in the wind. The textures of Shrek's outfit are finely detailed and the marks and slight stubble of his chin add to the verisimilitude.

The animation of the human characters has elegance in both broad comedy (such as when the mob go to get Shrek at the beginning of the film) and more subtle emotion as played out by the character of Fiona. That is not to say Shrek is without subtlety too. There is a stand-out scene late in the film where Fiona and Shrek eat and talk to one another. A series of close-ups on them suggest something deeper at work and when Shrek fails to speak from the heart a wide shot nicely reveals his look of dismay and his clenched fist of frustration.

The animation of Donkey is endlessly engaging and funny, from his walk to his heavy eyelids and endearing grin.

Details of sunlight reflecting off armour and even firelight reflected in Shrek's eyes enhance the believability of the illusion.

The film excels with its intricately detailed backgrounds and lighting effects. Scenes set in moonlight are especially affecting and the glow of fire and firelight add menace and warmth as appropriate. There is even a nice heat ripple rolling over Donkey when the dragon blasts him with her fire. Donkey flambé . . . almost.

CHARACTER SKETCH: Shrek starts out as very dismissive of the fairy-tale concept – after all, it is he who reads the film's prologue and then shuts the book, bored with the tone of it. Shrek might think he is happy alone in his trunkhouse, but his friendship with Donkey and his love for Fiona make him a rounded, softer character.

Donkey is the film's comic chorus. He occupies the classic sidekick role, so excellently established by Jiminy Cricket way back in *Pinocchio*. Like Jiminy, Donkey advises Shrek on matters of the head and heart. Donkey is a streetwise kind of character who also has his role to play in the adventure; he is the most human character.

Princess Fiona is both an old-school and a new-school heroine, in love with the notion of a charming prince who will rescue her but also tough talking and tough acting – as her encounter with Robin Hood and his Merry Men proves. When Fiona sings happily in the forest it recalls Snow White singing in the Disney version, until the moment when Fiona's voice reduces a bird to just smoking feet.

Lord Farquaad is an almost nasty villain, more interested in preening himself than anything else. His attempt to marry above his station is his undoing.

TOON TUNES: The film opens with a gorgeous English-pastoral-sounding orchestral motif and the orchestral score continues throughout the film.

Composers Harry Gregson-Williams and John Powell also scored *Antz* and *Chicken Run* for DreamWorks. Gregson-Williams has also scored *The Borrowers* and *The Replacement Killers*, among others.

Two soundtracks were released, one featuring the songs from the film, the other the orchestral score. Both soundtracks are listed here:

Shrek (Songs): 'Stay Home', 'I'm a Believer', 'Like Wow, It Is You', 'Best Years of Our Lives', 'Bad Reputation', 'My Beloved Monster', 'You Belong to Me', 'All Star', 'Hallelujah', 'I'm On My Way', 'I'm a Believer', 'True Love's First Kiss'.

Shrek: (Orchestral Score): 'Fairytale', 'Ogre Hunters/Fairytale Deathcamp', 'Donkey Meets Shrek', 'Eating Alone', 'Uninvited Guests', 'March of Farquuad', 'The Perfect King', 'Welcome to DuLoc', 'Tournament Speech', 'What Kind of Quest', 'Dragon!/Fiona Awakes', 'Saving Donkey's Ass', 'Escape from the Dragon', 'Helmet Hair', 'Delivery by Shrek/Making Camp', 'Friends' Journey to DuLoc', 'Starry Night', 'Singing Princess', 'Better Out Than In/Sunflower/I'll Tell Him', 'Merry Men', 'Fiona Kicks Ass', 'Fiona's Secret', 'Why Wait to Wed', 'Ride the Dragon', 'I Object', 'Transformation/The End'.

TOON TALK:

Donkey to Shrek: 'You definitely need some Tic Tacs or something.'

Shrek to the Seven Dwarfs (when they put Snow White in her coffin on his table at home): 'Dead broad off the table.'

Magic Mirror on Snow White: 'Although she lives with seven other men, she's not easy.'

Shrek to Donkey: 'For your information there's a lot more to ogres than people think.'

OTHER SIMILAR FILMS: As the computer-animated movie has found its feet in the late 1990s it is worth comparing *Shrek* with the other movies created in essentially the same way, such as the Pixar films, *Ice*

Age (Carlos Saldanha, Chris Wedge, 2002) and *Antz* (Eric Darnell, Tim Johnson, 1998), by the same animation studio as *Shrek*.

So popular was *Shrek* that it first led to a short theme park film called *Shrek 4D*. The film picks up immediately after the feature with Shrek and Fiona on honeymoon. Fiona is kidnapped and Shrek and Donkey go to the rescue. They team up with the Lady Dragon from the feature and

go up against a nefarious dragon that comes to life from statue form. Lord Farquuad appears as a ghost.

Given *Shrek*'s huge popular success, *Shrek 2* is on its way in summer 2004. Shrek returns along with Fiona and Donkey. The premise is that Shrek and Fiona go to visit Fiona's parents who are less than happy that Fiona has married him. The film is regarded as a nice bridge between the original feature and the forthcoming sequel. *Shrek 2* is directed by Kelly Asbury and Conrad Vernon from a screenplay by Joe Stillman and Andrew Stanton. Mike Myers, Cameron Diaz and Eddie Murphy reprise their original roles. The story begins with Shrek and Fiona going to visit Fiona's parents King Harold and Queen Lillian, voiced by Julie Andrews. Puss in Boots features in the sequel (voiced by Antonio Banderas) and he develops a rivalry with Donkey. In a publicity conference Jeffrey Katzenberg said, 'So, it's a little bit of *Guess Who's Coming to Dinner?* meets *Shrek*.'

Complicating the set-up is the fact that Princess Fiona was meant to have married Prince Charming (Rupert Everett). Shrek's intervention has thrown fate off course.

The film's original screenwriters Ted Elliott and Terry Rossio departed the project after commencing script duties.

RECOGNITION: 'Beautifully written, gloriously animated and tastily subversive' wrote *Empire*, while the *LA Times* described *Shrek* as 'A gleeful piece of wisenheimer animation' and the *Guardian* felt the film had 'A zany, fractured unreality . . . The great rolling fields that Shrek crosses reminded me of the road to Oz.'

AWARDS: *Shrek's* commercial fireworks were matched by its showing at awards time. Most significantly, *Shrek* was the first animated film to win the Best Animated Feature Oscar in 2002, beating *Monsters, Inc.* The film was also nominated for Oscars in Best Writing for a Screenplay based on Previously Produced or Published Material. *Shrek* won the award for Best Animated Film at the National Board of Review awards

and also the Los Angeles Film Critics Association Awards for Best
Animation. In 2002, it was nominated for the American Film Institute
award for Best Animation. The film was nominated for a Saturn award
for Best Fantasy Film, Best Music, Best Supporting Actor (Eddie
Murphy) and Best Writing.

At the 2002 Grammy awards it was nominated for Best Compilation
Soundtrack Album and won the Hugo for Best Dramatic Presentation.
At the Annie awards the film won Best Animated Theatrical Feature,
Directing, Effects Animation.

At the Golden Globes it received a nomination for Best Picture,
Musical or Comedy. At Cannes in spring 2001 Shrek was nominated for
the Palme d'Or. The Las Vegas Film Critics Society Awards awarded the
film the Sierra Award for Best Animated Film. At the BAFTA awards,
the film won Best Adapted Screenplay and was nominated for the
Anthony Asquith Award for Film Music and was also nominated for
Best Achievement in Visual Effects, Best Film, Best Sound and
Supporting Actor.

COMMENT: 'All four main characters are organised around the
concept of self esteem.' Terry Rossio.

VERDICT: *Shrek* is a very knowing film, even post-modern. This is most
evident in its storyline around the evicted fairy-tale characters. They are
very recognisable – the Three Bears, Pinocchio, Snow White and so
forth.

Unlike its computer-generated contemporaries produced by the Pixar
Studio, Shrek is a little more 'streetwise' which is fun up to a point but
which threatens to puncture the reality of the fantasy world that has
been so lavishly designed.

The film has a nice softness of tone to it and its principle concern with
appearances not being what they seem is appealing. In less weighty terms
there is much to be enjoyed in the film's energetic action sequences,
notably the high adventure involved in rescuing Fiona from the dragon's
lair.

Rather like the *Toy Story* movies, *Shrek* is rooted in the buddy movie
as Shrek and Donkey bicker and help one another out. Watch the scene
of Shrek and the Donkey walking through the sunflowers when Shrek
tries to explain that ogres are multi-layered.

Mavericks

As with any field of endeavour, there are those who step outside certain establishments and work more independently in terms of the choices they make. Animation has its share of independent minds, some working in very accessible formats, others in less popular forms.

Don Bluth, Brad Bird and Jan Svankmajer are the feature animation directors that will be looked at in detail but it is also worth acknowledging the contributions of others, too. For example, one cannot overlook contributions by animation directors such as Michel Ocelot who broke through to wider public appeal with his animated feature *Kirikou and the Sorceress*, which tells of an African baby and the attempts to rid his village of an evil sorceress named Karaba.

Some notable British-based animators working in the stop-motion arena are The Brothers Quay based in London. Their creative timbre is very different from the Aardman style.

The work of The Brothers Quay is far more akin to the work of Jan Svankmajer and his progenitor Wladyslaw Starewica. The Brothers Quay use animation to explore metaphor and the unconscious. They are less driven by the mechanics of what can be called classical narrative. Discussing their work, The Brothers Quay have stated that 'Puppet films by their very nature are extremely artificial constructions, even more so depending at what level of "enchantment" one would wish for them in relation to the subject, and above all, the conceptual *mise en scène* applied.'

Heavily influenced by Eastern European culture, they put the associative over the narrative. For many The Brothers Quay's finest hour was their short film *Street of Crocodiles* (1986). Film directors Murnau, Kirsanov, Tarkovsky and writer Franz Kafka are all informing sources for their shadowy, uncertain animated worlds where the concrete, bright, peppy and optimistic do not necessarily underpin their narratives.

Like Aardman and many other animation houses, The Brothers Quay have also worked on music promos for names such as His Name Is Alive, Michael Penn, Sparklehorse and they contributed to Peter Gabriel's *Sledgehammer* video. More recently they have worked on a collaboration with composer Steve Martland, making four short films for a live event at Tate Modern. They are also in preproduction on their second feature with the amazing title *The Piano Tuner of Earthquakes*.

Graduates of the Royal College of Art, Stephen and Timothy Quay began working in 1980 alongside fellow student and subsequently producer Keith Griffiths. The Brothers Quay have produced an arresting and startling body of work (predominantly short form) that offers a refreshing and fascinating alternative to the more classically styled work of their contemporaries in Britain and North America. The whole creative impulse is radically different, owing more creative inspiration to literature, dance and music than the vaudevillian spirit, though their work is vividly anti-realistic in many ways.

Like so many of their contemporaries and antecedents, The Brothers Quay infuse their work with a fairy-tale sensibility. But it is the darkness and ambiguity of image that they amplify, rather than the sense of hopeful resolution or of some 'cute' relationship between humans and animals.

The Brothers Quay work on a small scale, creating the puppets, sets and costumes themselves for their stop-motion work. They even go so far as to suggest that they also consider their camera as a puppet and hence a character, playing its part in describing the story. Tellingly, the decor and set design often leads the eventual design of characters and in their films it is hard to deny the impact and intricacy of their sets; they are very much more than just backgrounds that support the drama played out in front of them. The backgrounds often source the drama, intrigue and resonance.

Three of their short films function as a vivid introduction to their work, namely *The Unnameable Little Broom*, *The Cabinet of Jan Svankmajer* and *Street of Crocodiles*. Their work might be seen as extremely bizarre and unfamiliar yet, watching their work closely, it is frequently a purer form of animation than much that is produced. It is certainly beautiful and redolent with a dream quality. The Brothers Quay are major fans of Jan Svankmajer and also of Eastern European literature such as the work of Bruno Schulz. Their work also suggests Franz Kafka and Latin American writer Jorge Luis Borges.

The Unnameable Little Broom began as a pilot episode for an animation series for British TV which never received its funding. The film is based on *The Epic of Gilgamesh*, the ancient Babylonian myth. Typically playful at titling their work, this short's alternative title is *Little Songs of the Chief Officer of Hunar Louse, Tableau II* 'being a largely disguised reduction of the epic Gilgamesh'.

The film centres on its Gilgamesh character, a Punch-like character who rides around on a bike. The world he patrols, a decaying room, outside of which stands a menacing forest, is intruded upon by the

Gilgamesh tale character of Enkidu, a wild man of the woods. In this piece of work the character resembles a bird and the sound of its flapping wings is used to eerie and unsettling affect. The Gilgamesh character lures Enkido and eventually kills him, dismembering him with scissors (scissors recur in *Street of Crocodiles*). The film has no dialogue and an insistent music score. The film amplifies the emotional potency of shapes and the power the camera has of not showing everything so that the audience can comprehend either immediately or never fully. The film feels more like a game, and certainly like a contraption and a puzzle. The images might be considered grotesque. To the uninitiated, who feel that animation is just for kids, the work of The Brothers Quay will most likely promote a reaction of scorn and revulsion.

Texture and a sense of decay runs through their work and is certainly evident in this film, which is maybe at its most arresting when the animation includes chunks of raw meat appearing amidst the animated contortions. The film is suffused with sexual imagery and an overwhelmingly abrasive quality. Shadow, mystery and the undefined lend the film a dreamy menace. There is also a debt to the silent film tradition with the use of intertitles.

In contrast to *The Unnameable Little Broom*, *The Cabinet of Jan Svankmajer* is a more playful film, its title not only honouring the great Czech animator but also referencing the German Expressionist film *The Cabinet of Dr Caligari* (Robert Wiene, 1919). *The Cabinet of Jan Svankmajer* was originally a series of brief animation interludes included in a documentary about the filmmaker, where their action was given more context. Pieced together the film has a free-flowing quality, prompting the audience to rearrange the order of the story any way they like.

The film animates perception and the main character is an abstract puppet representing Svankmajer, made evident up front. For his hair he has the pages of an opened book fanning out gloriously. Again, dialogue plays no part in the film and the music is a vital part of the storytelling. The character goes on an odyssey of sorts, helped at points by a boylike doll.

As with *The Unnameable Little Broom*, there is a sense of violence in the images, but also a welcome and refreshing sense of free association based around the logic of images. The film's sections include *An Unexpected Visitor* and *Pins for Loose Geographies*, *Pursuit of the Object* and *The Child's Divining of the Object*. In ways they recall titles for modernist music by composers such as John Adams and Steve Reich. The key sequence is perhaps the one where the protagonist and the boy investigate a room comprised solely of drawers that overflow with items and objects.

In contrast to *The Unnameable Little Broom*'s brown pallor, this film is marked by a wintry grey. The film feels post-modern with its emphasis on knowledge. The ending suggests the boy's thought and perception being reconstituted by the Svankmajer puppet, animation being used to open up our sense of perception.

The Brothers Quay most celebrated short is widely regarded as *Street of Crocodiles*, based on the story by Bruno Schulz that was originally titled *Cinnamon Shops*. Schulz is noted for his intense short stories and erotic fiction, and his longer-lasting legacy may not be his literature but a series of murals that he painted during the Second World War and the Holocaust. Schulz was living and working in his hometown of Drohobycz in Poland when the Nazis invaded. Schulz was protected by a Nazi officer who ordered Schulz to paint the Nazi officer's son's bedroom walls with fairy-tale murals. These murals were only uncovered in 2001.

The story of *Street of Crocodiles* is set around a district of Prague named Street of Crocodiles. The film begins with a middle-aged man (live action) going and looking into a kinetoscope at a provincial library. A drop of the man's saliva animates the puppet characters. The world concocted by the film is very much a subterranean one of passages, doorways and shelves. Music, played predominantly on a violin, remains insistent in the film. A sense of sinister magic pervades from the outset as screws loosen themselves from decaying window frames. A doll-like child examines the free-moving screws, engaging with them, attuned to their magic. The man appears and is less at ease in this world. Indistinct and distorted voices are heard on the soundtrack, contributing to mood but not making what could be considered narrative sense.

Reality slips and slides furiously in the film and the camera lovingly tracks around the spaces. Dolls with shining eyes confront the puppet man. One of the dolls conducts the other to life and they remove the man's head and create a new character. A map is pulled apart and a slab of meat appears. The illusion of the animation process is foregrounded and delighted in by The Brothers Quay. Anatomy and history are key to the film which ends with an excerpt from Schulz's text despairing of contemporary life. For The Brothers Quay, Schulz's defiance is emblematic of their stance in relation to the received idea of animation. They boldly plough a genuinely maverick furrow with their work, creating what they regard not so much as dream worlds but alternative realities.

In 1995, The Brothers Quay produced their first feature-length film that combined live action and animation. This was called *Institute Benjamata* and was based on the work of proto-Surrealist writer Robert Walser's book *Jakob von Gunten*. This was followed by a BBC commission for their Sound on Film International project whereby filmmakers put visuals to existing music. This is how the Quays typically worked, commissioning music for their animated shorts which they would then build their visuals around. The twenty-minute film they produced for the BBC project was called *In Absentia* and was based around a piece of music called *Zwei Paare* by Karlheinz Stockhausen. The narrative that the Quays devised was based on a woman in a psychiatric hospital writing to a man outside. The film was lit almost exclusively with available, natural light. This was designed to give some sense of the divine to the images in a tip of the hat to one of their key non-animation heroes, Andrei Tarkowsky, who made films such as the stunning *Andrei Rublev* and *Solaris*.

John and Faith Hubley are regarded as principal figures in the American independent short form of animation. John Hubley worked in animation between 1935 and 1977 and went for a visual design that ran contrary to the prevailing taste for realism made popular by the Disney style. Hubley began by working at the Disney studio (as an art director on *Bambi* for example) but eventually left when creativity seemed to be curbed.

In contrast to these male-dominated animated high jinks, there is the long-lasting, quality work of the late Faith Hubley, a real star of the accessible short form animated film. When she married her husband, the late John Hubley, they had just two vows: to eat dinner with their children and make one independent animated film every year. They worked prodigiously.

The project that caused Hubley perhaps most consternation was his animated film *The Brotherhood of Man* which was regarded as pro-Communist. Partly because of the reaction to this project, Hubley's independent work was affected and Hubley became involved in commercials, creating numerous animated pieces and winning countless awards. At the same time, he and Faith produced one-off pieces as independents, notably *Moonbird*, *The Adventures of an* * and *Everybody Rides the Carousel*.

In the opinion of some animation historians, Faith Hubley was perhaps undervalued as a collaborator of her husband, animation having long been dominated by men. The last film Faith made with her husband was *A Doonesbury Special* based on the Gary Trudeau cartoon strip. In the wake of her husband's death, Faith continued working with great success. Her first solo film was *Women of the World*. She also made a film called *My Universe Inside Out* about child abuse and a fractured childhood.

Faith Hubley was less concerned with linear narrative and much more with tone and something more impressionistic. Her film *Seers and Clowns* (1994) married the spoken word of Native American Chief Seattle with images of human achievement and failure. *Witch Madness* (1999) was about the treatment of women and *The Big Bang and Other Creation Myths* (1981) celebrated her love of mythology. Faith Hubley died in 2001, having been widely celebrated and honoured at the Cannes, Venice and London Film Festivals. In 2000, she was awarded The Golden Gate Persistence of Vision Award at the San Francisco International Film Festival.

Other mavericks of the animation form include Lotte Reiniger who worked almost always alone creating magical silhouette animation often based on old folktales. French animator Michel Ocelot is another notable figure with films such as *La Princesse Insensible*, *La Reine Cruelle* and *Les Trois Inventeurs* which uses paper cut-outs in relief. The Leeds Animation Workshop has produced socially committed, simply designed animation. By contrast, and maybe a little more in keeping with the Eastern European tradition, is the work of British animator Dave Borthwick, whose most famous work is *The Secret Adventures of Tom Thumb*. In it, live action and stop motion meet with the actor being moved one frame at a time. Wendy Tilby is a star of Canadian animation with films such as *Strings*, which had images composed from progressive paintings on glass.

DON BLUTH

The Secret of Nimh (1982)

(82 minutes)

Directed by Don Bluth
Written by Don Bluth, Will Finn, Gary Goldman, John Pomeroy

Produced by Don Bluth, Gary Goldman, John Pomeroy
Executive Producers: Mel Griffin, Rich Irvine, James L Stewart
Music: Jerry Goldsmith
Cinematography: Bill Butler, Joe Jiuliano, Jeffrey Melquist,
Charles Warren
Sound: Walter A Gest, Stan Levine, Kevin O' Connell, John
Roesch
Special Effects: Dorse Lanpher, Tom Hush, Bruce Heller
Animation: Will Finn, Heidi Guedel, Emily Jiuliano, Skip
Jones, Dan Kuenster, Linda Miller, David Molina, Lorna
Pomeroy, Dave Spafford, Kevin M Wurzer

BUDGET: $7 million

BOX OFFICE: $10 million

RELEASE DATE: June 1982

CERTIFICATE: G U

VOICES: Elizabeth Hartman (*Mrs Brisby*), Derek Jacobi (*Nicodemus*), John Carradine (*Great Owl*), Dom DeLuise (*Jeremy*), Arthur Malet (*Mr Ages*), Hermione Baddeley (*Aunt Shrew*), Peter Strauss (*Justin*), Shannon Doherty (*Teresa*), Will Wheaton (Martin), Paul Shenar (Jenner)

TAGLINE: Right before your eyes and beyond your wildest dreams.

STORYLINE: A dark room and candlelight. A gnarled hand writes in an ancient book in a shining, fiery script. 'Our world is changing. We cannot stay here much longer,' intones a wizened voice.

A farm and the field beyond it. A rusting old combine harvester is home to Mr Ages, an old but wise and bumbling inventor and potion maker. Into his makeshift home comes a mouse, Mrs Brisby, asking his help for her son Timmy, who is suffering from a fever. Mrs Brisby lives as a single mother with her children in a stone on the edge of a field that will soon be ploughed. Mr Ages diagnoses Mrs Brisby's son as having pneumonia and concocts a medicine for her to take to him.

On her way home, Mrs Brisby untangles a bumbling, fast-talking crow called Jeremy. Her situation is imperilled when Jeremy riles the farm cat who gives chase. Mrs Brisby drops the medicine but it is retrieved by

Jeremy. A new friendship is formed. Mrs Brisby gives Timmy the medication. Auntie Shrew arrives at the Brisby home to announce that moving day is very near. The field will be ploughed and the home is under threat.

At the farmhouse the farmer's wife talks to her husband about a phone call they have had from NIMH (National Institute of Mental Health) about the rats on their farm and whether they are displaying any odd behaviour.

The next day, Mrs Brisby sees the tractor heading across the field and towards her home. Racing to get to Timmy and her other children Mrs Brisby is entangled on the plough though Auntie Shrew rescues her and knocks the tractor out of commission just in time. Mrs Brisby is sad and she longs for the company of her husband, Jonathan. Auntie Shrew says that Mrs Brisby should go to see Great Owl for advice. It is a dangerous-sounding mission.

Mrs Brisby, with Jeremy as pilot, flies to a ravaged and frightening forest and into the tree where the Owl lives. When she explains who she is, and hence her marriage to Jonathan, the Owl seems more willing to help her sort out where she can move to. He advises her to go to the rosebush on the farm and see Nicodemus. The rosebush is home to the super-intelligent rats.

Mrs Brisby goes to the rosebush and ventures inside. A rat tries to block her progress. Mr Ages takes Mrs Brisby to a council meeting. It emerges that the rat Jenner is keen to take power. He wants the rats to stay in the rosebush and continue stealing electricity and resources; Nicodemus wants the rats to move to Thorn Valley and live from their own efforts. Jenner plans to kill Nicodemus. Mr Ages takes Mrs Brisby to where Nicodemus resides and he tells Mrs Brisby the secret of Nimh and of how the rats were transformed from city rats to super-intelligent when they were used for medical experiments. Several mice were also experimented on, of which one was Jonathan. It was he who made their escape from the facility possible. Nicodemus gives Mrs Brisby an all-powerful amulet.

Mrs Brisby prepares to return home for the move somewhere safer, out of the harmful way of the tractor. She is then caught by the farmer's son and she is put in a cage. She overhears a phone call in which she discovers that NIMH will arrive the next day and destroy the rosebush. Mrs Brisby escapes and goes to tell the rats. The rats are busy moving Mrs Brisby's house to safety. Jenner murders Nicodemus during this and is then confronted by Chief Guard, Justin. Jenner perishes. Mrs Brisby's home, her children inside, begins to sink in the mud, but the power of the amulet saves the day. The rats go to Thorn Valley and Mrs Brisby and her family start life again in a new part of the field.

THE DRAWING BOARD: Famously, in the late 1970s the Disney animation studio experienced testing times as it struggled to maintain its focus on creating strong animated features in the aftermath of Walt Disney's death. On 13 September 1979, three animators, followed by another fourteen artists, resigned from the studio, unhappy with the quality of the work being produced at the studio. The three animators who led this departure were Gary Goldman, John Pomeroy and Don Bluth. During their time at Disney and in an effort to keep their love of animation alive, these three men worked on their own animated short in Bluth's garage. That project was called *Banjo the Woodpile Cat*. Bluth's commitment was a desire to 'preserve this valiant art form'. He felt that Disney, while investing in technology, were not investing as much energy in narrative.

In January 1980, with financing in place from Aurora (an outfit that had been formed by two ex-Disney animation executives), Don Bluth Productions began production on their debut feature *The Secret of Nimh*. Reading articles from the time of the film's release in 1982 (see **RECOGNITION**) it is fascinating just how excited animation fans were that a classically animated feature had been made. The film was regarded as heralding a renaissance in animation. Had it ultimately proved more commercially popular this might have been the case but *The Secret of Nimh*, aimed at family audiences, was released the same summer as *ET: The Extra-Terrestrial*.

Bluth had read Robert C. O'Brien's novel *Mrs Frisby and the Rats of NIMH* when at Disney but the book was rejected as a possible basis for an animated feature. Bluth had a supporter at the studio in Ken Anderson. The novel had won a Newbery Award and Bluth, Pomeroy and Goldman were sure it would make a compelling feature. Twenty years on the film has a cult following.

The film was released by MGM/United Artists to a real fanfare in publications like *Starlog*, *Fantastic Films* and the much-missed *Comics Scene* magazine.

At the time of the film's release Bluth commented that, 'The world needs heroes now more than ever . . . I animate because it brings joy to people, and joy, when it's shared, is absolutely explosive.'

After *The Secret of Nimh*, Bluth went on to make animated features such as *An American Tail* (1986), *The Land Before Time* (1988) and

Thumbelina (1994). When *An American Tail* was released in December 1986 it was the highest-grossing animated feature ever. The film was as fluidly animated as *The Secret of Nimh* but was less dark, perhaps resulting in a more commercial venture.

In the mid-1980s, Bluth transferred his base to Dublin. At the time of *NIMH*, Bluth proposed an intriguing follow-up that has never come to pass: a post-apocalyptic piece in which animals and humans work together for the future. Another project that was put into development was Robert Towne's *Little Blue Whale*. This project was developed during the period Bluth was investigating video games with *Dragon's Lair* and *Space Ace*. *The Pebble and the Penguin* (1995) was a movie Bluth did make, but it was poorly received due to changes at MGM during its production which resulted in the project being affected in terms of production value. *Anastasia* (1997) was a relatively successful feature release and certainly Bluth's favourite after *The Secret of Nimh*. Bluth is now based back in the United States.

INSPIRATIONS: Bluth's key informing source is the classical animation of the Disney studio from the 1930s and 1940s. The rich watercolour backgrounds to be found in *Snow White and the Seven Dwarfs*, *Pinocchio* and *Bambi* inspire similarly rich environments in *The Secret of Nimh*. Like these Disney films, Bluth's effort is strongest in its darkest, moodiest moments.

TOON TEAM: Don Bluth's lifelong association with animation began when, as a child, he was overwhelmed by Disney's work. In 1956 Bluth got a job as an assistant animator at Disney working under John Lounsberry on *Sleeping Beauty*. After eighteen months at the studio, Bluth took some time out to teach in Argentina for the Mormon Church and then went to Brigham Young University to study English. In 1967 he joined Filmation as a layout artist in Saturday morning animation. In 1971 he returned to Disney where they had established a new animation training programme. Bluth worked on *Robin Hood* (1973) and *Winnie the Pooh and Tigger Too* (1974). Bluth was a directing animator on *The Rescuers* (1977) and director of animation on *Pete's Dragon* (1977). Bluth also directed and produced a short for the studio called *The Small One* (1978) set around the Nativity and a donkey. He served as an animator on *The Fox and the Hound* before finally leaving. At the time of the release of *The Secret of Nimh*, Bluth commented that, 'Animation is a beautiful art form that is in danger of dying out.'

VOCAL TALENT: The vocal cast for *The Secret of Nimh* includes Derek Jacobi, Hermione Baddeley and Dom DeLuise.

Derek Jacobi's other screen credits include *Little Dorrit* (Christine Erzardt, 1988), *Henry V* (Kenneth Branagh, 1989), *Dead Again* (Kenneth Branagh, 1991), *Cadfael* the TV series (1994), *Gladiator* (Ridley Scott, 2000) and *The Revenger's Tragedy* (Alex Cox, 2002). Elizabeth Hartman had starred in *You're a Big Boy Now* (Francis Ford Coppola, 1966) and was Oscar-nominated for *A Patch of Blue* (Guy Green, 1965). Arthur Malet had appeared in *Mary Poppins* (Ken Anderson, 1964), *Ace Eli and Rodger of the Skies* (Bill Sampson, 1973), *Young Frankenstein* (Mel Brooks, 1974), *Halloween* (John Carpenter, 1978), *Hook* (Steven Spielberg, 1991), *Toys* (Barry Levinson, 1992) and *Anastasia* (Don Bluth, 1995).

Dom DeLuise had come to mind for Bluth, Pomeroy and Goldman independently of each other. He had starred in his own American TV show in the late 1960s. He had appeared in *Blazing Saddles* (Mel Brooks, 1974), *Smokey and the Bandit* (Hal Needham, 1980), *The Cannonball Run* (Hal Needham, 1981), *Haunted Honeymoon* (Gene Wilder, 1987) and the animated features *All Dogs Go to Heaven* (Don Bluth, 1989) and *An American Tail: Fievel Goes West* (Simon Wells and Phil Nibbelink, 1991).

Hermione Baddeley had appeared in *Scrooge* (Brian Desmond Hurst, 1951) and *Mary Poppins*. John Carradine had appeared in *The Grapes of Wrath* (John Ford, 1939), *Boxcar Bertha* (Martin Scorsese, 1972), *The Shootist* (Don Siegel, 1976), *The Howling* (Joe Dante, 1980) and *Peggy Sue Got Married* (Francis Ford Coppola, 1986).

INK, PAINT AND HARD WORK: Production on *The Secret of Nimh* ran from January 1980 until June 1982. The film is noted for the richness of its colour scheme. More than 600 colours were deployed in the film and over 1,000 backgrounds were created. All the backgrounds were created and screened alone within the story continuity so that the filmmakers could decide if more of less of a certain tone was needed.

In keeping with the project's fervent commitment to rich and believable animation, three-dimensional sets were built to allow the team to block out the most dynamic movement. Background paintings were done in wash, tempera and some acrylics.

Roughly a third of the film was storyboarded in colour but time prevented that. The storyboards were shot in continuity with the dialogue track playing. Each character was animated in a key pose, with a position for every eighth frame. A rough test with a line drawing of the character was then made of every other frame of movement. These tests were refined into a sequence that was ready for the in-between work and a film test was shot of the pencil drawings on paper.

THEME: At the heart of this very gentle adventure film is a story about the capacity for courage.

The value of community and selflessness also underpin the endearing fantasy and there is an ecological aspect to the film that is rooted in man's insensitivity to the fragile world underfoot.

The world is also shown as having potential for magic, so that what is unseen is as important as what is seen. Ultimately, the film follows a classic birth-of-the-hero storyline.

STYLISH TOONS: The fluidity and personality of movement was not the only level of commitment displayed in the film. Also evident is a richness in the application of various lighting and other effects that had not been deployed much in animated features for many years. Dorse Lanpher was the artist charged with the responsibility of achieving these effects. Lanpher explained the concept: 'What we've attempted to do is give the picture a lot of depth by using heavy colour and a lot of animated shadows.' The film employs extensive backlighting and also a particular illusion of fire. Fire is not only painted in *NIMH*, but also cut out as a design with a coloured gel placed over it which is then backlit with a strong light. The film is then passed over the backlight a second time with the lens out of focus which makes the fire appear hotter and with a halo effect.

Split exposures were used to create shadows and translucent images. Six months were spent designing two new cameras, as existing cameras could not achieve the necessary multiplane camerawork. It took fourteen months to build the new cameras.

To create realistic motion for some of the objects in the film speed photography of models was used. A model would be shot at 96 frames per second in order to get the maximum possible sharpness for the movement, and every fourth frame would be printed optically and rotoscoped to provide the basis for the art. This process was used with the boat, the lantern elevator and the bird cage. It did not work for the model of the tractor as it did not look believable.

Details are all. Flames were outlined in red or yellow rather than black. Jeremy was outlined with grey to distinguish the parts of his black-feathered body.

One shot contained twelve separate elements, redolent of the richness found in *Pinocchio*. The scene in question in *NIMH* included a background, two characters, their shadows, a Bunsen burner flame, a rope and bubbles rising to the surface of a liquid.

There is a lovely shot where the camera widens out to show the Brisby family, minute in their little home. The silence and gentility of the moment recalls several similar moments in *Snow White and the Seven Dwarfs* when the camera widens out to reveal the dwarfs' cottage in its bucolic and peaceful setting.

The richness of the colour palette is matched by the naturalism of the character animation. Consider Mrs Brisby's anxious face in the moment before she leaps to her escape from the cage in the farmer's house. Or the tender pat the gnarled hands of Nicodemus make on the box containing the amulet at the beginning of the film.

The film's cinematic pans and tilts and fast cuts for action invest it with a rhythm. The scary scenes are indeed menacing and the contrast between the rich, orange glows of home contrast with the greys and blues of the Owl's tree. Colour codes the emotions: when Justin and Jenner duel, the sky is a bloody red; Nicodemus is crowned by soft pastel colours.

The sincerity of the film is very winning. It is clearly a family film and its very positive message of courage and community is a useful one for kids to pick up on, but it does not feel preachy.

A nice shot of the Brisby family framed by the window of their home widens out to suggest their loneliness in the big world.

CHARACTER SKETCH: To create the right colour scheme for each character ten to twelve different colour models were made.

Mrs Brisby is a soft-hearted, single mother mouse for whom the adventure brings out strength and capacity for courage, partly through her own endeavour but also through the memory and legacy of her husband's bravery.

Jeremy is comic relief – the classic sidekick who helps Mrs Brisby out on her adventure, his good nature and eagerness to please outweighing his clumsiness.

Great Owl and Nicodemus are the stand-out, showy characters, both of them menacing and benevolent.

Jenner is efficiently nasty and Justin, the rat with whom Jenner duels, is given a romantic leading man persona that Mrs Brisby is drawn to.

Mr Ages is a typically bumbling old fuddy duddy with immense spectacles.

TOON TUNES: Jerry Goldsmith's lavish, magical and often intense score lends drama and richness to the film. It recalls his other score of 1982 for the film *Poltergeist* (Tobe Hooper) with its choirs and brass. In keeping with the film's sincerity and focus it has not been conceived as a musical. Instead it works very well with a straightforward, sincere score. Goldsmith's long career has yielded countless classic scores that include *The Blue Max* (John Guillermin, 1966), *Chinatown* (Roman Polanski, 1974), *The Omen* (Richard Donner, 1976), *Alien* (Ridley Scott, 1979), *Legend* (Ridley Scott, 1985), *Total Recall* (Paul Verhoeven, 1990), *Mulan* (Tony Bancroft and Barry Cook, 1998) and *Looney Tunes Back in Action* (Joe Dante, 2003).

Goldsmith's rich score for *The Secret of Nimh* anticipates his work on *Legend* (Ridley Scott, 1985). Goldsmith had not scored an animated feature before but approached it just as he would a live-action feature, giving the music a density and maturity. Goldsmith's score was performed by the National Philharmonic Orchestra and augmented by the Ambrosian Singers. Paul Williams wrote and sang the song 'Flying Dreams'.

The Secret of Nimh soundtrack listing: 'Main Title', 'Allergic Reaction/Athletic Type', 'Flying Dreams – Lullaby', 'The Tractor', 'The Sentry Reel – The Story of NIMH', 'Escape from NIMH – in Disguise', 'Flying Dreams', 'Step Inside My House', 'No Thanks', 'Moving Day', 'The House Rising', 'Flying High/End Title'. This soundtrack listing refers to the 1996 reissue, which arranges the original track recordings in the order they appear in the film.

TOON TALK:

The Wise Owl: 'You can unlock any door if you only have the key.'

Auntie Shrew: 'Oh rats!'

OTHER SIMILAR FILMS: Don Bluth's follow-up was the Steven Spielberg-produced *An American Tail* (1986), also featuring a mouse far from home. His other output is *The Land Before Time* (1988), *All Dogs Go to Heaven* (1989), *Thumbelina* (1994), *Titan A.E.* (2000). In the early 1980s Bluth had attempted to develop an adaptation of *Beauty and the Beast*; in the months following its being shelved, the *American Tail* project came to Bluth.

Bluth's involvement in *An American Tail* came about because Spielberg had expressed an interest in working with him after watching *The Secret of Nimh*. It had been Jerry Goldsmith, working on Spielberg's production of the Tobe Hooper film *Poltergeist,* which Goldsmith scored, who urged the director-producer to watch Bluth's great labour of love. The film opened on 21 November 1986 and its budget of $9.6 million returned $47.5 million at the box office. Spielberg's involvement was in suggesting amendments to sequences and, as it was his first production, he was tentative. *An American Tail*'s story had been written by Judy Freudberg who also went on to write the storyline for *The Land Before Time*. The success of *An American Tail* arguably encouraged Disney to roll their sleeves up and get back into animated features.

After the production of *An American Tail*, Bluth continued to collaborate with Steven Spielberg on *The Land Before Time* (initially *The Land Before Time Began*). This time George Lucas, the director of *THX 1138* (1971), *American Graffiti* (1973) and *Star Wars* (1977) joined as a co-executive producer with Spielberg. The project represented their enthusiasm for creating movies for young people – in this case very young people – though some critics complained the child lost and found was a little too familiar after the previous film. The now-familiar Bluth richness of colour and environment was in place.

The Land Before Time was released in November 1988 and tells the story of five young dinosaurs journeying to find the paradise-like sanctuary of The Great Valley. The leader of these dinosaur kids is Littlefoot, a Brontosaurus. His pals are Cera, a plucky and feisty triceratops, Spike, the dim-witted stegosaurus and Ducky, an Anatosaurus. Their journey also teams them up with an orphan Pterodactyl called Petrie. *The Land Before Time* was produced in Ireland at Sullivan Bluth Studios.

The original story idea for *The Land Before Time* came from Spielberg in April 1986 and the storyline was developed by Bluth, Lucas, John Pomeroy and Gary Goldman. The screenplay was written by Stu Krieger. John Pomeroy also served as directing animator on the project. Lucas's role was initially fine-tuning Spielberg's ideas – for example, it was Lucas who suggested making Cera a tough little girl rather than a tough little boy. In May 1987 there was a screening of the half-finished film in London for Lucas and Spielberg. The session resulted in certain characters being refined. A two-day story session with Lucas ensued, out of which came 80 per cent of the final narrative. One of the significant changes made to the film on Spielberg and Lucas's input was the softening of some of the more intense material, such as the Sharptooth attack which they felt would most likely terrify young children.

One of the animation challenges of the film was the creation of subtle and delicate expression in characters who did not have hands. Thus everything was expressed facially and through the tilt of a neck. All the film's backgrounds are in lush watercolour. Browns, yellows and reds create a harsh environment for the dying world and the Great Valley is dominated by soft, bright pastel colours and shades.

For the death of Littlefoot's mother, the team researched heavily to achieve as much emotional effect as possible. The sequence was almost dropped, but psychologists were consulted and their advice led to the creation of a character called Rooter who befriends Littlefoot after his mother's death.

As is so frequently evident, animation yields fine opportunities for lush, melodic music and *The Land Before Time* is no exception. The film eschews a musical format with the only song being a Diana Ross tune called 'If We Hold on Together' which runs over the end credits. The film's music is very classical and expansive, running for much of its duration. The soundtrack was again composed by James Horner and is a high-water mark of his animated film score body of work. The choir for the film was from King's College School, Wimbledon who had also supplied fantastic choral accompaniment on the film score for *Willow* (Ron Howard, 1988) also composed by Horner.

By the mid-1980s, James Horner was well established as a new composing talent and his work is to be found on many films, including a run of films *StarTrek II: The Wrath of Khan* (Nicholas Meyer, 1982), *Cocoon* (Ron Howard, 1985), *Field of Dreams* (Phil Alden Robinson, 1989), *Glory* (Ed Zwick, 1989), *The Rocketeer* (Joe Johnston, 1991), *Legends of the Fall* (Ed Zwick, 1994), *Casper* (Brad Silberling, 1995), *Balto* (Simon Wells, 1995), *Jumanji* (Joe Johnston, 1995), *Titanic* (James Cameron, 1997).

After the success of *The Land Before Time*, billed as a Lucas/Spielberg presentation, Don Bluth went on to make *All Dogs Go to Heaven*, *Anastasia*, *The Penguin and the Pebble* and *Titan A.E.* but sadly none of these films made as much of a popular or artistic impact as his 1980s projects. Bluth is currently considering a movie based on the popular *Dragons Lair* computer game of the 1980s.

RECOGNITION: The reviews for the film tended to mention its importance in the greater scheme of animation: 'It's a spectacular return to the shimmering, mesmerising deep focus animation associated with Disney's classic period . . . and the villains are as primally terrifying as cartoon villains should be' (*Time Out*); 'A richly animated and skilfully structured film that should test whether there still remains a family audience for new Disney-type pictures.' (*Variety*); and 'An animated feature that Disney should be making.' (*Starburst*).

AWARDS: In 1983 *The Secret of Nimh* won the award for Best Animated Feature at the Academy of Science Fiction, Horror and Fantasy awards.

HOME VIEWING: *The Secret of Nimh* has quite a cult following. The film is currently available as a very bare-bones DVD, the only supplementary material being the original trailer. Given the film's importance in the revival of classical feature animation in the 1980s, one might hope for a 'special edition' at some time.

COMMENT: 'In this Age of Realism and Naturalism, what too many people don't see I think is that the truth isn't just physical facts; it's also feelings.' Don Bluth.

VERDICT: *The Secret of Nimh* is a compact, tightly structured film whose ambition to function as a compelling and serious piece of work shines through as brightly as the fiery script written at the beginning of the film. Its rich colours and detailed backgrounds enhance the drama. The voice work is very strong and varied and there is an emotional impact to the material, though the closing few moments after the climax don't quite have the emotional completeness that makes all that has preceded it so satisfying.

BRAD BIRD

The Iron Giant (1999)

(86 minutes)

Directed by Brad Bird
Screenplay Brad Bird (Screen Story), Tim McCanlies
(Screenplay) based on the novel *The Iron Man* by Ted Hughes
Produced by Allison Abbate, Des McAnuff
Executive Producer: Pete Townsend, John Walker
Original Music: Michael Kamen

Cinematography: Steven Wilzbach

Editor: Darren T Holmes

Production Design: Mark Whiting

Art Direction: Alan Bodner

Sound Recordist: Chad Algarin

Sound Effects Editor: Beau Borders

Effects Department Head: Allen Foster

BUDGET: $48 million

BOX OFFICE: $23,154, 305

RELEASE DATE: August 1999

CERTIFICATE: U

VOICES: Jennifer Aniston (*Annie Hughes*), Harry Connick Jr (*Dean McCoppin*), Vin Diesel (*The Iron Giant*), James Gammon (*Marv Locah/Floyd Turbeaux, General Sudokoff*), Cloris Leachman (*Mrs Lynley Tensedge*), Christopher McDonald (*Kent Mansley*), John Mahoney (*General Rogard*), Eli Marienthal (*Hogarth Hughes*), M Emmet Walsh (*Earl Stutz*)

TAGLINE: It came from outer space!

STORYLINE: Outer space, 1957. The Sputnik satellite arcs through the sky and passes Earth. A moment later the silence of space is filled by a roaring fireball that plummets towards Earth.

Off the coast of Maine it is night and a fishing boat is caught in stormy seas. The pilot of the boat watches a fireball strike the sea somewhere.

The next day young Hogarth Hughes rides through Rockwell town and visits his mother at work in the local diner. Hogarth talks about wanting a pet but his mother is reluctant. Hogarth gets chatting with local beatnik Dean McCoppin and he and Hogarth strike up a friendship. At home later that evening, Hogarth's mother calls. She is going to work late. Hogarth goes out on to the roof and looks at the forest (his torch beam weakening the further it shines). He goes and investigates.

Hogarth comes across a power plant and he gets a glimpse of the visitor as he watches the Iron Giant being electrocuted by the power lines. Hogarth intervenes and saves the Giant.

Intrigued, the next day Hogarth returns to the forest but there is no sign of the Iron Giant. A government man named Kent Mansley turns up to investigate what has been going on but he is sceptical. Hogarth finally meets the Iron Giant again and they befriend one another.

Realising that the Iron Giant feasts on scrap metal, Hogarth takes his new friend to Dean's scrapyard. Hogarth asks if Dean can hide the Iron Giant. Dean is reluctant, though he is intrigued by the 'creature'. Mansley sets about trying to find the Iron Giant, regarding it as a threat to American citizens. Mansley interrogates Hogarth about the Giant, having found evidence that the boy knows about it. Mansley calls in the military.

Hogarth and the Iron Giant play and Hogarth and Dean realise that the Giant reacts aggressively – and destructively – in self-defence.

The Iron Giant finds himself rescuing two boys from a rooftop in town. The public look on in wonder and in the next moment The Iron Giant is subjected to a volley of fire and artillery. Hogarth and Dean run to try and ensure the safety of their friend. Mansley suggests that the nuclear bomb would be the best way to despatch the Iron Giant, who converts himself into an astonishing robotic arsenal of firepower in self-defence. In a moment of terror, Mansley orders the missile fired at the Iron Giant. Hogarth and the Giant say goodbye as the missile closes in. The Iron Giant rockets into the sky and intercepts the bomb, both objects exploding. The town is spared.

THE DRAWING BOARD: In the summer of 1999 when George Lucas's *Star Wars: Episode 1 – The Phantom Menace* was released, another fantasy film sneaked out but without much fanfare. It has since gone on to garner a real cult following and is acknowledged as one of the best animated features of the new era, reminding audiences of the charm and expressive warmth of classical, hand-drawn and painted animation.

The Iron Giant began as an animated feature when it was taken to Warner Brothers as a musical based on Ted Hughes's novel, *The Iron Man*. When Warner Brothers decided not to pursue the *Ray Gunn* project (about a gun with a soul) they asked Bird what he might be interested in from their development slate. For Bird the image of the giant and the boy was compelling. Before his death, Ted Hughes read and loved a script for the film that Bird sent him.

Warner Brothers, though, were concerned about their commercial prospects with animation because their previous animated feature, *Quest for Camelot,* had not been popular.

Subsequently, Bird was given a year less than a typical animated feature of this type would normally be allocated, and about a third less the budget of comparable movies from the Disney and DreamWorks studios. At one point, Warner Brothers had encouraged Bird to include several new characters to expand the film's merchandise potential but Bird stood firm that this was the story.

Inevitably, there are differences between screenplay and finished film. Thus, one draft has the Iron Giant's parts distributed in India after the explosion, where a young boy gets an elephant to haul what is thought to be a meteorite out of a crater. The little boy discovers it is the head of the Iron Giant. A closing image shows one of the Iron Giant's hands orbiting Earth and finally reaching back towards it.

Another planned sequence would have served as something of an origins sequence, showing a planet full of Iron Giants at war. This material could have been intercut with the power station and deer scenes, creating some sense of a dream the Iron Giant is lost in.

INSPIRATIONS: Ted Hughes's source novel *The Iron Man* is the most obvious inspiration, notably with its theme of regeneration. The concept of the boy becoming father to the giant was a key point of interest.

TOON TEAM: *The Iron Giant* was directed by writer–director Brad Bird, a contemporary of Tim Burton and John Lasseter whose career has perhaps taken a little longer to hit the so-called big time. Bird recognised his love of animation as a child growing up in Oregon. When he was fourteen he sent Disney his version of *The Tortoise and the Hare* and became Milt Kahl's protégé.

In the mid-1980s Bird had made a short called *Family Dog* (drawn by Tim Burton) which aired as an episode of Steven Spielberg's uneven but intriguing *Amazing Stories* anthology series of 1985–87. Bird also co-wrote the live-action, special-effects fantasy **batteries not included* (directed by Matthew Robbins in 1987 for Spielberg's Amblin Entertainment) and served as executive consultant on *The Simpsons*. **batteries not included* relates to *The Iron Giant* as it too is about two magical high-tech strangers from another galaxy who befriend characters in need of help.

The Iron Giant marked Bird's feature debut. In the mid-1980s, Bird had been offered several other opportunities by Spielberg but decided to follow other avenues, which included the ill-fated movie *Little Monsters* (Richard Alan Greenberg, 1989). Spielberg had been interested in doing

Family Dog as a series, but this was before *The Simpsons* hit big and a TV series was still an untested format. One of Bird's other concepts had been a feature called *Ray Gunn,* an action film noir that has yet to be made. Bird also went to work on *The Simpsons* as key animator for any episodes involving Krusty the Klown.

The screenplay for *The Iron Giant* was written by Tim McCanlies from the original story. Many of the animators had worked on Warner Brothers' previous animated feature *Quest for Camelot.*

The design for the Iron Giant himself was by Bird's old friend, Joe Johnston, a veteran of Industrial Light and Magic where he had worked as a designer on the original *Star Wars* trilogy (1977–83). Johnston's design was slightly amended by Mark Whiting, the film's production designer, and Steve Markowski, the lead animator.

VOCAL TALENT: Jennifer Aniston is most well known for her great comic work on the long-running, era-defining sitcom *Friends* where she played Rachel. She has also appeared in *She's the One* (Ed Burns, 1996) and *Bruce Almighty* (Tom Shadyac, 2003).

Harry Connick Jr has appeared in *Memphis Belle* (Michael Caton-Jones, 1990) and *Copycat* (Jon Amiel, 1998).

Christopher McDonald (Mansley) is most noted for his comic role as Darryl in *Thelma & Louise* (Ridley Scott, 1991).

Vin Diesel, who voices The Iron Giant, got his breakthrough with a role in *Saving Private Ryan* (Steven Spielberg, 1998) before going on to *The Fast and the Furious* (Rob Cohen, 2001) and *xXx* (Rob Cohen, 2002).

INK, PAINT AND HARD WORK: The Iron Giant was a computer-animated character while the other characters were cel animated. The design philosophy was that the computer-animated character should look 2-D and not the 2-D characters made to look computer-generated.

A program was written to make the computer character's lines wobble almost infinitesimally to allow them to be less obviously computer generated.

The Iron Giant was shot in CinemaScope, emphasising the widescreen lushness of the visual design. Bird's rationale behind this was that the story was set in the 1950s and CinemaScope had been a staple of 1950s spectacles.

Critical to the project was planning, perhaps even more so than usual, given the film's restricted budget. Animatics for the film were created early on, allowing the team precisely to nail the dynamics of scenes beyond just static storyboards.

THEME: Maybe Brad Bird's big theme with *The Iron Giant* is the question of what constitutes heroism. The film also brings out, just enough, the 1950s American fear of anything non- and un-American and demonstrates how damaging such ignorance is. Hogarth is open, innocent and imaginative and these traits are all considered positive.

The film is a timely reminder of how cultural difference can become cultural diffidence and there is a powerful anti-military and anti-gun strain to the film. *The Iron Giant* is about peace and the value of difference. Living as a unique person is key to the film and one shot of Dean in his house/workshop includes a photo of Jack Kerouac on the wall in the background. Jack Kerouac was the figurehead of the Beat literary movement that promoted freedom and youthfulness and was regarded as a counter-cultural movement. Hogarth befriends Dean and they are characters who celebrate being a little bit outside the mainstream.

Rather like some of the Japanese anime films, but with a very different, more playful tone, *The Iron Giant* expresses an interest in the idea of the soul and whether it is possessed by machines. Of course, one of Brad Bird's other concepts for a feature is *Ray Gunn* about a gun with a soul. The conversation between Hogarth and the Iron Giant on this subject takes place in the junkyard under the stars, emphasising the eternity of their questions.

STYLISH TOONS: There is a very welcome gentility to the film that bears out Bird's opinion that too many films adopt a frantic pace as 'an attitude of panic . . .'

In the film's favour is the absence of a cute and funny sidekick or a villain who is too melodramatic for their own good.

The Iron Giant is a computer-animated character and this stylistic choice integrates well with the classically animated (ink and paint) human characters.

The film's autumnal time frame results in rich auburns and golds as the story unfolds largely around the forest of Maine. While it is easy to focus on the immense Iron Giant bestriding the Maine forests, another successful detail of the film is its lighting effects. Watch the scene when Hogarth goes into the forest at night with his torch on, or the scene when Mansley interrogates Hogarth.

That sense of joy that is so central to animation is well in place in *The Iron Giant*, which delights in the difference in size. Two of the most emotional moments are based on small but immense gestures. The first is when Hogarth and the Iron Giant see a deer in the forest; the Iron Giant lowers his huge hand to the deer who puts its nose to the Giant's finger. At the end of the film, there is a similar gesture, with Hogarth saying goodbye to the Giant. The sequence in the woods with the giant and the deer is a critical scene as it introduces the theme of hunter and hunted to the film in a nicely understated way.

The film mocks the whole Red Scare ethos present in American society during the 1950s. The film features a fictional bomb-drop information film and Hogarth is shown reading a comic called *Red Scare*.

One of the best visual jokes in the film, which is also laden with mystery and menace, is when the sailor in stormy waters thinks he sees a lighthouse beam. He is shocked when the beam seems to turn and double so that two shining eyes look down at him from the top of an unidentified towering frame standing in the sea.

Of animation and his aim for it, Brad Bird has said, 'I'm interested in showing that animated films are films first, and animation second.'

CHARACTER SKETCH: Amidst the fluidity of animation, strength of tone and shifts in tone and atmosphere, *The Iron Giant* is all the stronger for its terrific vocal characterisations.

Hogarth Hughes is a confident and smart but lonely boy, but he does not revel in self-pity. He is a little spiky and very assured and through his adventure he comes to understand a little more about the wider world when it 'invades' his hometown.

The Iron Giant is indeed a gentle giant whose loneliness matches Hogarth's.

Dean McCoppin is a nicely cool character, or 'cat', as he might refer to himself. His stubble, goatee and turtleneck sweater mark out his bohemian, peacenik credentials.

Annie Hughes, Hogarth's mother, is a stressed-out single mum whose loneliness is finally resolved by the end of the film.

Kent Mansley, the government agent, is richly drawn as a slightly buffoonish and certainly patronising government man who, by the end of the film, reveals a far more insidious side. Though funny on the surface his manner is far from appealing, especially when he tries to infect Hogarth with his blindness and prejudice motivated by fear of the unknown.

TOON TUNES: Established film music composer Michael Kamen created a very dramatic and far from cute score for the film that only enhances the drama. Like the rest of the film, the score is restrained and does not go for the easy emotional effect. Kamen's other credits include *Lethal Weapon* (Richard Donner, 1987), *Robin Hood: Prince of Thieves* (Kevin Reynolds, 1991), *X-Men* (Bryan Singer, 2000), *Open Range* (Kevin Costner, 2003) and the TV series *Band of Brothers* (various directors, 2001).

The Iron Giant's soundtrack: 'Eye of the Storm', 'Hogarth Hughes', 'Into the Forest', 'Giant Wakes', 'Come and Get It', 'Cat and Mouse', 'Train Wreck', 'You Can Fix Yourself?', 'Hand Underfoot', 'Bedtime Stories', 'We Gotta Hide', 'His Name is Dean', 'Eating Art', 'Space Can', 'Souls Don't Die', 'Contest of Wills', 'Army Arrives', 'Annie and Dean', 'He's a Weapon', 'Giant Discovered', 'Trance Former', 'No Following', 'Last Giant Piece'.

TOON TALK:
Dean: 'If we don't stick up for the kooks who will?'

OTHER SIMILAR FILMS: For all their tonal differences, perhaps the most analogous films are Japanese features such as *Akira* and *Ghost in the Shell* in that they all share an apocalyptic strain and a sense of the corruption in military power without responsibility. Closer to home, the story of an outsider finding their place in a world that is not always accommodating recalls *James and the Giant Peach*.

RECOGNITION: *Time Out* felt *The Iron Giant* was 'As entertaining as it's intelligent.'

AWARDS: Although it was only modestly successful commercially, *The Iron Giant* was instantly recognised for its creative strength. At the 2000 Annie Awards it won virtually every award, namely for Best Animated Theatrical Feature, Character Animation, Directing, Effects Animation, Music, Production Design, Stroyboarding, Voice Acting (Eli Marienthal) and Writing. At the 2000 BAFTA Awards it won the Children's Award and at the 2000 Hugo Awards was nominated for Best Dramatic Presentation. In 1999 it won the Los Angeles Film Critics Association award for Best Animation and in 2000 won the Las Vegas Film Critics Society Award for Best Animated Film.

HOME VIEWING: *The Iron Giant* is available on both VHS and DVD. At the time of writing a special edition DVD is imminent but is already available as a Region 3 disc. The special edition features an alternative opening sequence, feature-length commentary, thirteen branched featurettes, *The Voice of the Giant* featurette, analyses of the Annie Meets Kent scene and the Duck and Cover scene. There is also a still gallery, trailers and Easter Eggs.

COMMENT: 'I was and am willing to look foolish in an attempt to get you to feel something.' Brad Bird.

VERDICT: This film is too great to have been so little seen by people. It is a real animated film that spikes its sentiment and cuteness with parody and a sharp and simply drawn critique of American isolationism. *The Iron Giant* is a very small-scaled story that appeals so readily to the audience's understanding of what it is to be alone. In this way, it has similarities to *ET: The Extra-Terrestrial* (Steven Spielberg, 1982), *Lassie* (Daniel Petrie, 1994), *The Red Pony* (Lewis Milestone, 1949) and *The Black Stallion* (Carroll Ballard, 1979), though *The Iron Giant* is more political.

The animation is so simple and unfussy and delights in movement, sunlight and autumn colours. Also of note is the emotional impact of the voice-overs.

This is a really complete film and an example of classical, American animation at its best. The sunny, funny fantasy of the premise is nicely rooted in a more serious sense of what popular animation can be.

JAN SVANKMAJER

Acclaimed as a genius filmmaker, animator and a proponent of the form for forty years, Svankmajer is criminally unknown beyond real cineaste and animation circles. He has a following that includes Tim Burton and Terry Gilliam yet, in America especially, where so much animation is produced, Svankmajer is a relatively unknown quantity. When Svankmajer's and The Brothers Quay's work was toured they were given the collective title *The Alchemists of the Surreal: The Films of Jan Svankmajer and The Brothers Quay*.

Based in Prague, Svankmajer is a surrealist filmmaker for whom surrealism is not an aesthetic but a psychology. He is also a poet,

243

ceramicist and sculptor for whom animation is a way to explore the human psyche with a form and tone of animation that for some may shock, so far removed as it is from what most people would consider animation. Most of Svankmajer's career has been engaged with animated shorts. In 1988 his first animated feature was released, an adaptation of Lewis Carroll's *Alice in Wonderland* story. He followed this up with a feature-length animated piece based on the Faust legend.

Svankmajer is held in high regard for his engagement with the form, but Czech censorship has limited his audience beyond the keenest animation fan and cineaste. Svankmajer began his career working in the theatre but ultimately found he was unable to reach a public that would respond to his work. By some degree of chance he became involved with Laterna Magika where he first encountered film. Soon after this he became aware of a studio that had funds for a short film. The director who was due to make the short film pulled out. Svankmajer wrote a script which the studio approved and he made his first short, called *The Last Trick* which featured puppets and also actors in masks. One of his other celebrated shorts is *Down to the Cellar*. In the 1960s he produced ten animated shorts and won 21 international festival prizes with films such as *The Last Trick* (1964), *Punch and Judy* (1966) and *The Flat* (1968). In 1990 he was nominated for a BAFTA with his film *The Death of Stalinism in Bohemia*.

Svankmajer has been likened to David Lynch in the richness he finds in the logic of dreams. Svankmajer plumbs the richness of childhood imagery and feels that civilisation suppresses so many childhood impulses.

Svankmajer also taps into a folkloric heritage still conspicuous in Eastern Europe, just as his compatriot the composer Leos Janacek was influenced by his native Moravia and the folkloric modes of that region. So there is a tradition at work. Svankmajer's work taps into a *fin de siecle* sensibility that defined the twentieth century, namely an interest in the Gothic.

Svankmajer's work expresses allegorical images that centre on cellars, decay, menace, the hidden and the abnormal and certainly *Alice* oozes with such images and predilections.

Svankmajer's more recent film *Little Otik* tells of a log that is adopted by a couple who are unable to conceive a child. The film then charts the intense and darkly amusing effects of the log's coming to life with a taste for human flesh. Animation it is for sure, but is also a horror movie based on a Czech folktale. Of his work Svankmajer says, 'My creative work is not didactic, nor is it an attempt to make the viewer a better person.'

For Svankmajer, 'Objects conceal within themselves the events they've witnessed. I don't actually animate objects. I coerce their inner life out of them.' With this approach in mind it may come as no surprise that he finds computer animation a paradox, claiming that because none of the animated figures ever really existed as objects they bear no marks of real life. For Svankmajer, computer animation only pretends to be from this world.

Many of Svankmajer's films have been banned or limited in exhibition and his projects are hard to market and distribute. He has been labelled the Alchemist of the Surreal.

Svankmajer has been a member of the Czech Surrealist Group since 1970, the group having been established in 1934. For Svankmajer computer animation is an aberration in that 'the objects are created artificially and have no content or soul as objects'.

Rather like Ray Harryhausen (working at the other end of the animation spectrum with his monsters and dinosaurs rampaging through tried and true stop-motion genre pieces), Svankmajer sees something paranormal in animation saying that 'I can characterise animation shortly as magic . . . I try to make objects alive in the real sense of the word.'

Svankmajer's work is invested with rich psychological associations and demands the audience construct the meaning and symbolic value of the images.

Svankmajer's films are noted for their investment in Gothic tone and images. Several of the short films he made prior to *Alice* explicitly adapt touchstones of the Gothic literary genre to the screen. Horace Walpole's *Castle of Otranto* (1764) was made into *Ostransky Zamek* (1973/79) and Edgar Allan Poe's *The Pit and the Pendulum* became *Kyvadlo, jama a nadeje* (The Pendulum, the Pit and Hope, 1983).

A project that Svankmajer was contemplating making in 2002 and beyond was called *Madness*, a combination of live action and animation based on the writing of Edgar Allan Poe and the Marquis de Sade. Svankmajer termed the project 'a kind of philosophical horror film' when discussing it in 2002 with indieWIRE.com.

Svankmajer is a filmmaker of world renown who keeps the flame of Czech animation alive. It is a form with a rich heritage that appeals to a folk sensibility that capitalism has not quite erased. Other Czech animators of note include Karel Zeman and Jan Trnka who made a stop-motion version of *A Midsummer Night's Dream* (1961) and the less whimsical piece *The Hand* (1965). Czech animation flourished under the

Communist state of the 1960s through to the start of the 1990s but it may be that a certain level of productivity and financing has passed for the moment. The thought of the Communist administration was that animation was without much value and was not much more than eye candy.

Zdenka Deitch, head of Prague studio Bratri vs Triku said in September 2003, 'You have to give children respect in animation. What you give to kids in these films will be returned by them when they grow up ... Everybody wants to have computer animation today, but classic animation comes from the heart.' One of the studio's most enduring shorts is *The Mole*.

With Svankmajer ever more celebrated, a newer animator with a strong profile is Jiri Barta whose films include *The Last Theft* (1987), a live-action film for the most part but directed as though featuring puppets. *The Ballad of Green Wood* (1984) is also notable as is *The Pied Piper* (1985). Barta is currently producing *The Golem* and has even collaborated with S4C to create the short *The Tyrant and the Child*.

Of course, perhaps the last thing to say here is that Svankmajer himself would most likely object to having his work classified as animation and included in a book on the subject, but his work does engage with the process and offers a relatively accessible step into a world of animation that to the general reader and animation fan would not necessarily be well known. Like other creators of animation, Svankmajer engages with the power of fantasy, but does so with less sentimentality and nostalgia than can be found in much animated material.

Alice (1987)

(86 minutes)

Directed by Jan Svankmajer
Animator: Bedrick Glaser
Cinematography: Svatolpluk Maly
Editor: Marie Zemanova
Art Direction: Eva Svankmajer and Jiri Blaha
English-version supervisor: Larry Sider
Executive Producers: Keith Griffiths and Michael Havas
Producer: Peter-Christian Frueter
Produced by Condor Features

RELEASE DATE: 1987

CERTIFICATE: PG

CAST: Kristyna Kohoutova (*Alice*)

TAGLINE: Inspired by Alice in Wonderland by Lewis Carroll.

STORYLINE: A sunlit forest and a stream. Sitting on the bank is a young girl, Alice, and an adult whose face is not shown. When Alice looks through the book that the adult is reading she is slapped.

At home, Alice lies in her room, surrounded by toys, objects and even a stuffed rabbit in a glass box. The rabbit comes to life and gets dressed in a red coat and white gloves. The rabbit smashes a hole in the glass cabinet and rushes out. Alice runs after him.

Outside on some very muddy and dead ground the rabbit heads on. Alice follows and comes to a desk. She opens the drawer and disappears inside it. She enters a sinister-looking corridor. Alice sees the rabbit eating. He sees Alice and runs on. She falls through a hole and finds herself in a lift that is descending past a range of ominous-looking levels.

Alice lands on top of a heap of autumn leaves. Looking around she sees a door and then a smaller door within it. She looks in on a magical world and sees the rabbit. Alice drinks from a bottle of ink and shrinks in size. She tries to grab the rabbit and he reacts violently. Alice cries and her tears are enough to flood the room. Alice is exiled from the building in a torrent of water that takes her downstream. She clambers up on to the riverbank where the rabbit orders her to go and fetch new scissors, which she does.

Alice enters another room and finds a house made of toy bricks. She goes inside and finds some scissors. She drinks more ink and grows back to full size. The rabbit shows up and tries to get at Alice. Alice pushes him away. The rabbit calls in some terrifying-looking creatures in an attempt to get Alice. They succeed and encircle her. Alice gets away again and continues her exploration; the rabbit attempts to get to her again, this time using an axe.

Alice finds herself in an eerie room filled with jars of pickled items. She goes to another room and sees caterpillars made of socks rushing around. One of the caterpillar socks talks to Alice.

Alice goes to the tea party with the March Hare and the Mad Hatter. After this she finds herself playing croquet with the Queen of Hearts.

Alice is put on trial and is to be beheaded. Alice awakes from her dream. All is back to normal and she is lying in her room, surrounded by many of the objects that have featured in her journey. She looks startled across the room: the rabbit is not back in its glass case and the glass is smashed.

THE DRAWING BOARD: A key concept that Svankmajer works with in this film is where dream and reality merge and how the impulses and emotions of childhood inform adulthood. Svankmajer uses found objects to animate and draw the life from. Dead animals, vegetables, minerals, artefacts are all ripe for animation and reinterpretation as objects. Svankmajer collects and hordes objects in his Czech studio. An atmosphere of death and decay permeates the work. This is not the bright and streamlined, happy-ending world of the animation most audiences will be used to. Critically, Svankmajer never calls himself an animation filmmaker because he says he is not interested in animation techniques or creating a complete illusion. Instead his interest is in 'bringing life to everyday objects'.

INSPIRATIONS: Svankmajer's movie-making heroes are Buñuel, Fellini and George Melies and the most significant influence on his approach must be his own commitment to the Surrealist aesthetic. In adapting Lewis Carroll's work Svankmajer draws on the source material's debt to English nursery rhymes which contain their share of violence and anarchy. Carroll, however, was apparently unaware of the nihilistic tone of the Wonderland he had created. Svankmajer's avoidance of the didactic in his work contrasts with Carroll's own tendency to preach.

TOON TEAM: Svankmajer's working methods are concentrated and small scale as the production credits for his films indicate – the 'Toon Team' is minimal.

VOCAL TALENT: The only voice heard – infrequently – in the film is that of Alice.

INK, PAINT AND HARD WORK: Much of the film was shot on location in a bakery in Prague.

THEME: *Alice* celebrates the exploration of the way images can be made to thrive on juxtapositions that only forms of animation could allow for. The film has no apparent moral centre or character who dispenses any kind of ethical message, which in the context of much feature animation, is unusual. The film's interest in the darker, less upbeat and sunny tendencies of childhood imagination is perhaps more adult than child-friendly.

As the character of Alice narrates at the start of the film, the process of seeing is as dependent on imagination as literal vision. Her voice-over introduction ensures that the audience is primed for something that will be different to the usual fairy-tale inspired animated film when she says, 'Alice thought to herself "Now you will see a film for children."' There is a pause and she adds the word, 'Perhaps.'

STYLISH TOONS: Significantly, simply narrating what happens in Svankmajer's film does not do justice to the intensity of the images and action. Alice is a film that is strong on atmosphere, no matter how unsettling it may be.

The film emphasises not just the image but the power of sound to be disturbing and unsettling, from the repetitive sound of sugarcubes being thrown into a cup of tea through to the thrashing of a bird's wings and the scraping sound of the lift carrying Alice down into a very dark Wonderland.

Alice is very much a horror film presented through stop-motion animation. It has a bleak pallor to it and the enclosed world only adds to the sense of being trapped. It is a film very far removed from the bright adaptation of Lewis Carroll's book that audiences would be familiar with from the Walt Disney version.

Violence marks much of the action, sometimes humorously – such as when the sailor mouse considers Alice's head an island he can camp out on.

The film's cascade of images of violence and strangeness include the rabbit smashing out of its glass box using a pair of scissors, jam containing tacks, a baguette that sprouts nails, and a sardine tin with no sardines, just the key.

CHARACTER SKETCH: Alice says barely anything throughout this essentially silent film, though several close-ups on her mouth reveal her narrating elements of the story. The sound is disconcertingly out of synch, matching the jarring effect of so many of the images. Alice journeys through Wonderland looking either afraid or unsure, but never really happily enchanted. She is at her most frightening when she is encased in a doll's outfit and mask, her face truly horrifying at that moment as she becomes increasingly ensnared in the world.

For the rabbit, though he is always in a hurry, Svankmajer creates a stop-motion character who is abrasive, nasty and often horrific, always clearing the sawdust out from its stomach.

The other 'characters' that inhabit the world that the rabbit has led Alice into are freakish, sometimes unsettling and highly imaginative fusions of forms, appropriately stitched together. When the rabbit calls the creatures in to capture Alice they are led by chickens pulling a carriage and neighing like horses. The carriage is driven by a fish skeleton with the skull of a bird, capped with a hat like that worn by a Punch puppet.

The building in which the action happens is very much a character too, as are all the objects glimpsed or more fully animated. They do feel as though they have come to life more through magic than human intervention.

The overall tone of the film is abrasive and chilling, everything tainted with decay and fracture. Seeing this film, it is easy to recognise the influence on The Brothers Quay. As in their short film *The Unnameable Little Broom*, a bird's wings flap violently (the sound more intense than the image) and scissors are central and very violent in Svankmajer's film.

TOON TUNES: As a silent film, there is much use of music throughout that veers from the eccentrically playful to the more menacing. If anything one could argue that Svankmajer uses sound effects as the music of the film. It is filled with clattering, skittering, knocking, tapping, insistent and spooky.

TOON TALK:
Alice (to the film's audience at the start of the film): 'Now you must close your eyes, otherwise you won't see anything.'

OTHER SIMILAR FILMS: Since *Alice*, Svankmajer has made a version of Goethe's story *Faust* and also *Little Otik*.

Faust (1994) is Svankmajer's attempt to bring the romantic story back to a common-man frame of reference. The film draws on Christopher Marlowe's plays, Johann Wolfgang von Goethe's plays, a novel about the character by Christian Dietrich Grabbe, old Czech puppet versions and also the opera by Charles Gounod. As with *Alice*, live action and animation interact to startling effect. The film includes a claymation baby on an alchemist's desk. The baby has a skull with eyeballs staring out from it at one point as the baby transforms to resemble the Faust character, a man living in contemporary Prague. At another point, the film animates a Golem figure. The Golem is a mythical beast synonymous with Prague.

Inevitably, a director's earliest efforts often enrich the viewing of their later films. The bizarre and darkly playful worlds of Svankmajer's films began with his short film *The Last Trick* (1964) in which two puppets have an intense rivalry. The puppets are portrayed by live actors within life-size marionettes.

RECOGNITION: 'Here, as always, Svankmajer's methods are hugely enjoyable in their perversity', said *Time Out*.

AWARDS: Won Best Film – Animated Feature at Annecy Film Festival 1988. In 1989 was nominated for Best Film at International Fantasy Film Awards.

COMMENT: 'Carroll was a precursor of the Surrealists, so mentally we're on the same side of the river; also, we are both infantile, which in normal society is an insult.' Jan Svankmajer.

VERDICT: *Alice* can be considered as an accessible introduction to Svankmajer's quixotic and bold approach to animation. There is no attempt to create a classically styled story world or indeed too strong a narrative. Instead, the emphasis is on the textures of the image and the suggestions that associations made between objects can achieve. The film asserts the power of animation to work way beyond its most familiar, comforting forms and it does indeed have the power of suggestion to it.

RICHARD WILLIAMS

For many, Richard Williams is the classical animator's animator and his name is legend. He has created some of the most impressive pieces of classical animation and yet tragically his life's work was the victim of commercial misjudgement (not his). After thirty years in the UK, Williams relocated to his native Canada.

Richard Williams has won three Oscars and an Emmy as well as numerous awards for commercials. He provided the animation for *Charge of the Light Brigade* (Tony Richardson, 1968) and directed one of the best adaptations of Charles Dickens's *A Christmas Carol* (1972).

His most high-profile project, though, was his work as director of animation on *Who Framed Roger Rabbit?* On the back of the success of that film it looked as though Williams would finally be able to complete his animated feature *The Thief and the Cobbler* which began life for Williams way back in 1964 when he read a series of Sufi folktales.

Soon Williams was collaborating with a writer called Idires Shah and, around 1965, Williams illustrated a new publication of these stories called *The Exploits of the Incomparable Mulla Nasrudin*. In 1967, the film project sparked by the tales began, under the title *The Amazing Nasrudin*. Sean Connery, Anthony Quayle, Donald Pleasance and Vincent Price all lent their vocal talents to the project. The film went on to be retitled *The Golden City*. Finances became tight and Williams worked on a thirty-minute commission of *A Christmas Carol* with the assistance of Chuck Jones, the director of countless brilliant *Road Runner* cartoons.

In 1972 a copyright infringement case loomed when Idires Shah's sister claimed she owned the stories. Williams departed the project, taking his images with him, and at that moment *The Thief and the Cobbler* took form. In 1973, all the work so far done was re-done by Williams. After working on other commissions, Williams struggled to restart the project in 1976. In 1978, Prince Feisal invested $100,000 but Williams missed the deadline. Test footage on the project was completed in 1979 for about $250,000. In the late 1970s a full, complete animated feature would have cost $8–9 million. The test footage was of a huge battle scene. In 1980 Prince Feisal withdrew his financing. By the 1980s, Williams was again making commercials and the project was re-dubbed *The Thief Who Never Gave Up*. In 1984 Gary Kurtz, riding high as a fantasy movie producer after *Star Wars* (George Lucas, 1977), *The Empire Strikes Back* (Irvin Kershner, 1980) and *The Dark Crystal* (Jim Henson and Frank Oz, 1982), was able to secure a little funding for the project. Robert Zemeckis saw some footage at the time when he was considering directing *Who Framed Roger Rabbit?* and, sure enough, Williams was hired.

In the afterglow of *Who Framed Roger Rabbit?* further investment came Williams's way for *The Thief*. In late 1992, the Disney film *Aladdin* opened to great success. Williams kept pushing on with his movie, *Aladdin* having amplified the Arabian aesthetic that Williams had been working on for so many years. In June 1992, Williams screened the nearly finished film (about fifteen minutes of animation remained to be done).

Financial woes continued when the Completion Bond company fired everyone including Williams. Fred Calvert, a long-standing TV animator, was hired to finish the film. In early 1994 a version of the film, truncated and altered, was released in Australia and South Africa.

In early 1995, Miramax bought the film and reworked the material that bit more. The narrative order was changed and more dialogue was inserted. Certain scenes remained unaltered, for example the war machine sequence and ZigZag's card tricks. Williams's concept was evidently for a near-silent film. The character of the witch is completely removed. Miramax released the film as *Arabian Knight* and it was a commercial failure.

Williams's dream of creating the *War and Peace* of animation fell victim to the obvious, literal thinking behind so much commercial endeavour.

More recently, Disney put out a call for lost material to be sent to them, allowing for a legitimate restoration of the film.

Appendices

Two animated features were made in what might come to be regarded as something of a 'late' period of classically animated movies, given the massive popularity of computer-generated images at present. The two films both share similarities in their narratives and represent high benchmarks in this part of animation. Interestingly, both films were supervised by Jeffrey Katzenberg, so perhaps he is the true guiding light.

The Lion King

Written by Irene Mecchi, Jonathan Roberts and Linda Woolverton, the film was directed by Roger Allers and Rob Minkoff and produced by Don Hahn. Indicative of its interest in 'big themes' was its tagline, 'Life's greatest adventure is finding your place in the Circle of Life.' The film became one of the most commercially successful films ever made, sealing the Disney studio's animated-feature renaissance.

As well as its stunning animation, it would be reasonable to suggest that the film's classic, hero's journey narrative gave it such widespread appeal. One of the principal inspirations for this original story must be what has come to be referred to as the hero's journey. It was a template marked out by writer Joseph Campbell in the 1930s in his now very famous book *The Hero with a Thousand Faces*. Campbell recognised a recurrent pattern in myths from around the world. They were all telling essentially the same story. A young hero's adventure begins at home from where he responds to 'the call to adventure'. Initially reluctant, some force compels them to undertake the mission. En route, the hero's worth and stamina are tested and at a critical point the hero experiences a submersion, a moment of profound bleakness from which they are then retrieved.

Able to locate whatever their mission asks, the hero returns home with the 'treasure' that will benefit their entire community. The journey brings out of the hero their finest qualities and also prompts them to face their failings. Ultimately, the hero's journey template is an affirming way to frame the experience of being alive – his journey is the journey every person undergoes in their own particular way – and *The Lion King* (like *Star Wars* (George Lucas, 1977), *ET: The Extra-Terrestrial* (Steven Spielberg, 1982), *It's a Wonderful Life* (Frank Capra, 1946), *North by Northwest* (Alfred Hitchcock, 1959)) articulates these concerns. *Dumbo* and *Pinocchio* are more specific Disney features of old that cover some of the same territory in terms of a protagonist seeking to find their place in the world.

With a voice cast featuring Matthew Broderick (*Simba*), Joseph Williams (*Simba, singing*), Jonathan Taylor-Thomas (*Young Simba*), Jason Weaver (*Young Simba, singing*), James Earl Jones (*Mufasa*), Jeremy Irons (*Scar*), Moria Kelly (*Nala*), Nikete Calame (*Young Nala*), Laura Williams (*Young Nala, singing*), Ernie Sabella (*Pumbaa*), Nathan Lane (*Timon*), Robert Guillame (*Rafiki*), Rowan Atkinson (*Zazu*), Madge Sinclair (*Sarabi*), Zoe Leader (*Sarafina*), Whoopi Goldberg (*Shenzi*), Cheech Marin (*Banzai*), Jim Cummings (*Ed/Gopher*), Sally Dworsky (*Nala*), *The Lion King* had a rich vocal palette that matched the stunning images and action.

Of historical significance was the fact that *The Lion King* was the first Disney feature to be generated in-house rather than being based on a fairy tale or children's story.

In 1989 the Disney studio had been discussing the prospects of an animated feature set in Africa. At another conceptual level, Jeffrey Katzenberg, the studio executive overseeing animation, had a desire to tell a story about growing up, a classic hero quest story. At the time of the film's release in the summer of 1994, Don Hahn said, 'It's a combination of Moses-Hamlet-King Arthur meets Elton John in Africa.'

For animated features, once production has begun, changes can be massively expensive. Paper is cheap and film is expensive, so much time in animation is typically spent developing the characters and story. Unlike live-action filmmaking, animation does not allow for material to be found at the editing stage.

In late 1991, the original director of *The Lion King*, George Scribner (who had directed the modestly successful *Oliver and Company* (1988) a canine reworking of Charles Dickens's novel *Oliver Twist*) was no longer involved in film. Sadly, he had reached a creative impasse with the studio who regarded his take on the story as too ponderous and sombre. Starting from scratch in many ways it was decided to make the film a musical of sorts in keeping with films such *The Little Mermaid* and *Beauty and the Beast*.

At the studio some animation staff regarded *The Lion King* as a less interesting prospect than another feature in development, *Pocahontas* (1995).

With Scribner no longer involved, the project took on two new directors, Roger Allen and Rob Minkoff, who had directed the energetic

and very funny *Roger Rabbit* shorts of the late 1980s and early 1990s
(see **Who Framed Roger Rabbit?**).

By April 1992, the screenplay for *The Lion King* was in serious need
of repair. The studio felt there was insufficient comedy and that its
thematic basis was not coming through. As had happened before, the
team had to start afresh. Don Hahn, Roger Allen, Rob Minkoff, story
supervisor Brenda Chapman, Kirk Wise and Gary Trousdale (fresh from
their *Beauty and the Beast* success) got into a creative huddle and
reworked the story over two intense days. The resulting outline then
became the one that was turned into the film by screenwriters Irene
Mecchi and Jonathan Roberts.

One of the key breakthroughs for this story overhaul was that Simba
was made a more sympathetic hero character. Early on in the story
concept, Simba had been in the care of Scar after the death of Simba's
father Mufasa. Subsequently, it was felt that this made Simba look weak.
Another issue was finding a way to lighten the tone of the film after the
tragic death of Mufasa. Rob Minkoff suggested sending Simba into exile
immediately after his father's death. This did two things: it freed Simba
of his lineage and later on made his endeavour to restore his family all
the stronger. It also allowed the emotional intensity of his father's death
to be countered by humour, in the shape of Timon and Pumba. By
August 1992, even with its new story shape, the material did not seem to
be working.

In April 1994 and with 20 per cent of the animation remaining to be
coloured, a test screening was held in Pasadena and the film went down
very well, boding well for its summer release.

The phenomenal success of *Beauty and the Beast* was to be superseded
by the global success of *The Lion King*, one of the most successful films
ever made and certainly the most commercially popular animated
feature at the time of its release. With *The Lion King* it seemed as though
the Disney studio and animation in general could do no wrong. The film
was a narrative classic proving popular in a way that the *Star Wars*
narrative does. *The Lion King* producer Don Hahn said at the time, 'We
wanted to tell the whole 'Circle of Life', life-affirming hero's story . . .
and we didn't want to whitewash it.'

Whilst the film was credited for its ecological sensibility, when it was
released in summer 1994 it came under fire for what some perceived as
racial stereotyping. The film did present a range of animals living
together as part of a harmonious Circle of Life but the villanous hyenas
were set apart from this and were voiced by minority ethnic actors.

Alan Menken, who had been so vital to the success of *The Little Mermaid* and *Beauty and the Beast*, was already at work developing material for Disney's *Pocahontas* project and so could not commit to *The Lion King*. *The Lion King*'s first director George Scribner had wanted an African soundtrack to the film he was envisioning but at the time that was not necessarily the route that the studio was prepared to take.

Tim Rice was brought on board *The Lion King* and he suggested that perhaps Elton John should be approached. The studio was unsure if the singer-songwriter would be interested. John was keen to be involved. Initially, his song 'Can You Feel the Love Tonight' was rendered entirely as a comic piece and John stood his ground in saying it needed to be treated seriously as the film's love theme.

Elton John composed his 'Circle of Life' piece for the opening of the film and Hans Zimmer treated it with more African instrumentation. Hans Zimmer was commissioned to write 65 minutes of underscore for the film in three weeks. The power of the opening musical sequence of the film was such that no dialogue was deemed necessary. Zimmer wrote Western music and had it sung by African voices.

The Lion King was successfully transferred to the theatre on Broadway with innovative designs that do not slavishly mimic the appearance of the characters in the film. The show was directed by Julie Taymor. It has also been showing in London since 1999.

The Lion King continued Disney's early 1990s success and prestige at awards ceremonies. Things got off to a good start when the Los Angeles Film Critics' Association awarded the film Best Animation. The film won the 1995 Oscar for Best Music, Original Score for Hans Zimmer's work. At the Oscars the film also won for Best Music, Song for 'Can You Feel the Love Tonight?' by Elton John and Tim Rice. Oscar nominations also went to the film for Best Music, Song for 'The Circle of Life' and Best Music, Song for 'Hakuna Matata'. At the 1995 BAFTA awards the film was nominated for the Anthony Asquith Award for Film Music and was also nominated for Best Sound (Terry Porter, Mel Metcalfe, David Hudson, Doc Kane). At the 1995, BMI Film and TV Awards the film won for Best Film Music and Most Performed Song from a Film for 'Can You Feel the Love Tonight?' At the 1995 Chicago Film Critics Association Awards the film won for Best Score and Best Motion Picture (Comedy/Musical) and Best Original Song for a Motion Picture for 'Can You Feel the Love Tonight?' The film was also nominated for best Original Score. The 1995 Grammys nominated the film for Best Instrumental Composition and Best Song Written Specifically for a Motion Picture or for Television for 'Can You Feel the Love Tonight?'

The Prince of Egypt

Several years later *The Prince of Egypt* was released, another film about dynasty and destiny. Sumptuously designed the film is significant for the scale of its classical animation ambition. Budgeted at $60 million it was the most expensive animated feature of the time. The film is especially noteworthy for the subtlety of its animation and its emotional impact. For DreamWorks SKG it represented their debut animated feature and was extensively promoted.

The film's life began before DreamWorks SKG had even been officially announced. Spielberg asked Jeffrey Katzenberg what would make a great animated feature and Katzenberg elucidated his opinion. Spielberg suggested *The Ten Commandments* met the criteria and Geffen suggested that should be the studio's debut animated feature. At the time of its production, 1995–1998, the film was the most expensive classically animated film in history. Katzenberg oversaw the production of the film.

A huge amount of research was put into Egyptian architecture, including a visit to Egypt and the Sinai Peninsula by lead staff members. Eighteen months were spent focusing on getting the narrative just right. One of the key concerns was in keeping Moses accessible and human.

The actors were video performing their dialogue recordings so the animators had useful reference in their character animation.

For Jeffrey Katzenberg, the project marked his first animated feature after his incredible success at Disney overseeing films such as *The Little Mermaid*, *Beauty and the Beast*, *Aladdin* and *The Lion King*.

To ensure the film's fidelity to the spiritual truth of the Biblical and historical source material the production consulted two Biblical experts, Everett Fox and Burton Visotzky. It is important to remember too that the film was the launch animated feature for the new DreamWorks studio and its voice talent is notably comprised of high profile actors such as Val Kilmer, Michelle Pfeiffer, Ralph Fiennes, Steve Martin, Jeff Goldblum, Sandra Bullock, Martin Short and Danny Glover.

The drawings of Gustave Dore, especially his sketchings of Biblical scenes, were a key inspiration to the film as were the paintings of Claude Monet and the epic dramas of film director David Lean such as *Lawrence of Arabia* (1962).

In a break from classical, narrative animation, where faces are divided into thirds, *The Prince of Egypt* design effort rendered human faces as being shorter at forehead and chin and longer in their midsection. Thus the proportions were more 30 per cent/40 per cent/30 per cent. This elongation of the mid-face area allowed for more expression.

To ensure realism of movement the production even had costumes made that could serve as references for the animators.

The overall concept of the film was to depict something of a hero's journey. The film featured 885 painted backgrounds and for the three miracle scenes, two live-action special-effects artists were involved, Henry LaBounta and Doug Ikele. Their job was to find powerful ways to represent the Burning Bush, the Plagues and the Red Sea parting. Ten digital artists worked on the Red Sea sequence, which runs about seven minutes and for which 318,000 hours of computer rendering time were required.

The film made a key technological breakthrough in its fusion of computer-generated three-dimensional models and traditionally drawn two-dimensional characters and settings using the exposure tool. Thus, for the chariot chase between Moses and Rameses the human characters were 2-D classically animated but the chariots were three-dimensional models built in the computer. The film also features a very live-action-styled crane camera shot as the camera apparently lifts up and pulls through scaffolding to reveal the expanse of the Egyptian Empire.

Colour is emotion and a distinct palette was created to develop an emotional texture in terms of décor, costume and environment. The Midianites were dressed in very vibrant colours, befitting their zest for life. In contrast, the Hebrew homes were rendered in earthy tones and the Egyptian environments in white and light pastels.

In keeping with the Exodus story, there was the necessity for scenes containing vast numbers of people. About twenty stock characters and figures were created as a database. To begin, a character was traditionally drawn by hand. It was then modelled on the computer in 3-D. This character was then reshaped to produce four key characters. Varying percentages of these four models were combined to create twenty generic crowd characters. For the final epilogue shot, 146,000 computer generated characters were brought to life.

The Prince of Egypt contains a range of songs written by Stephen Schwartz (he had also worked on *Pocahontas* (Mike Gabriel and Eric Goldberg, 1995) and *The Hunchback of Notre Dame* (Gary Trousdale and Kirk Wise, 1996)). The score was written by Hans Zimmer who had worked with Katzenberg before on *The Lion King* to great success. Of his score for *The Prince of Egypt*, Zimmer commented, 'I worked rather to create a musical path through the emotions of the story, while remaining true to the two cultures as far as we know.' Some of the actors, such as Ralph Fiennes, Michelle Pfeiffer, Steve Martin and Martin Short also sang.

The Israeli singer Ofra Haza sang the lullaby as Moses's natural mother sends him downriver in the basket. Haza sang the song in seventeen other languages for the foreign versions. Broadway star Brian Stokes Mitchell sang the song 'Through Heaven's Eyes'. The Hebrew language was incorporated into the Hebraically themed music of the film. The song 'Deliver Us' that commences the film was the first completed ahead of the start of production.

Of *The Prince of Egypt*, Jeffrey Katzenberg commented that 'Our goal was to be faithful to the text without always being literal – to embrace the themes and the fundamental aspects of the story as they are presented in the Bible.'

The Animated Short

Before there were animated feature films there were animated shorts and it is animation in this format that people are perhaps most familiar with. Today, the animated short continues as a compelling form and it was the short form that allowed animation to make the transformation and graduation towards a viable art in the early years of the twentieth century. In his book *Animation: A Guide to Animated Film Techniques*, Roger Noake writes: 'for the first time an animated film went beyond the mere insertion of tricks into live action material or extension of music hall routines into the cinema'.

The Brothers Quay made their reputation with work in this form and Nick Park at Aardman Animation came to the fore of British animation with short projects. Most audiences might immediately think of the short cartoons of animation directors such as Chuck Jones and Tex Avery but there are countless other practitioners working in a range of styles. The short form, for example, has been a rich source of material for feminist filmmakers and the computer animation success story of Pixar animation had its roots in a series of one-off shorts.

Countless highly detailed studies of the form exist, notably the brilliant book *7 Minutes: The Life and Death of the American Cartoon Short* (1993) by Norman Klein which expounds on the aesthetic, industrial and pop culture charms and significance of the American animated short. Today the seven-minute short is less prevalent than the twenty-minute series episode of *The Simpsons* or *South Park* or *Ren and Stimpy*.

What follows is an overview of some of the more well-known practitioners of the format. The number of animated cartoons that run anywhere from a minute to twenty minutes numbers thousands worldwide. In the 1920s the validity of the short proved itself. Up to then it had still been very allied to its progenitor, the comic strip, so that the action ran left to right or up or down. Eventually, perspective and spatial depth became part of the technique and the scope for stories expanded and enriched. Otto Mesmer's *Felix the Cat* was a big hit until the coming of sound, when the character's chosen voice failed to engage audiences. Clearly, sound was as harsh as it was kind. Of course, many animated stories were enhanced by sound and suddenly there were two levels at which humour could operate, namely what was seen and what was heard. Think back to *Dumbo*, where so much of the humour comes from the sound of Casey the train chugging along, as well as its movement and suppleness.

As the 1920s unfolded, the idea of transparency and illusion became central to the conception of the animated short. Realism became increasingly important. Between 1929 and 1940 much was written on the subject of animation but only in the 1980s did this interest rekindle.

Undeniably, the American short cartoon powerfully established a template for the short, initially based around the chase scenario and also the laughter mileage present in scenarios based around man's hapless relationship with machines. The spirit of American vaudeville also set the tone for so many minutes of animated visual humour; sight gags as they would be named, in keeping with the birth of live-action cinematic humour courtesy of geniuses such as Buster Keaton, Harold Lloyd, Charlie Chaplin, and Laurel and Hardy.

Walt Disney began with the short form before breaking into feature production. His short successes were the *Alice in Cartoonland* series and the *Silly Symphonies*. The Fleischer Studio, Disney's biggest commercial rivals, produced the *Out of the Inkwell* series. In the 1940s the animated short really hit its stride with the Warner Brothers shorts starring Bugs Bunny, and in the 1950s MGM began producing a lot of memorable characters, notably Tom and Jerry, and Droopy. Droopy was the creation of Tex Avery, considered – alongside Chuck Jones – as one of the titans of the format.

Fred 'Tex' Avery grew up in Texas, home state of the tall tale, and this propensity for exaggeration seems to have fed his imagination. Screwy Squirrel, a frenetic squirrel, and Droopy a slow moving pooch with heavy eyelids and a deadpan expression were Avery's most enduring creations. He had also created Bugs Bunny and given the 'wascally wabbit' his famous catchphrase, 'What's up, Doc?' which had been a saying in Tex Avery's hometown. In his book *Tex Avery: King of Cartoons*, author Joe Adamson writes, 'No artist in any century, on any continent, in any medium, has ever succeeded in creating his own universe as thoroughly and overwhelmingly as Tex Avery.'

Between 1941 and 1954, Avery ran the animation unit at MGM and, even though he aimed at a family audience, his humour was never far from a more adult sensibility with cartoons such as *Red Hot Riding Hood* which revelled in sexual innuendo. Avery is famous for the eyes on stalks at the sight of a pretty girl and the (literal) wolf whistling that accompanied such ocular gymnastics.

Avery's great creation Droopy debuted in 1943 in *Dumb Hounded* and *Drag Along Droopy* (1954) is considered a classic. Avery, then, was the animator of absurdity. No physical contortion was too much for his characters and his films moved so fast they could almost have exploded with energy. One of Avery's ambitions was to have as many 'black-out' (short, self-contained) jokes as possible in each seven-minute animation. He loved the visual humour available in differences in size and in his film *King Size Canary* a dog, cat, bird and mouse all inflate to huge sizes. Avery also enjoyed jokes about the film process itself and in his film *The Magical Maestro* at one point a character reaches out to remove what is apparently a rogue hair trapped in the camera's field of vision. After his incredible contribution to animated shorts (he also created Daffy Duck), Avery found a successful career producing animation for commercials. His legend lives on today, continuing to inspire animators.

In contrast to his contemporary and one-time colleague Tex Avery, Chuck Jones's animation is defined by the rich characterisation he poured into his animated shorts. The time he spent when young watching Chaplin and Keaton comedies infuses his work.

Jones went on to animate Bugs (initially a crazier-looking hare-brain than in his later, more familiar Jones overhaul appearance), Daffy and others but his most enduring pieces of work are most likely to be the *Road Runner* series of shorts in which a hapless but admirably determined Wile E Coyote attempts to catch the effervescent Road Runner.

Jones gets immense humour out of Coyote's Sisyphus-like trauma, endlessly trying to catch the Road Runner and failing. In contrast to Avery's rapid-fire humour, Jones enjoyed the pause before the joke occurred and in the Road Runner series this was always most evident and cherished in the look that Coyote would typically give the camera of resigned failure before plummeting to his doom after another failed attempt at ensnaring the 'meep meep-ing' bird.

The format for the *Road Runner* cartoons was dazzlingly contained. The stories were always set in the American southwest desert, the Road Runner always stayed on the road and the Road Runner never fought back at the Coyote. As Jones said, 'The Road Runner is really a force. He's the Coyote's Holy Grail.' Such was the pathos of the Coyote's plight that in the 1960s a club was set up by some students at Stanford University in America to cheer only for the Coyote when a *Road Runner* short was screened.

Jones's main period of work in shorts ran from 1938–1961 and for many his greatest achievement was a one-off called *What's Opera, Doc?* starring Bugs Bunny and his nemesis Elmer Fudd. Staying in their characters, Bugs and Elmer perform Wagner's *The Ring* in a period of around seven minutes. The retention of their classically American accents jars hilariously with the Teutonic, European grandeur of the opera's setting as the short parodies the operatic tradition.

For others, though, *One Froggy Night* is the great one-off animated short of Jones's career. Certainly Steven Spielberg regards it as the *Citizen Kane* of the form – the story centring on an all-singing, all-dancing frog discovered by an entrepreneur. The problem is that the frog only performs when nobody is watching. Such was Jones's standing that for the first-ever public screening of *Star Wars* in May 1977, George Lucas ran *Duck Dodgers in the 24th Century* prior to the movie. The cartoon short featured Daffy Duck as a space ace. Like Bugs Bunny and Woody Woodpecker, Daffy's original appearance was similarly crazed, and Jones toned him down from loon to prima donna. Yosemite Sam reflected the spirit of Fritz Freleng the legendary producer of shorts at Warner Brothers.

In the mid-1960s, with the studios closing down their animation units, Jones moved into television and features. Jones was disdainful of most Saturday morning animation, and he focused on half-hour specials of which one of his most notable pieces of work was an adaptation of Dr Seuss's *How the Grinch Stole Christmas*. Jones's adaptation stayed faithful to the Seussian curves and certainly the look of Seuss's picture-book character, even though Jones and Theodore Geisel (aka Dr Seuss) tussled over the character's final appearance. Jones's adaptation is a landmark in TV animation history. When it premiered on 18 December 1966 on CBS TV in North America, 38 million people tuned in, making it one of the most watched specials in TV history. Geisel and Jones were old friends though Geisel took a degree of convincing that an adaptation would be a valid project. Geisel, like Jones, invested fantasy with a real American sense of humour and a universal emotional palette as sharply drawn and richly coloured as their images. Enhancing the visuals was the voice-over by Boris Karloff, who also voiced the Grinch to great effect.

Expanding the book, Jones introduced two songs to the story: 'You're a Mean One, Mr Grinch' and 'Welcome, Christmas'. The short also amplified the role of the Grinch's dog, Max, a pooch committed to unconditional love. Jones's animation team were tried and trusted colleagues Maurice Noble (Jones's long-standing layout supervisor), Auril and Richard Thompson, Hal Ashmead and Phil Roman.

The Grinch adaptation certainly has an affinity with The Nightmare Before Christmas and that film's creator and producer, Tim Burton, has cited the Jones influence. Watching the film one can also see the Road Runner visual humour in those moments when the Grinch or his dog Max look to camera before something goes terribly wrong. The sleigh ride down the mountain recalls the energy of the Road Runner shorts and the physical humour as the Grinch wrestles to stop the sleigh and presents falling off the mountain is redolent of Wile E Coyote's exertions and stresses. There is a nice sense of the ridiculousness of the Grinch's plan when a wide shot shows the enormous boulder-like sleigh and sack being pulled by tiny Max.

Chuck Jones also adapted Norton Juster's stunning children's fantasy novel The Phantom Tollbooth (1969), a fascinating combination of freewheeling fantasy and rich psychological resonance. It was the only animated feature Jones made but it failed to find an audience, perhaps because it trod a precarious line between fun and education. This ethos was in keeping with the spirit of Juster's terrific book, which sadly seems unknown in the UK. Another of Jones's shorts that is notable for its accessibly experimental approach is The Dot and the Line. A Christmas Carol followed (1972) on which Jones collaborated with animator Richard Williams. Jones also produced several more modernist, non-narrative shorts. Jones was directing animated shorts right through until the mid-1990s.

In 1994, Chariots of Fur was the first Wile E Coyote/Road Runner short in thirty years. Jones's stature was confirmed by the three Academy Awards that he won and the Lifetime Achievement Award (1996) he received. Perhaps more significantly Jones was one of the three inductees into the Animation Hall of Fame. He was in terrific company: Winsor McCay and Walt Disney were the other two. Jones once said 'Animation isn't the illusion of life; it is life.' Jones, who died in 2002, is the most collected animator, fans buying up cels and images of his work.

Chuck Jones' legacy of over 250 animated shorts was in refining his action to an absolute essential that could be endlessly varied. Jones was also committed to making the short form as emotionally engaging as possible. One of Jones's heroes was Mark Twain, whom Jones charmingly resembled in his later years and whose crazy tales almost always remained on a human scale for all their fantasy and adventure. *Huckleberry Finn* and *A Connecticut Yankee in King Arthur's Court* are notable examples. Jones worked repeatedly with his tried-and-trusted layout artist Maurice Noble and all of Jones's stories held the torch high for the anarchic in animation.

In 1944, Jones wrote, 'If the motion picture producer, writer or musician believes the end purpose of the cartoon to be the cartoon short of today, then it must follow that the end purpose of easel painting is the comic strip.' It is a reservation that has currency even today.

In such a visual medium one of the most famous names was that of a voice artist named Mel Blanc who apparently shared the same throat muscle construction as Enrico Caruso.

Blanc only became widely recognised for his contribution to animation in the 1960s. His first regular character had been Porky Pig and to nail the voice Blanc spent a few hours on a farm listening to pigs. Blanc was a mainstay of the Jack Benny show on American radio in the 1930s and 1940s and also worked with Abbott and Costello, George Burns and Gracie Allen. Blanc had originally been the voice of Woody Woodpecker.

It was animation producer Leon Schlesinger who gave Blanc his break and, when he would not increase Blanc's fee, Blanc negotiated and secured an on-screen credit that read 'Voice characterisation by Mel Blanc'. Blanc went on to voice Bugs Bunny, Fred Flintstone and even Twiki on the *Buck Rogers* TV series of the 1970s. Originally, Blanc would record the voice for a cartoon in one linear block, leaping between characters. This would be expensive if a mistake was made midway. Blanc had a better idea that was taken up – to record each character separately and have the sound editors cut the tracks together in story order. Often Blanc's voices were mechanically treated to alter their pitch and pace.

A lesser-known name is Jay Ward who was responsible for *Crusader Rabbit* in collaboration with Alexander Anderson Jr. The show ran in 1948 and was Anderson's creation. When his project was turned down at Terry Toons he turned to his real-estate pal, Ward, for funding and Ward became heavily involved. The animation was limited in its story of a wised-up rabbit (voiced by Lucille Bliss) and his tiger pal, Rags, as they deal with the bumbling bad guy, Dudley Nightshade. The series was a precursor to the more successful *Rocky and Bullwinkle* series of

1959–1961 which had a fast thinker (Rocket J Squirrel) and a less fast thinker (Bullwinkle J Moose) grappling with resident villains, Natasha and Boris. June Foray voiced Rocky and Natasha, Bill Scott voiced Bullwinkle and Paul Frees voiced Boris. Again, the animation was limited but the character designs are memorable and simply drawn and the show's witty scripts earned it a cult following that endures.

Dudley must have been a favourite moniker of Jay Ward as his other enduring character is virtuous, beaming Mountie, *Dudley Do-Right*. Ward collaborated with Bill Scott in this series that parodied melodrama. The show ran in 1961 and had an earlier incarnation in 1948 in a *Crusader Rabbit* episode called *The Comic Strips of Television*. Scott actually created Dudley and Jay Ward helped develop the character and scenario. Again, June Foray voiced Nell, Hans Conreid (who had voiced Captain Hook in Disney's *Peter Pan*) voiced Snidely Whiplash and Paul Frees voiced Inspector Fenwick. Bill Scott voiced Dudley.

Despite the modest success of Jay Ward's work he had two intriguing-sounding concepts rejected: *Fang the Wonder Dog* and *Hawkear*, which followed the adventures of a Native American scout in the Old West.

William Hanna and Joseph Barbera first met at MGM and their studio output of the late 1950s onwards continues to be broadcast today and their characters are as recognisable and familiar as many of the Disney icons.

Their greatest achievement must have been *The Flintstones*, a cartoon spin on the sitcom *The Honeymooners*.

Joseph Hanna and William Barbera began as co-directors with the MGM animation unit in 1939. One of their first successes was the Academy Award-winning *Puss Gets the Boot* (1940) which introduced a cat called Jasper and an unnamed but plucky and inventive mouse who would go on to be named Jerry. Jasper would be renamed Tom and a legendary love–hate relationship in 2-D was born, running to over a hundred episodes. In their MGM tenure Hanna and Barbera won seven Oscars for Best Animated Short. (Back then, animated shorts were theatrically released – only in the 1960s and beyond did they become a staple of television.)

Hanna Barbera's second production was *Huckleberry Hound* and soon enough their stable of memorable and humorous characters became a staple of television programming. The names include *Scooby Doo, Quick Draw McGraw, The Jetsons, Top Cat* and *Hong Kong Phooey*.

To keep costs down and productivity up, the Hanna Barbera studio introduced planned animation whereby characters, to some degree, took on the quality of background elements. If they were talking only their mouth would move and the rest of their body would remain essentially static. Walk and run cycles were re-used in numerous instalments of a given character series and the backgrounds repeated within an episode. At an aesthetic level this could be regarded as a retrograde step, and was seen as minimising the potential for maintaining one of animation's key charms – namely its antic spirit. The vaudevillian energy was lost.

However, the studio also ventured successfully into feature animation, taking its TV stars to the big screen. Their first project was *Hey There, It's Yogi Bear*. Others followed such as *The Man They Called Flintstone*, *Yogi's First Christmas* and *The Jetsons Meet the Flintstones*. In the 1960s Chuck Jones directed several Tom and Jerry shorts. In 1957, MGM shut down their animation facility and the Hanna Barbera phenomenon was born. Within months of leaving MGM, Hanna Barbera had a new series on TV called *Ruff and Ready*, inspired to some degree by *Crusader Rabbit*.

Perhaps the other key name in the pantheon of the worldwide popularity of the American cartoon is Walter Lantz, the producer of the *Woody Woodpecker* shorts. Woody Woodpecker was the bright blue bird with a rich yellow beak, bright red hair and a laugh somewhere between hilarious and annoying.

Lantz became known as the dean of American animation on account of the length of his career. He had been good friends with Walt Disney whom, in a 1985 interview, he devotedly referred to as 'Mr Disney'.

As with pretty much all the big names in any field, there were achievements and adventures prior to hitting the so-called big time. Walter Lantz began producing animation in 1929 under his own studio name at Universal. Born a year before Disney, he began working as an animator at the age of eighteen, writing, directing and animating his own shorts that owed a creative debt to the *Out of the Inkwell* series of the Fleischer studio. Soon Lantz was working for JR Bray. When Bray's studio shut in 1927, animation was going through a downtime and Lantz left New York and went to Hollywood.

For a period Lantz worked in live action with comedy auteurs Hal Roach and Mack Sennet. Lantz ended up as head of Universal, Carl

Laemmle's chauffeur and when the studio aimed to start up a new animation arm, Lantz was there for the taking at the age of 28.

Prior to this, Carl Laemmle had wanted to streamline the supply of animation and decided an in-house unit would be best. Up to then the studio had gone to independents such as Walter Mintz, who supplied them with shorts such as *Oswald the Lucky Rabbit* (originally a Disney character). Lantz and his assistant, Bill Nolan, pulled together an animation team at Universal, beginning with new *Oswald the Lucky Rabbit* shorts. In 1934, inspired by the Disney studio's successful Silly Symphonies series, Lantz began producing the Cartune Classic series of which *Jolly Little Elves* (1934) was the first title. It was Lantz's first animated short in colour.

In 1935, Lantz negotiated with Universal and became a separate entity. It was when *Oswald the Lucky Rabbit* began to feel outdated that Lantz sought to create a new character and thus Woody Woodpecker was born, becoming the studio's most successful product.

Woody made his debut in an Andy Panda cartoon called *Knock Knock* (1940) with a script by Ben 'Bugs' Hardaway. Ben's personality fed in greatly into Woody's and it was Mel Blanc (seemingly the voice of an entire nation of animated characters) who voiced the redheaded bird. Woody Woodpecker's own series of shorts began in 1941 with *The Cracked Nut* and it was the short in which he was actually named as Woody Woodpecker. Two Woody shorts were Oscar nominees, namely *The Dizzy Acrobat* (1943) and *Musical Moments from Chopin* (1947). 3 October 1957 was the date of Woody Woodpecker's TV debut, symptomatic of the shift the animated short made from the big to the small screen. Woody even shows up in *Who Framed Roger Rabbit?* Woody was a sparky, upbeat and energetic character with an outrageous trademark laugh who had begun with a more maniacal look and two teeth. By 1945 Woody possessed something more akin to a duck's bill and in 1950 his look was finalised. It was refined a little more in 1960 to make him cuter. In 1972 the studio finally closed.

In 1979, Lantz received a Special Achievement Oscar for his contribution to American animation. He died in 1994.

John Kricfalusi is most famous for his *Ren and Stimpy* animation series. For Kricfalusi, the animator Bob Clampett was the inspiration. What is notable about Kricfalusi is that he is a model example of creator-led animation. Kricfalusi created *The Ren and Stimpy Show* for Nickelodeon but ran into issues around censorship with the network. After *Ren and Stimpy*, Kricfalusi moved into commercials. His characters Sody Pop, George Liquor and Jimmy the Idiot Boy can still be viewed online. Kricfalusi attempted to launch a feature called *The Ripping Friend* but to no avail.

Animation has been central to Canada's film culture and a figurehead of the form was Norman McLaren. He was commissioned to establish an animation studio in Canada in the 1950s by the great British documentary filmmaker John Grierson who had run a study about the state of Canadian filmmaking. McLaren is regarded as mentor to the first generation of Canadian animators. His own passion was less for narrative, character-based animation than for something more akin to the sensory. He produced a range of scratch films such as *Lines Vertical* (1960) and *Lines Horizontal* (1961) and, in 1952, he created the Academy Award-winning animated short *Neighbours* which ran eight minutes and powerfully explored the futility of aggression. McLaren's abstract interests connect him to Stan Brakhage, who died in 2002, and was perhaps the chief proponent of scratch film, a very pure form of animation whereby the scratches are made on the film itself. It's a long way from *Pinocchio* and *Wallace and Gromit*.

Another avant-garde animator is Russian, Yuri Norstein who, rather like Svankmajer perhaps, considers himself more a magician than an animator. Certainly, animation is well suited to the avant-garde and experimentation as it can so easily contain various materials and forms. Norstein made what is considered one of the great animations, *Tale of Tales*.

In Britain in the 1970s, the wobbly TV characters of Bob Godfrey came to the fore. His notable creations were *Roobarb and Custard* (1975) about a cat and a dog. The characters were drawn in felt tip. *Henry's Cat* in 1983 was similarly popular, this time combining cel animation and felt-tip-drawn characters. Godfrey won an Academy Award in the early 1970s for his fast-paced biotoon of Isambard Kingdom Brunel called *Great*. Advertising on television also yielded rich talent and image-making in animation.

In the late 1980s and early 1990s, British short form animation was crowned by the stop-motion efforts of Aardman Animation with the *Creature Comforts* short and then the *Wallace and Gromit* thirty-minute shorts. Both of these projects are a fair way from one of Aardman's earlier shorts, *Down and Out* which took documentary sound recorded at a Salvation Army hostel and then put animated clay figures to the soundtrack in a very affecting way. More regularly produced highlights emerged courtesy of the Cosgrove Hall studio in Manchester where Brian Truman's great scripts for *Dangermouse* were endlessly inventive. *Dangermouse* was a spoof of a kind of James Bond figure. Voiced by David Jason, Dangermouse was a world-weary eyepatch-wearing plucky rodent aided by his bumbling pal Penfold, voiced by Terry Scott. Dangermouse's nemesis was Baron Silas Greenback. Our heroes were based underneath a red postbox.

In the 1990s animation on TV continued with real success. Steven Spielberg oversaw the series *Tiny Toons*, which pitted the junior version of Warner Brothers classic characters against the world. Following this was a very popular all-new show called *Animaniacs*, about two brothers and a sister who lived in the Warner Brothers studio lot water tank and got involved in all sorts of self-referential adventures. Spielberg had also established his own animation company in London in the early 1990s but it only yielded a handful of films: *An American Tail*, *Fievel Goes West*, *We're Back!* (based on the Hudson Talbot story about dinosaurs in modern-day New York city) and *Balto*, based on a real event about a heroic wolf in Alaska.

Bob Kane's comic book character *Batman* was also realised powerfully in a very popular series that was inspired by the Fleischer *Superman* series of the 1940s. Writer Paul Dini was key to the development of the animated TV series in the 1980s and 1990s, particularly through his work on the very noir-like *Batman* series that found great success.

In the 1980s George Lucas presented *Ewoks* cartoon series and *Droids* but neither quite worked. In autumn 2003, the Cartoon Network produced *The Clone Wars* cartoon series, three-minute episodes made by the people behind *Samurai Jack*.

In the mid-1990s *South Park* proved a cult favourite, even resulting in a feature simply called *South Park: The Movie*. With its abrasive humour and violence the show was marked by a refreshing sense of subversion and proved hugely popular in its stories of four friends living in Colorado. Perhaps the most distinctive aspect of the show, however, was its apparently crude animation that suggested cut-outs rather than anything more fully drawn.

Undoubtedly, though, the definitive animated series like no other has been *The Simpsons*. Initially beginning as a series of animated breaks for the Tracey Ullman show, the concept proved so popular that a series began. Matt Groening, series creator, had been invited by Tracey Ullman's producer James L Brooks to submit an idea. Groening sketched the concept fifteen minutes before the meeting, naming the characters after his parents and sisters. Bart was an anagram of brat.

The show was immediately popular. President Bush even said the American public should aspire to be more like the Waltons than the Simpsons. The show is now in its fourteenth season and looks set to run through to a sixteenth. It is the longest-running prime time animated series since *The Flintstones* and the longest-running comedy series, breaking the record of American sitcom *The Adventures of Ozzie and Harriet*. For several years now there has been talk of a feature-length *Simpsons*, but one senses caution on the part of Matt Groening who is aware of how well the current format works. There have been 250 episodes produced over twelve years with 60 million viewers in 60 countries. Disillusionment with the world and the celebration of ignorance and underachievement clearly touches a worldwide chord. The underlying cynicism of the show has its roots in Groening's comic strip *Life in Hell* (still syndicated in around 250 alternative newspapers) which tells of two rabbits, Binky and Sheba, as they grapple with existentialist matters. For Groening, what *The Simpsons* alerts audiences to is the fact that, 'Your moral authorities don't always have your best interests in mind.' *The Simpsons* encapsulates that anarchic, coyote spirit that has forever been part of the animation medium, whatever the nationality of its producer.

Groening's follow-up series, a science-fiction spoof called *Futurama*, could never match the seismic impact of *The Simpsons* but it has the same invention and combination of satire and warmth. In visual terms it is very much from the same imagination. It tells the story of a twentieth-century pizza delivery boy named Fry who is accidentally thrown forward in time by several hundred years into a retro futuristic world of flying cars, mile-high skyscrapers and clunky robots. The show even manages to make a one-eyed alien woman sexy.

Animating the Future

The future of animation looks bright, particularly for computer animation. Beyond the range of the animated film, live-action movies continue to turn to animation in the creation of illusions. With his new film *The Polar Express*, director Robert Zemeckis seems about to blur the line even more between photography and the painting process of computer-generated images. New from Disney is the classically animated *Brother Bear*. The final episode in the *Star Wars* prequel trilogy will no doubt further prove Lucas's ambition to make live-action–animated movies.

The Pixar studio has a raft of projects ready to entertain audiences. The first of these is a project created, written and directed by Brad Bird, director of *The Iron Giant*.

The Incredibles is the story of an everyday family who also happen to be superheroes. Production began on 15 April 2002 and the film is due to be released on 5 November 2004. Initially there were creative challenges to be met when Bird brought his 2-D animators into the 3-D computer-animation world. The film's budget is quoted at around $91 million. John Lasseter has served as producer on the project.

The Incredibles are a dysfunctional family of superheroes who have been put into anonymous suburbia on the Witness Protection Programme to protect them from their arch enemy. As they do heroic battle, the family must contend with family bust-ups and complications.

Mr Incredible is voiced by Craig T Nelson, the square-jawed Everyman dad from *Poltergeist* (Tobe Hooper, 1982) and an early-days possibility as Indiana Jones. Mr Incredible's arch enemy has been voiced by Samuel L Jackson. Holly Hunter also lends her vocal talents to the film alongside Jason Lee, Wallace Shawn and John Ratzenberger.

Bird had brought his project *Ray Gunn* to Pixar but they opted for *The Incredibles*, which Bird conceived way back in 1993. Many of the character designs have been done by Tony Fucile (an *Iron Giant* veteran) and Teddy Newton. A teaser trailer for the film was screened with Pixar's *Finding Nemo*, showing the Incredibles' phone ringing and lighting up in a drab office festooned with ageing magazine covers of younger days. Mr Incredible, overweight and middle-aged, attempts to squeeze into his archetypal bright red hero suit with comic results. The

273

overall character design is a variation on the Pixar look established in their films so far. John Barry is composing the score.

November 2004 will see another major leap in the live action and animation arena. It is a Robert Zemeckis film, filmed between March and May 2003, that offers a return, in some ways, to the driving spirit behind *Who Framed Roger Rabbit?* – the impulse to see what happens when actors and animation are combined.

The Polar Express is based on the Chris Van Allsburg picture book of the same name. As the original was only 35 pages long, the screenplay evidently expands the basic premise. Zemeckis has worked on the screenplay with William Broyles, with whom he worked on the brilliant *Cast Away* (2000). *The Polar Express* stars Tom Hanks as the conductor of a train, The Polar Express, which takes a boy, who still believes in Santa Claus, to the North Pole. The film has been shot on high-definition video and has utilised a lot of green screen so that the Van Allsburg-inspired environments can be 'painted' in postproduction.

Furthermore, Hanks and the other actors will be represented on screen by computer-animated versions of themselves. Hanks's face has been scanned, as have pictures of him as a boy so that his adult character can be shown as a kid. The film could be one of the most expensive ever made. Doug Chiang, a former LucasFilm concept designer on the *Star Wars* prequels, among others, is also on board.

Hanks has said of the film, '(We're) using his art as the storyboards for the movie. It's got all sorts of elements to it. There's doubt, there's a journey, there's a quest. There are monumental moments that everyone can relate to.'

In November 2003, a teaser trailer was released, proving just how faithful the adaptation promises to be to the look of its source material. The heavily nostalgic images looked utterly magical, hanging somewhere between the photographic and the illustrative. As with *Who Framed Roger Rabbit?* director Robert Zemeckis is not afraid to move his camera through the new animated world of computer-generated images so that there is a bold live-action feel to the material (the teaser trailer is a segment from the opening of the story). The little boy lies asleep and is awoken by a rumbling sound as his toys rattle and fall. A blast of golden light fills his moonlit room and he scrambles to see what is happening. The camera booms up slowly behind him as he opens the door of his house to see the magical train pulling up and a warm golden light bathes the inviting face of Tom Hanks (looking a bit like Mark Twain) as the

Conductor, smoke clearing around him and beams of light slicing through the night. The final flourish of the trailer shows the full extent of the train as it thunders off to the north Pole. The trailer ends, assured in its combinatin of naturalism and the heightened reality that animation has always so beautifully offered.

Brother Bear, released in autumn 2003, is a classically animated feature from the Disney studio about North American bears. Originally titled *Bears*, it tells the story of Kenai, a teenage bear who must regain human form after he is transformed into a bear.

DreamWorks has *Shrek 2, Over the Fence, SharkTale* and *Madagascar* on the way. *Shrek 2* details what happens when Shrek meets Fiona's parents. *Over the Fence* is based on a cartoon strip and tells of a raccoon and a turtle living it up in suburbia. Shark Tale is a gangster spoof with sharks, the Mob and even the voice of Martin Scorsese. *Madagascar* tells of zoo animals from Central Park zoo that get shipwrecked on the island of *Madagascar*. The film's luscious backgrounds are inspired by the paintings of Henri Rousseau, while the computer-generated animation eschews a more naturalistic look for the characters, making them more obviously 'cartoony' and angular.

French comic book artist and concept designer, the legendary Jean 'Moebius' Giraud, has a computer-animated feature in development called *Through the Moebius Strip* in which a scientist gets trapped and lost in a space-time portal he invented. His son must come to rescue him. Giraud's designs are vivid, featuring blue-skinned giants and space outfits that are at once bulky but beautiful in their intricacy. Giraud's densely detailed design work has graced costume designs for *Tron* (Steven Lisberger, 1982), *Willow* (Ron Howard, 1988) and *The Abyss* (James Cameron, 1989). Moebius's clean, bold lines in his comic books, *Blueberry, The Airtight Garage of Jerry Cornelius, Arzach* and so forth recall the work of Winsor McCay.

In Britain, animated features continue to be produced such as development work on *Flushed Away* at Aardman about a rat who learns to enjoy sewer life (original script by Ian La Frenais and Dick Clement, of *Porridge, The Likely Lads* and *Auf Wiedersehen, Pet* fame). Dave Borthwick is directing a new feature version of *The Magic Roundabout*. The film is being realised with computer-generated animation. The film features the voices of Jim Broadbent, Kylie Minogue and Joanna Lumley.

ANIMATED FILMS Animating the Future

Another CGI fantasy being produced in Britain is *Gnomeo and Juliet*, produced by Elton John's Rocket Pictures and directed by Gary Trousdale who accomplished so much with *Beauty and the Beast*. Terry Pratchett's *Bromeliad* trilogy is also in development with PDI/DreamWorks animation. Nick Park is currently at work on the Wallace and Gromit feature, a chilling horror movie by all accounts, currently titled *Wallace and Gromit and the Curse of the Were-Rabbit*. Another British project, from Silver Fox Films, *Water Warriors*, is a computer-animated fantasy about frogs defending their pond from water-hungry aliens.

And in this age of evolution in movie-making, digital technology continues to expand the palette of possibility for the rebel filmmaker. The word on the street is machinima, a computer-generated animation format derived from computer gaming. The material can be distributed online, split into its component parts and rendered in real time: www.machinima.com

The future of animation is as exciting for audiences and enthusiasts today as it must have been to those first dreamers at the beginning of the twentieth century. They recognised the magic in making the impossible real and in encouraging audiences to exclaim, 'Wow, look at that. It's amazing!' That's the miracle of animation.

Index of Quotations

Grant, *The Encyclopedia of Walt Disney's Animated Characters*, Hamlyn, 1987

40 'mixture of . . .' Walt Disney quoted by John Grant, *The Encyclopedia of Walt Disney's Animated Characters*, Hamlyn, 1987

41 'The greatest moving picture . . .' Westbrook Pegler, *New York World Telegram*, December 1937, reprinted in Grant, op. cit.

41 'If you miss Snow White . . .' Frank Nugent, the *New York Times*, reprinted in Grant, op. cit.

41 'Motion picture . . .' Edwin Schallert, *LA Times*, reprinted in Grant, op. cit.

41 'A generally cute fantasy . . .' Geoff Andrew, *Time Out Film Guide*, Ninth Edition, edited by John Pym, Penguin Books, 2001

41 'He's just put all your . . .' Munro Leaf, reprinted in Grant, op. cit.

42 'I saw . . .' Walt Disney, quoted in Grant, op. cit.

Pinocchio

45 'Woe to those boys . . .' Carlo Collodi, *Pinocchio*, Penguin Books, 2002

51 The power of the . . .' Roger Ebert, *Chicago Sun-Times*, 1992, www.suntimes.com

51 'Disney's second cartoon . . .' Geoff Brown, *Time Out Film Guide*, Ninth Edition, op. cit.

52 'What I will . . .' Walt Disney quoted by Leonard Mosley, *The Real Walt Disney*, Future, 1985

Dumbo

58 'just the . . .' Andreas Deja on *Dumbo* DVD documentary praising Timothy Mouse

60 'the most genial . . .' Bosley Crowther, the *New York Times*, quoted by Grant, op. cit.

60 'One of the best animated features . . .' W Stephen Gilbert, *Time Out Film Guide*, Ninth Edition, op. cit

60 'The first time . . .' Ward Kimball, quoted in Grant, op. cit.

Beauty and the Beast

64 'The Disney film . . .' Marina Warner, 'Beauty and the Beasts', *Sight and Sound*, volume 2, issue 6, October 1992

64 'gives us . . .' ibid.

64 'When Disney does a fairy tale . . .' Glen Keane quoted by Kim Masters, 'The Mermaid and the Mandrill', *Premiere*, November 1991

70   'Fragmented as it is . . .' Jonathan Romney, *Sight and Sound*,
      volume 2, issue 6, October 1992

70   'The film is as good . . .' Roger Ebert, *Chicago Sun-Times*,
      22 November 1991, www.suntimes.com

70   'There's enough . . .' Peter Bradshaw, the *Guardian*, 2002

71   'This is the closest . . .' Jeffrey Katzenberg, 'The Mermaid and the
      Mandrill', *Premiere*, November 1991

Stop-motion Miracles

76   'King of the . . .' Phil Tippett quoted by Stephen Lynch, *Working
      on the Threshold of Animation, Projections 8*, Faber and Faber,
      1998

The Nightmare Before Christmas

85   'I wanted . . .' Danny Elfman quoted by Frank Thompson, *Tim
      Burton's The Nightmare Before Christmas: The Film, the Art, the
      Vision*, A Roundtable Press Book, 1993

86   'Restores originality and daring . . .' Peter Travers, *Rolling Stone*,
      issue 669

86   'This beautifully realised confection . . .' Tom Charity, *The Time
      Out Film Guide*, 2001, Ninth Edition, op. cit.

87   'I see *Nightmare Before Christmas* as a positive story . . .' quoted
      by Frank Thompson, *Tim Burton's The Nightmare Before
      Christmas: The Film, the Art, the Vision*, A Roundtable Press
      Book, 1993

James and the Giant Peach

91   'a landmark fusion . . .' Mark Cotta Vaz, 'A Giant Peach in the Big
      Apple', *Cinefex 66*, June 1996

95   'an imaginative combination . . .' *Box Office Magazine*, 1996
      www.boxoffice.com

95   'an enchanting, at times, ghoulish appeal . . .' Wally Hammond,
      Time Out Film Guide op. cit.

95   'I like to do outlandish . . .' Henry Selick quoted by Mark Cotta
      Vaz, 'A Giant Peach in the Big Apple', *Cinefex 66*, June 1996

Britoons

101   'how you manage . . .' Nick Park from *Chicken Run* press kit, 2000

101   'Park and company . . .' Simon Louvish, 'Henzappopin', *Sight and
      Sound*, volume 10, issue 6, June 2000

Watership Down

106 'Certain demands . . .' Martin Rosen quoted by Richard Adams, *The Watership Down Film Picture Book*, Penguin, 1978

Chicken Run

111 'smoothness is rather low . . .' Peter Lord quoted by Kevin H Martin, 'Poultry in Motion' *Cinefex 82*

114 'You come to care greatly . . .' BBC online review by William Gallagher

114 'You realise just how much . . .' Kim Newman, *Sight and Sound*, August 2000

114 'This upmarket production . . .' J Hoberman, *Village Voice*, 21–27 June 2003, www.villagevoice.com

115 'It had to be chickens . . .' Nick Park and Peter Lord, *Guardian* online, 14 July 2000

Japanimation

118 'at times it seems . . .' unnamed reviewer on *Spirited Away* at www.filmjournal.com

118 'a style that is pure . . .' Nick Park, the *Guardian*, 1 August 2003

119 'To depict what constructs . . .' Hayao Miyazaki notes

Akira

124 'just let . . .' Otomo on the *Akira* DVD production documentary

127 'In the manner of contemporary . . .' Richard Harrington, *Washington Post*, 15 December 1989 – online

127 'Features some of the most mindblowing animation . . .' Geoff Andrew, *Time Out Film Guide*, Ninth Edition, op. cit.

127 'Akira seems to have attempted . . .' Fred Patten, quoted by Andrew Osmond, 'The Anime Debate', *Animation World*, issue 5.9, December 2000

Ghost in the Shell

133 'Extraordinarily artful . . .' Barry Walters, *SF Examiner*, SFGate.com

133 'The *Blade Runner* . . .' Nigel Floyd, *Time Out Film Guide*, Ninth Edition, op. cit.

133 'The kind of film James Cameron . . .' Clark Collis, *Empire* magazine, April 1996, www.empireonline.co.uk

160 'After about a decade . . .' Jonathan Rosenbaum, *Chicago Reader*, quoted by Norman Kagan, *The Cinema of Robert Zemeckis*, Taylor Trade Publishing

160 'Robert Zemeckis' multidimensional free-for-all . . .' Desson Howe, *Washington Post*, 24 June 1988

161 'The one I'm proudest of . . .' Steven Spielberg commenting on his favourite film as producer to *Starlog*, June 2001

161 'The idea of mixing . . .' Robert Zemeckis explaining the appeal of the movie on the *South Bank Show* TV profile of his career, ITV, October 1992

The Digital Toon

166 'When I saw . . .' Dennis Muren quoted by Don Shay and Jody Duncan, *The Making of Terminator 2 – Judgment Day*, Titan Books, 1991

169 'The heart of the story . . .' Steven Spielberg in *Empire*, September 2001

173 'a rich kid's toy . . .' Thomas G Smith, *Industrial Light and Magic: The Art of Special Effects*, Columbus, 1986

Star Wars: Episode 1 – The Phantom Menace

178 'I specifically . . .' Rob Coleman, quoted by Ron Magid, *CG Star Turns, American Cinematographer, Star Wars Special Edition*, volume 80, no. 9

183 'the biggest problem . . .' Andrew O'Hehir, *Sight and Sound*, July 1999, www.bfi.org.uk

183 'Writing the script . . .' George Lucas quoted by Laurent Bouzereau and Jody Duncan, *The Making of Star Wars: Episode 1: The Phantom Menace*, First Edition, Ebury Press, 1999

Toy Story

187 'We wanted . . .' John Lasseter quoted by Rita Street, 'Toys Will Be Toys', *Cinefex 64*, December 1995

187 'because of the richness . . .' John Lasseter in interview with Jonathan Ross, the *Guardian,* 19 November 2001

192 '*Star Wars* simmered . . .' John Lasseter quoted by Estelle Shay, 'Beyond Andy's Room', *Cinefex 81*, April 2000

193 'One of the things that's different . . .' John Lasseter quoted by Estelle Shay, 'Beyond Andy's Room', *Cinefex 81*, April 2000

193 'The characters . . .' Christine Jones, *Box Office Magazine*

218 'All four main characters . . .' Terry Rossio, *Creative Screenwriting*, volume 8, no. 3, May/June 2001

Mavericks
219 'Puppet films by their very nature . . .' Suzanne Buchan, *Shifting Realities: The Brothers Quay – Between Live Action and Animation*, www.awn.com

The Secret of Nimh
227 'preserve this valiant . . .' Don Bluth, *The Secret of Nimh* 1982 press release notes
227 'The world needs heroes . . .' ibid.
228 'Animation is a beautiful art . . .' Don Bluth quoted by David Hutchison, 'Don Bluth: Meet the man and the studio that may change the direction of today's animated movies', *Comics Scene*, May 1982
230 'What we've attempted to do . . .' Don Bluth quoted by Paul Mandell, 'Good old-time cel animation finally meets its makers as former Disney artists unite to re-establish The Golden Age, an interview with Don Bluth and Dorse Lanpher', *Fantastic Films*, spring 1982
234 'It's a spectacular . . .' David Pirie, *Time Out Film Guide*, 1991
234 'A richly animated . . .' *Variety*, June 1982
235 'An animated feature . . .' Richard Hollis, *Starburst*, October 1982
235 'In this Age of Realism and Naturalism . . .' Don Bluth, *The Secret of Nimh* press release, 1982

The Iron Giant
240 'an attitude of panic . . .' Brad Bird quoted by Bob Miller in 'Lean, Mean Fighting Machine: How Brad Bird made The Iron Giant', *Animation World Magazine*, issue 4.5, August 1999
241 'I'm interested . . .' ibid.
242 'As entertaining . . .' Wally Hammond, *Time Out Film Guide*, Ninth Edition, op. cit.
234 'I was and am willing to look foolish . . .' Brad Bird quoted by Michael Sragow, 'Iron without Irony', *Salon* magazine, 5 August 1999

Alice
244 'My creative work . . .' Jan Svankmajer quoted by Daniel Steinhart in indieWIRE.com 8 January 2002

Appendices

Two Classically Animated Features: The Lion King and The Prince of Egypt

The Animated Short

Animating the Future

Bibliography

Adamson, Joe, *Tex Avery: King of Cartoons*, DaCappo Press, 1985

Bettelheim, Bruno, *The Uses of Enchantment: The Importance and Meaning of Fairy Tales*, Penguin Books, 1977

Bouzereau, Laurent and Duncan, Jody *The Making of Star Wars: Episode 1 The Phantom Menace*, First Edition, Ebury Press, 1999

Clements, Jonathan and McCarthy, Helen, *The Anime Encyclopedia: A Guide to Japanese Animation since 1917*, Stonebridge Press, 2001

Grant, John, *The Encyclopedia of Walt Disney's Animated Characters*, Hamlyn, 1987

Johnston, Ollie and Thomas, Frank, *The Illusion of Life: Disney Animation*, Hyperion, 1995

Jones, Chuck, *Chuck Amuck*, Farrar Straus & Giroux, 1989

Jones, Chuck, *Chuck Reducks*, Time Warner, 1991

Kagan, Norman, *The Cinema of Robert Zemeckis*

Klein, Norman, *7 Minutes : The Life and Death of the American Cartoon*, Verso Books, 1995

Lyons, Christopher, *The International Dictionary of Films and Filmmakers: Directors*, Macmillan, 1984

McCarthy, Helen, *Hayao Miyazaki: Master of Japanese Animation: Films, Themes, Artistry*, Stonebridge Press, 1999

Miyazaki, Hayao, *The Art of Spirited Away*, Viz Graphic Novels, 2002

Poitras, Gillies, *The Anime Companion*, Stonebridge Press, 1998

Pym, John (ed.), *Time Out Film Guide*, Ninth Edition, Penguin Books, 1988

Schroeder, Russell, *Disney: The Ultimate Visual Guide*, Dorking Kindersley, 2002

Sibley, Brian and Lord, Peter, *Cracking Animation*, Thames and Hudson, 1998

Smith, Thomas G, *Industrial Light and Magic – The Art of Special Effects*, Columbus, 1986

Taylor, Richard, *The Encyclopedia of Animation Techniques*, Focal Press, 1999

Vaz, Mark Cotta and Duignan, Patricia Rose, *Industrial Light and Magic – Into the Digital Realm*, Virgin Books, 1996

Zipes, Jack, *The Oxford Companion to Fairy Tales*, Oxford university Press, 2002

Web Resources

www.filmcomment.com: website for one of the best film magazines out there, a place of genuine film criticism and appreciation rather than monthly marketing hype

www.animationmagazine.net: the online version of the splashy American monthly print version

www.cinefex.com: the Holy Grail of visual effects publications, typically showcasing three major visual-effects films with each issue plus shorter sideline articles

www.aardman.com: the website for the creators of *Wallace and Gromit* and *Chicken Run*

www.pixar.com: the website for the producers of the *Toy Story* films

www.vinton.com: the website for the claymation production company

www.awn.com

www.toonopedia.com: another all-embracing resource covering shows, films, creators, studios

www.ilm.com: the official website of the visual-effects company whose work since 1977 has proved the often poetic power of a visual effect

www.chuckjones.com: the official website for Chuck Jones giving filmography, biography and also a merchandise area

www.animated-movie.net: an incredible listing of detail for the animated films most people are familiar with; trivia, images, interviews

Picture Credits

The following pictures are from the Ronald Grant Archive:
Page 1 (bottom); Page 2 (top); Page 4 (top) © Disney; Page 5 (top) courtesy Nepthene Productions; Page 7 (top) courtesy Studio Ghibli.

The following pictures are from the Kobal Collection:
Page 1 (top) courtesy Walt Disney Pictures; Page 2 (bottom) courtesy Columbia; Page 3 courtesy McCay Productions; Page 4 (bottom) courtesy Touchstone/Burton/Di Novi; Page 5 (bottom) courtesy DreamWorks/Allied Filmmakers/Aardman; Page 6 courtesy Amblin/Touchstone; Page 7 (bottom) courtesy Warner Brothers; Page 8 (top) courtesy DreamWorks and Page 8 (bottom) courtesy Amblin/Universal.

Index